ROGER WILLIAMS

ROGER WILLIAMS

Witness Beyond Christendom

1603-1683

JOHN GARRETT

The Macmillan Company

Collier-Macmillan Ltd., London

f
82
.W7732

The Macmillan Company
866 Third Avenue, New York, N.Y. 10022
Collier-Macmillan Canada Ltd., Toronto, Ontario

Library of Congress Catalog Card Number:
76-109449

First Printing

Printed in the United States of America

Contents

Contents

Preface

T HIS STUDY OF Roger Williams was made possible by an invitation to spend a semester as a visiting scholar at Union Theological Seminary in the City of New York in 1967. I have to thank the seminary—and especially President John C. Bennett, Dr. Robert S. Handy and Associate Professor Robert F. Beach and the members of his library staff—for much interest and kindness.

I am also indebted to the Massachusetts Historical Society Library, the Andover Harvard Library, the John Carter Brown Library at Providence, and the Rhode Island Historical Society Library in the same city. In England, I have been helped by staff members at the Institute of Historical Research at the University of London, the British Museum, the Library at Friends' House, the Bodleian Library at Oxford, and the Essex County Records Office at Chelmsford.

Personal help has been given by Professor George Yule of Melbourne, Professor George Hunston Williams of Harvard, Dr. Robert S. Paul (then of Hartford), Mr. Bradford F. Swan of Providence, Rhode Island, Dr. Geoffrey F. Nuttall of London, Dr. Christopher Hill of Balliol College, Oxford, and Dr. James

S. Vendettuoli, Jr., of Groton, Connecticut. My friend Robert S. Lecky has carefully checked and improved the whole book. My thanks go to them all, but any errors and faults remaining are my own.

I have usually modernised spelling and punctuation in quotations, but have left titles and some shorter quotations unaltered for the sake of flavour. Williams's characteristic "&c" has been included at intervals because it is a mark of his style, however inelegant. In most cases I have quoted from Volume VI of Williams's Complete Writings in citing letters, but a new and critical text of the letters is needed, and comparison with manuscripts has been required. In Chapters 7 and 8 I have included many long quotations for the benefit of scholars who need textual evidence on difficult points. I have tried to make them clear also, however, for the general reader who wants to come to know Williams better.

My wife and family have helped me with the writing of this book in many ways. My wife's careful study of the manuscript and the discerning criticisms of the late F. E. Baguley and Mrs. Baguley while I was writing in their welcoming Essex home have greatly improved it at numerous points. The hospitality and friendship of Fred and Ming Baguley, extending over many years, explain the dedication.

JOHN GARRETT

Pacific Theological College
Suva, Fiji Islands

ROGER WILLIAMS

1
The Elusive Roger Williams

AMERICA HAS COME to think of Williams as a banished man. The magistrates of Boston certainly expelled him from their jurisdictions by order of their general court in October 1635. Yet long before, his friends in England had loved his honesty and hated his impetuous ways. "Divinely mad,"[1] they called him. It is a good description as long as the accent is on the adverb. In looking into his letters and books to find his secret one discovers a Calvinist Puritan who became a runaway and preferred the rough wilderness of dissent to the tidy gardens of the conventional clergy. The logic of his banishment is prefigured in the English society that brought him to young manhood. His understanding of the meaning of the Bible for the Church and its task in the world had radical implications for the state church systems of the older Christendom. His founding of the community of Rhode Island was a frontier experiment among wild men; but it held the seeds within it for formal separation of church and state elsewhere. Williams was not a "revolutionary" born in advance of the Boston Tea Party or Bastille Day. He was profoundly different from the men of the Enlightenment. The Bible was his daily bread.

The late Perry Miller and others have insisted that theology
is the key to Roger Williams's mind.[2] Their effort of sympathy
has related him to his fellow-Puritans in colonial New England
and in England and continental Europe.[3] We recognise him
as a marginal lone wolf who came out of the fellowship of the
godly English preachers—William Perkins, William Sibbes, William Ames, John Preston, William Gouge.[4] For these "old
Puritans" we have no distinguishing party name. Their aim
was further reformation in the light of the Bible and under
the guidance of the Spirit. Their methods of preaching and
controversy were determined by the new logic of Ramus; they
were devoted to the plain style and the use of homely simile,
so as to fire the earthy imagination of God's Englishmen in
the task of bringing more reformation to the Church. The
disclosure of this thought-world has been an impressive venture
in the history of ideas.

The Puritans themselves would have been intrigued, but
still annoyed, by this type of dissection of Williams and other
Puritans, which revealed Perry Miller's own detachment as
well as his deep interest in the people he was studying. It is
as though all the fish in an aquarium are properly displayed
in something like their original habitat; but the specimens
themselves are more aware of a common element which gives
them life. The Puritans felt this about the Bible, its power
and influence. To each of them the text of the Bible spoke directly
every day. In showing what they have in common, even what
parties among them share, Miller's analysis of many other influences in the intellectual history of their time is instructive.
But in understanding one of them—and Williams has left us a
large body of writings to help—we have to pore over particular
books of the Bible. The interaction of a variety of recurrent
biblical themes enables us to share imaginatively in the way
Roger Williams felt about his personal pilgrimage and the
worlds of life and thought that were fused in his more than
eighty stormy years.

Those years happen to coincide with the main events in

the reigns of James I, Charles I, Oliver Cromwell, and Charles II. Although he has been claimed with justice as a herald of what America would become, Williams lived and died a loyal Englishman and a constitutional monarchist. All his life, though part of his heart was in the heavenly Jerusalem, another part was in London. Like his clerical adversary, John Cotton, he saw what was happening in New England as a premonition and a hope for old England's fuller reformation. He and many others dared to expect that old England would be the stage for the first act in the millennium, when Christ would consummate the Reformation by taking up His personal rule in the world. The time and manner of such an event became subjects of differing interpretation and judgment, but the great curve of excitement among Englishmen, roughly coinciding, as it begins, with the defeat of the Spanish Armada in 1588, rising to its peak in the frenetic aftermath of the execution of Charles I in 1649, and subsiding in the prudence and dashed hopes of the Restoration of 1660, is like a fever chart which anxious watchers interpreted in the light of the books of Daniel, Revelation, and the Song of Solomon.

Within the historical developments of those years, we shall try to explain the social forces (and his own reading of the Bible texts) that made Williams what he was—a forward-looking reactionary and a backward-looking revolutionary. Once we begin to understand him this way the writings of Williams speak for themselves.

As a writer Roger Williams does not endear himself to those who like good editing. There is plenty of concealed art in what Perry Miller called the "formidable terrors" of his style,[5] but Williams had preoccupations other than fine writing. Three ingredients in his manner may be detected as a guide to reading him. Each corresponds with an important phase in his career. Each reflects an aspect of English society that drew him to use particular expressions and vocabulary.

The first of these is plain speaking, with earthy metaphors drawn from trade and daily life. It enabled him to identify with his own family background among the London merchants, with politicians and legal pleaders, with the army, and with the lesser Puritan clergy who liked and used the down-to-earth manner of exemplary pastors like Richard Greenham of Dry Drayton and "godly Mr. Dod."[6] In his later career he could use this manner to appeal to the assorted religious and commercial adventurers of Rhode Island. Sometimes it took the form of racy abuse and banter. It must have been his speaking voice for religious and political gossip.

A second style is more "Elizabethan," with courtesies and conceits. Sometimes more or less Miltonic rhetoric pokes through. There are tags of Latin and allusions. Scripture is analysed, weighed, and applied. Here Williams tried hard to use what he learned at school and at Cambridge. At many points this "higher" style aligns him with John Cotton, with the university-trained black-coated clergy, the grandees of the Independent political party and highly literate lawyers like John Winthrop, Senior, who could have made their way at court if preferment had been their fortune. The gentry were accustomed to this kind of writing. Sometimes Williams used it to show his deference toward them. In his letters to John Winthrop, Senior, the honorifics give his style a pathetic tinge, though they are quite sincere. In the dedications of some of his books he sounds fulsome. The most embarrassing occurrence of this second mannerism is in a correspondence he conducted in 1629 with Lady Joan Barrington over his rejected suit for the hand of her niece, Jane Whalley.[7]

The third style is all his own—pointed, direct, and driving. With it he expounds and defends liberty. He lays bare the text of the Bible to try to show the falsity of defending the civil magistrate as an authority in the Church. All here is at white heat. Positively, Williams uses the same strong tone when he expounds parts of the Old Testament books of Isaiah, Ezra, and Jonah. For this type of utterance he has become known. He does not conform here to another way of life. He is free and speaks of the Christian Gospel and the person of Christ.

Any attempt to reduce these particular biblical expositions to general truths in either religion or politics means loss of the genuine Williams. Finally, as he developed his life's work and meditated more deeply, the first and second of the three voices of Williams became transmuted by the third. All three became unified into an admittedly "gnarled" prolixity; the influence of the Bible was the unifying force.

In seventeenth-century English literature Roger Williams is definitely a second-rank figure. It is necessary to fall madly in love with him to read him right through for pleasure. In historical context, though, he has his virtues and excitement. He should not be blamed for bad taste or lack of humour. Standards of taste and humour vary. Roger Williams, in many places and even in *George Fox digg'd out of His Burrowes*, the wordy tract that is often classified as a sign of his dotage, has a wry brand of humour. Its ancestry is in Chaucer,[8] the English translators of the French poet François Villon, some of Shakespeare's pit-pleasing scenes, and the Martin Marprelate tracts of the 1580's. It is not insignificant that he once befriended the royalist eccentric knight, Sir Thomas Urquhart of Cromarty, who was the translator of Rabelais into English.[9] If we care to listen for it, there is a deep chuckle beneath Roger Williams's most outrageous phrases. He laughed. So did his readers at the time. In the controversy with John Cotton in the 1640's and early 1650's we can find the joy of battle in this form. The otherwise dull pages of his attack on the Quaker leader, George Fox, show how he must have relished clobbering his opponents and making the bystanders laugh. Nothing pleased him more than tackling an establishment. He had done it when he fought Cotton. He did it again when he launched out against the socially powerful "junto of the Foxians"[10] in the Rhode Island of the early 1670's. Williams may have been tedious on that occasion. He was seldom puerile, never merely vulgar. He disdained bawdiness, but he made the Quakers figures of fun by a combination of exasperation and ridicule.

The literature of controversy written at this period can be

irritating because of its hidden allusions. What Williams said cannot be clarified without referring to the Bible and the pamphlets that preceded and surrounded his sallies into print. The provision of some contextual guidance can hardly make him palatable, but it might make him more digestible and nourishing.

2
Portrait of a Disciple

THE ROAD FROM Plymouth, in what is now Massachusetts, to Providence, Rhode Island, winds through small settlements surrounded by forest. Some of the villages date back to the late seventeenth century. A lonely Englishman named Roger Williams travelled the same way by snowy tracks in the first months of 1636. Friendly Indians of the Wampanoag tribe, whose language he already knew, were his guides. They helped him and his few companions, in a bitter winter, to reach the banks of the Seekonk River, near the present town of Rehoboth.

The traveller was a refugee. He had chosen exile from the young Massachusetts Bay colony and refused to submit to the uniformity of opinion and speech laid down by Puritan magistrates and clergy in New England's land of promise. Williams has become part of the American legend. School teachers like to depict him as pioneer and prophet of the rights enshrined in the American Constitution. Williams fails to fit the picture. He believed, unquestionably, in what he called "soul liberty." He desired a clear delimitation of the jurisdictions of church and state. But, unlike the architects of the Constitution, he thought of men as depraved and corrupt without hope of earthly remedy. Collusion of the powers of church and state struck him as more than simple tyranny. He saw man's ancient supernatural enemy, the Devil, sitting masked in the seats of supreme authority throughout the Christian world. This hideous usurper would be toppled from his throne only when Christ personally returned to renew His Church, finally to put down the mighty from their seats, and to inaugurate His universal reign of justice and peace. Williams was no optimistic "do it yourself Christian," with faith in America and the future. He looked on this life and everything in it as dross and worthless baubles and desired Eternity to be his business. He tackled practical commerce and politics without many illusions and regrets; but he wanted the Church to be virgin-pure.

All Puritans, by definition, wanted the Church purified. Roger Williams wanted it without spot or blemish, or any such thing. Shockable Christians and industrious Freudians find his favourite image of the Church's worship erotic. He derived it from passages in the Old Testament and the New. He thought of the washed and prepared bride coming with pleasure to the marriage bed of the splendid bridegroom, Christ. The groom, he taught, will arrange that the Word, prayer, praise, discipline, the ministry, and sacraments will be set in order, according to the specification in the "love letters" of the Scriptures, before Christ Himself comes to possess his bride on the approaching wedding night. Meanwhile, however, the scattered and disunited members of the Body of Christ, the Church, wander in the wilderness of this world. They must weep, and seek for the signs of their true married estate, listening for the voice of the beloved Bridegroom, whose marriage chamber is being prepared and whose fingers will soon rest on the handle of the door as he asks for entrance.

Williams drew the symbols surrounding this conception of the separated and prepared Church from an allegorised reading of the Old Testament Song of Solomon. He found New Testament parallels in Christ's parable of the Wise and Foolish Virgins, in frequent references of the apostle Paul, and in the

bridal imagery of the Book of Revelation. This last book of
the Bible, together with the Old Testament apocalypse of
Daniel, dominated much of his thinking and writing, from
his early association with the London Separatists until he grew
old as a farmer, trader, and politician among the assorted
adventurers in the Rhode Island colonies.

Theological conviction was always intimately related to
political achievement. Williams did not separate nature from
grace. He saw the political and ecclesiastical orders as distinct,
but united in the perspective of the anticipated final reign of
Christ. Like Luther, he regarded the political arena as a kind
of provisional space, providentially preserved from utter chaos
by compromises and legal adjustments. God the Father delegated
enough of His own power to the people to enable them to
make the most of politics as a "bad" job. Williams thought
the English Common Law a reasonably satisfactory instrument
for such purposes, so he used it. It served well for making
relative judgments. The absolute assurance of sacred support
for such judgments was another matter. When magistrates and
clergy together claimed to be agents of Christ's purpose, Williams resisted. He could not bear their claim that Christ endorsed
their all-too-human laws, whether governing claims to Indian
land or "enforced worships." The worldly Devil, he believed,
had a way of disguising himself as an angel of light, indeed
as Christ Himself. Williams scanned the otherwise benevolent
faces of governors and clergy, many of whom were his dear
friends, looking for hints of Satan's stratagem. It was embarrassing
for them, and it made it difficult to live with him. Yet he was
not merely negative. We cannot mark him off as a perpetual
angry young man. Many New England magistrates and ministers
testified to his zealous and constructive spirit. He became negative when he thought it was his duty to scour the Devil and
his hunger for more power out of the holy place, the Church.
If this could be done, it would follow that the Church would
not try to use the state to make itself comfortable; nor would
the state use the Church to give ambition and power-hunger

a veil of religious respectability. The vision was utopian, but the attitude brought results, in old England and New, in Williams's own lifetime. Church dignitaries and political eminences were cut down, on both sides of the Atlantic, to human size.

This was a byproduct. Williams was not aiming chiefly to make clergy less pompous and politicians more self-effacing. The wider aim of his impetuous life was to be a witness, to point others toward Jesus as the authority whose service meant liberation, joy in hardship, and calm in storm. The Christology of Roger Williams is the key to his motives. His radicalism does not stridently denounce false authorities; he asserts that the true authority is in the Man who, paradoxically, suffered an execution reserved for noncitizens and social outcasts. Williams fervently believed, with all the writers of the New Testament, that the infinite and eternal God, whose ways are apt to be otherwise unfathomable, had disclosed his nature in voluntary suffering and in the abnegation of "force majeure." He saw the pathway to divine, as distinct from human, power as lying along the way of rejection, misunderstanding, and distress, all gladly endured. His radical "servant Christology" gives the meaning of his codes of life and thought.

Who was this "divinely mad" Englishman? How did he come to make his journey through the wilds? What was the sequel?

Roger Williams, the son of a London merchant, was born, probably in 1603,[1] into a restless English society of lawyers, financiers, and men of affairs. In that year Queen Elizabeth I died and James I, the first of the Stuarts, came to the throne.

The London of Williams's boyhood was already tense with rivalry. Politics and religion were dividing Puritan lawyers, merchants, and gentry from the great families and place-seekers around the royal court. Little is known of the career of Williams until about 1616, when he became the protégé and scribe of Sir Edward Coke, the Lord Chief Justice of England. By that time he had passed through an experience

of conversion.[2] Later in life he remembered what happened
as a turning to "the true Lord Jesus." The characteristic phrase
implies that men may serve a "false" Lord Jesus as a means
of enhancing their prestige and power among the gods and
lords of this world.

The young Roger Williams was an accomplished shorthand
writer. The traditions of Rhode Island and the testimony of
Coke's daughter, Mrs. Ralph Sadleir, tell of his having caught
the eye of the great judge in the Holborn parish of St. Sepulchre
and being engaged as a recorder by Coke when the Chief Justice
presided in the court of Star Chamber. We have no way of
telling whether Williams acquired his skill in his father's business or in the busy commercial life of Smithfield, where the
family lived. A transition from his family background into the
law would hardly have been novel. Lawyers, merchants, and
country gentlemen were interconnected by marriages, invest-
ments, and Protestant sentiment.[3] Religious faith was inseparable
from the rest of life. Such people, in business or political
meetings, talked of saving grace; after common prayer they
discussed colonization and trade. They grumbled regularly over
the encroachment of royal and ecclesiastical prerogative on the
domain of the Common Law. Under James I the Parliament
was already functioning, in its own estimation, as a court of
justice, where commoners were skirmishing in accordance with
tactics they had learned under the first Elizabeth. Their leaders
aimed to fight their case against the King in the name of the
Lord—and win.

Sir Edward Coke was their greatest leader. Until his death
in 1634 the lawyers looked to his writings and his personal
counsel as a source of their strategy. His weight was all the
greater because he stood for loyalty to both throne and church.
In old age he blended conservative prestige with stubborn
defiance in the law courts and the parliament.[4] He irritated
the King and inspired a generation of rampant lawyers. This
great jurist, writing copiously, arguing, growling at his opponents, subject to passionate outbursts and to ribaldry, took

the young shorthand writer under his care. He became a second
father to Williams and called the boy his "son."[5] He sponsored
his entry into the recently founded Charterhouse School in
London[6] and his entry as Pensioner at Pembroke College,
Cambridge, where Williams graduated as B.A. in 1627.[7] From
Pembroke the young man went on toward holy orders, though
we have no surviving record of his ordination to the diaconate
or priesthood, this, however, being no proof that he was not
ordained. Many diocesan records of the period were destroyed
in the English Civil Wars.[8] Nor can we say whether he ever
served as a parish priest.

By 1629 he was serving as domestic chaplain in the household
of Sir William Masham at Otes, in Essex, some twenty miles
northeast of London.[9] The manor house of Otes was one of
many in that part of the country where young ministers with
Puritan views could find refuge from tightening episcopal
control. William Laud had become Bishop of London in 1628
and was insisting on subscription to the Book of Common
Prayer. Some ministers were quitting the country for the
Netherlands under Laud's steady pressure.[10] Many, up to that
time, had been "lecturers" at stated hours in parish churches,
but without induction to the cure of souls and the celebration
of sacraments in the parishes concerned.[11] Indoctrinated laity
like the Masham family[12] provided their livelihood. The office
of family chaplain to a large household, with its attendants,
visitors, and visiting relations, gave a further refuge to godly
dissidents. Roger Williams served in this capacity at Otes.
While there he rode up to London to watch the scene and
join in the gossip when Parliament remonstrated against royal
autocracy in 1629.[13] In the preceding year he would have heard,
with pride, of Coke's epic speeches in the old man's last turbulent
parliament. Lawyers and squires in East Anglia and the home
counties were glad to feel the ripples of that formidable discontent.

At Otes Williams fell in love with a young lady of good
family, only to have his suit rejected by the lady's adamant
aunt—the widowed Lady Joan Barrington, mistress of Barrington

Hall, Hatfield Broad Oak, not far from Otes.[14] In his frustration, he wrote Lady Barrington a tactically maladroit summons to watch for the eternal fate of her soul; but not long afterwards, on December 15, 1629, he married Mary Barnard, one of the maids-in-waiting to another ward of Lady Barrington.[15]

During his stay at Otes Williams had been an associate of ministers and squires from both East Anglia and the West Country—the men who planned the emigration of the Massachusetts Bay Company to New England in 1630.[16] He attended meetings held at Sempringham, the seat of the Earl of Lincoln[17] and was in touch with John Cotton, then incumbent of St. Botolph's Church, in old Boston.[18] John Winthrop, the squire of Groton, Suffolk, was then chafing[19] at the royal and episcopal confinement of their long range plans. Both Cotton and Winthrop had come to favour the setting up of an established Church providing for covenanted congregations in every parish, with royal patronage and protection. They felt frustrated because this was the last intention of King James and his court advisers. The Winthrops and Cottons of the countryside saw themselves unjustly excluded from the circle of the royal council and favourites. But they believed the Lord Himself would bring in the day when the current crop of royal appointees and sycophants would be moved out of the charmed royal circle to make room for themselves and their friends. Williams found himself in sympathy with their protest, though there were already signs that he regarded their goal as questionable and their methods as insufficiently drastic.

Winthrop sailed for Massachusetts with the main migration in 1630. Williams followed late in the same year. Cotton delayed. Perhaps he hoped for a compromise with his bishop that would enable him to remain in his Boston parish. Eventually he followed them, in June 1633. Williams's two honoured friends were to be among the "procurers of his sorrows"[20] when he was banished from Massachusetts, though Cotton denied he had a hand in it. He was, in fact, further to the left of the Puritan movement than they were before any of them sailed.

Bishop Laud's efficient scrutiny of nonincumbents was closing

in on Williams by the middle of 1630, forcing him to leave
Otes and to ride down with his wife to Bristol. They sailed on
the *Lyon* on December 10, 1630, and arrived off Nantasket on
the following February 5. Very soon Williams demonstrated his
leftward deviation from the leading men of the new Boston.
The Boston Church invited him to serve as its Teacher. He
declined, because he said he "durst not officiate to an un-
separated people."[21] It is hard to think the Separatist who
had landed was not a Separatist before he sailed. He meant
by his refusal that his precursors in Massachusetts had not been
willing to renounce the established Church of England, its
prayer book, and its "mixed assemblies" of regenerate and
unregenerate persons. He was, moreover, correct. John Cotton
had gone down to Southampton in March 1630 to preach a
farewell discourse to the migrants who saw their departure as
only a temporary and regrettable farewell to "their mother,"
the Church of England, and the people in the parishes there.[22]
Meanwhile they saw no crime in attending the parish churches
of their own party if they returned to England. Williams could
not agree. He wanted a complete break with the unholy medieval
alliance between Caesar and Christ. He did not believe the
true Church could again be seen in its pure lustre within
England's virtual continuance of that intact Christendom. Total
separation was his answer.

He went down from Boston to New Plymouth in 1631,
expecting to find more understanding of his Separatist conviction. The people there had by then enjoyed ten years of
"church estate" in the New World. They had been party to
the issues fought out in the London of his boyhood between
the godly moderate Puritans and a vocal minority of Separatist
brothers. Under Queen Elizabeth, in the 1590's, the followers
of Henry Barrow and John Greenwood had scarified the English
bishops as a "miserable compound, . . . neither ecclesiastical
nor civil."[23] They could not bear to see any royal appointee
sitting in a position of power over the Church, where, on
their view of the matter, none must rule but Christ through
His assembled saints. Some resisted to the death. Others, with

varying degrees of Separatist conviction, fled to the Netherlands.[24]
They included forerunners, members and founders of the New
Plymouth congregation—Henry Ainsworth, William Brewster,
William Bradford, and John Robinson. Those of them who
established the congregation at Leyden before their migration
to America tended to "come back half the way" out of Separatism
into a semiseparatist position. The Pilgrim Fathers submitted
an equivocating document through diplomatic channels to King
James in order to gain permission to emigrate in 1620. It shows
that they, like their London colleague, Henry Jacob, were ready
then to embrace more than a halfway loyalty to the Church
of England, bishops included.[25] Their appeal may have been
a frantic effort to wring assent from the English government,
but more than ten years later Williams found them still to
some extent disposed to "seek the Lord further,"[26] which implied
openness to his Separatist testimony. He preached among the
Pilgrims and earned their tribute as a good and earnest Christian
man.[27] At the same time he began his career as a missionary by
fraternising with the Algonquin Indians around Plymouth. He
put his linguistic gifts to use in acquiring their language and
made long-range plans to come to know them better and acquaint
them with the Bible and Christian teaching.[28]

In 1633 Williams accepted an invitation from the church
at Salem[29] to become one of its ministers. Many people there
responded to his ability and winning disposition;[30] they were
converted to his opinions, which were thought of as dangerous
by the magistrates and ministers at Boston. Danger threatened
all the Bay Colonies during the early 1630's because of the
attempts of James I and his advisers to forestall the development of a Puritan transatlantic stronghold against the home-
land's policies.[31] People like Cotton and Winthrop did not
want their colony to appear in blacker colours than it really
wore—as a nest of Separatism. They sought further reforms
of the Church of England, all in a loyal spirit. Williams, more
radical, was condemning the Church of England as in league
with the anti-Christ.

While he was at Salem, Williams circulated a manuscript

treatise[32] claiming that the royal Patent for the colony of Massachusetts, the basis of the colony's very existence, was not a document that could bestow genuine rights to the land held, which really belonged to the Indians.

Williams also sided, while at Salem, with members of his congregation who came to the conclusion after hearing him preach that the Cross of St. George should be removed from the quartering in the top left hand corner of the royal ensign then used in the colonies.[33] Williams saw the state as a providential human ordering of society rather than a sacral Christian institution. In any case, were not such representations of the cross images and "idolatrous" according to the commandment forbidding men to make any such thing? The Salem governor, John Endecott, saw force in the whole argument. He cut the cross out of the colours and precipitated a controversy that rent the colonies and led to the omission of a cross from all Massachusetts' flags until at least 1680.[34]

Another outbreak of primitive biblicism at Salem followed Williams's advocacy of the veiling of women in church.[35] He had probably studied the enigmatic advice given by Paul to the Corinthians—that they should cover their women's heads "on account of the angels" (*I Corinthians 11.10*). The custom had been far from general in the families of these exiled gentry, angels or no angels. Under the stress of this further irritant Williams, for all his native charm, was reckoned a "rigid" person.

All these Salem troubles coincided with a threat of English military action against the young colony. The colonists were already behaving like a state, when in fact they were meant to be an incorporated trading company.[36] They drilled troops and prepared for their defence. As this went on Williams invited more controversy by resisting the administering of an oath of loyalty to all freemen of the colony. He said an oath was an "action of God's worship."[37] A body politic had no right to require oaths; the state could not run the life of the Church. Imposition of oaths by the state used the name of God in vain; it was secular travesty of a spiritual solemnity.

The Reverend Cotton Mather, John Cotton's distinguished

grandson, was to give a description of all the bother created by Williams at Salem, when he came to write the *Magnalia Christi Americana*[38] in 1702. His ironic remarks about Williams's "quixotism" and cussedness reflect a general estimate among responsible leaders in the Massachusetts Bay Colony at the time of the strife. Roger Williams was difficult, mercurial, unyielding. Such people exasperate official theologians and patient administrators at any time, but especially when institutions are already under attack from elsewhere.

But by May 1635, Roger Williams, in spite of all the criticism from beyond Salem, had endeared himself to the people there. They installed him as their Teacher.[39] While he held the office, the Salem town community asked to be ceded some ground at Marblehead, adjacent to their boundaries.[40] Before he had been called to be Teacher and while still simply preaching occasionally at Salem, Williams had been summoned to give an account of himself before the magistrates at Boston.[41] At about the same time he had opposed regular meetings of ministers from various local churches as being a bad step towards an overarching presbytery.[42] On his second appearance before the Boston court he had become more accountable; he was now the Teacher of the Salem Church. Moreover he was still publicly defending the opinions on which he had undertaken to keep silent when he had been previously examined by the court. This time he was summoned more urgently, to give a full statement and satisfaction.[43] Naturally, his people at Salem could not separate the issue about the disposition of the land at Marblehead from what happened to the Teacher of their Church. By August he was ill and found himself psychologically isolated as a result of his having first renounced communion with the churches of the Bay, then having withdrawn from his own flock.[44]

It was a prelude to the breach that lay ahead. In October 1635, Williams was called finally before the general court with leading clergymen present. He was told to forego his errors. He refused, but asked for time to consider.[45]

The resultant exile has often been depicted as vindictive.

In reality the law as it stood left the magistrates little alternative. Winthrop and Cotton both showed mixed feelings about it, at the time and later. Their chagrin at having to resolve on the inevitable may be compared with John Calvin's unpleasant dilemma over the execution of Servetus in sixteenth-century Geneva. Williams dramatised the episode later as a case of persecution; but the punishment was to some extent self-willed. He had his eye already on the open country to the west of Plymouth for he felt a call to go among the Indians. A handful of friends proved ready to accompany him.[46] Land could be acquired for very little from the Indian sachems. Other dissentients and adventurers in the Bay were interested in expansion for farming and trade. As a preacher Williams felt drawn toward the frontier tasks of an "apostle," and he had seen enough of the bickerings of conventional congregations. None of them seemed to him authentic by his peculiarly lofty New Testament criteria. It seemed to him that God alone could again raise up a genuine Church with true sacraments —and that he was more likely to do it by a fresh start in the wilderness than by tinkering with the vestiges of the old order in Boston, Salem, or Plymouth.

At Boston, the authorities appear to have sensed the situation. They took a lenient view of the sentence of departure out of their jurisdiction, imposed on Williams by the general court on October 19, 1635.[47] They gave their miscreant three weeks, probably hoping he would relent and submit. Further illness overtook him. The period of grace was extended. He recovered from his sickness and was soon saying what he had said before— that Salem must separate from the "unclean" churches of the rest of the colony. When the court again met in January 1636, its hand was forced. A messenger brought Williams his final warning. He took the hint. By the time an agent had arrived to put him on board a ship for England, he had fled.

The route he took remains unclear. He may have travelled part of the way by boat and partly on foot through the woods. The men of Plymouth knew where he was. Back in Massachusetts, John Winthrop was interested in the prospect of getting new land for development.[48] When Williams and his few companions arrived at what is now Rehoboth, after fourteen weeks of travel in a harsh winter, the Plymouth leaders notified him that he was still within the limits of their grant. He promptly went further west and crossed the river, to land on the shore where he planted the settlement of Providence. According to reasonably well-attested local legend, the Indians who met the boat at Slate Rock, where he landed, greeted him with the words "What cheer, Netop?"[49] He was already a friend of the tribes; their own salutation together with the Shakespearian preface has a touch of likelihood. Williams had done his work of befriending the Indians well while he had lived at Plymouth.

The development of Roger Williams from 1636 onward may be traced in his letters and other writings. Before that date we can follow him only by internal evidence about the early years in his own books, and through fragmentary reconstruction based on the accounts of others. Williams's surviving letters and the early records of Providence Plantations describe how he made his band of adventurers into a civil community, the first in the modern Western world to be founded explicitly on separation of the civil and ecclesiastical powers.

In the early days of the new community Williams travelled tirelessly among the Indian tribes. From 1636 onward he corresponded with John Winthrop about their movements and rivalries.[50] His close relationship with the old Narragansett sachem Canonicus and his nephew Miantonoumi enabled him to act as adviser to the English of Massachusetts when the Pequot Indians were beaten in a bloodthirsty punitive raid on their main fort, near Mystic in coastal Connecticut. Williams did not act uncritically in dealing with the Indians. He knew they were much at war among themselves—Mohegans, Wampanoags, Shawmuts, Nipmucs, Narragansetts. He strove to keep peace, but when alliances shifted and violence was afoot he was ready to counsel the English about their most realistic course of action. In the Pequot War of 1637 he became a military adviser, relying on the accurate information he gathered from scouts about the Pequot positions at Mystic. When the slaughter of Connecticut colonists seemed imminent, he specifically appraised the type of ambush and killing that would be needed. The events of the Pequot War persuaded the men of Massachusetts that they had a shrewd agent in their exiled heretic. From the time of his going into the Narragansett country and his fruitless efforts to avert the tragic uprising of Indians in King Philip's War in the year 1676, he came as close to the peoples of those now-vanished cultures as anyone would ever be.

The town of Providence found its roll of fugitives from the Bay extended in 1638 by the arrival of Mrs. Anne Hutchinson with some of her followers.[51] She had been a prominent and admiring member of John Cotton's congregation at St. Botolph's in England and had followed him to the new Boston, where she and her adherents became embroiled in an obscure controversy about the place of the law and of good works in the obedience of the converted Christian. She and her circle were called Antinomians, because they were sufficiently *exaltés* to discount the evidential value of living up to the moral law in the process whereby forgiven sinners remained right with God. Her reliance on the gift of the Spirit put her in the company of those who downgraded the good works of the regenerate as a "nothing," whereas the moral casuists of central English Puritanism set some store by the hard grind of doing good, seeing it as an outward sign of an authentic rebirth.[52]

Here Williams was on the side of the official Calvinist Boston theology. His view of the person and saving work of Christ was always close to theirs so far as it concerned the change wrought in the life of the chosen by Christ's life, death, resurrection, and gift of the Spirit. He believed the predestinate would and should continue in good works. But predictably he did not let this stand in the way of his receiving this false female prophet, as entitled "in civil things" to the hospitality of Providence. Curiously, Mrs. Hutchinson's type of elevated piety united her for more than a short time, on both sides of the Atlantic, with John Cotton, her spiritual adviser. When she was condemned by cooler heads, Cotton drew back. To Williams she must have had the appealing quality of the eccentric and persistent. Such characters usually excited his sympathy—if they could think at all clearly. Mrs. Hutchinson, however, was to pass out of the Narragansetts country and perish at the hands of Indians in 1643 in the Dutch settlements to the north of Manhattan.[53]

Sweet news came to Roger Williams in 1640. The Long Parliament was meeting in England. The Scots were seeking closer alliance with English Puritans. John Pym's centre party was coming to effective power in the House of Commons.[54] The main actors in the parliamentary drama had known him when he was chaplain to the Masham family at Otes in 1629. The younger Harry Vane, who had been in New England and returned in a state of some disillusion after the Anne Hutchinson affair, was one of those who could be expected to show sympathy for the irregular enterprise of the Providence pioneers. The time had come for action. Providence Plantations could plead little legal status apart from *de facto* property claims ceded by Indians and the existence of a town compact. These qualifications did not amount to much in the eyes of the Council of Charles I, any more than Laud could be expected to consider Williams's co-sectaries to be a church. Parliament might be persuaded to judge otherwise, especially if legislation could be enacted to tolerate varying consciences on religious questions. Why not try to obtain a charter, or patent, for the Providence settlement, when news from England told him that his friends were likely at last to be in the ascendant? Williams probably knew from local intelligence that the Bay Colonists had designs of their own. He would have to go home and pull strings. He could do this among his old friends in the lobbies of the parliament and in country houses. Unless he went, he might be forestalled by Massachusetts, where two thoughts were abroad—the extension of the Bay's political authority to cover Providence, with the island of Aquidneck and the Narragansetts country, and the promotion of their own polity as a "model of church and civil power" in England. A Messianic hope underlay the second thought; they wondered whether they had been chosen by the Lord to prepare in New England a foretaste of the rule of the saints, the prelude to the millennium. John Cotton, in particular, believed the time might have arrived for this Western dawning to grow to full day in God's chosen England.[55]

Roger Williams sailed in May 1643, from one of the Dutch ports to the south. He spoke Dutch[56] and wisely chose this point of departure. Passage through hostile Boston would have been awkward if not impossible. During the voyage he put his first book in order for the printer in London. *A Key into the Language of America* could help to ingratiate him with all parties on arrival. He could, at the same time, have been musing on the theme of his second and most famous work, the long tract called *The Bloudy Tenent of Persecution for Cause of Conscience*. This book on the "bloody tenent" was more than a contribution to the pamphlet war already raging over liberty of conscience; it was a blow, struck by a representative of the underground Separatist tradition, against the vulnerable common front of the temporarily allied Presbyterian and Independent factions. They had jointly approved of the Westminster Assembly of Divines, called together by Parliament to prepare a restructured national Church.

Williams addressed his *Bloudy Tenent* to the Parliament. He followed it up with a searching pamphlet called *Queries of Highest Consideration*, addressed to the leaders of the Independent group in the Westminster Assembly. Between the lines he was telling the Parliament that a national church was no church. Only the elect could belong to the Church; nobody could be born or legislated into it. More explicitly, in his *Queries* he was questioning whether any set of "divines" could presume to know what form the Church should take. Christ alone could and would reveal right forms of worship and give the Church real power again, but this revelation had not yet been vouchsafed to any ecclesiastical party.

The Bloudy Tenent was burned by the hangman on the orders of a parliament still dominated by Presbyterians and was thus guaranteed a second printing and a wide circulation. Its anonymity deceived very few. It came hot from the most able spokesman of the Separatist religious underworld. Vituperative opponents took it to task. The English Independents, led by Thomas Goodwin and his fellow-authors of the *Apologeticall Narration*, looked on its argument with more cautious disfavour. The *Narration* they had written was addressed to the members of the Westminster Assembly in hope of a limited toleration that might give them time to erect a state-endorsed Congregational church polity instead of a Presbyterian.[57] They were in touch with John Cotton and earnestly sought in England what seemed to have arrived already in Massachusetts, a Congregational uniformity guarded by the civil magistrates. Williams aimed his *Queries* straight at them. He looked for permitted religious diversity, as found at Providence.

The radical from across the Atlantic turned out to be aligned with the winning side. Sectarianism, forced below the surface of English religious life in the reign of James I and of Charles I, was already re-emerging among certain powerful country families, in Parliament, in the City of London, and in the Army. Before he crossed the seas he had known London well, and he knew the radical sympathies of some of his former patrons and intimates in East Anglia. The Hampdens and Cromwells, their relatives and legal cronies, were already active behind the scenes. Forward families of merchants, known for their radical theological tendencies, were busy in what had been the world of his boyhood. Sir Harry Vane the Younger, the organiser of the emerging "war party" that prevailed after John Pym died on December 8, 1643,[58] gave him hospitality. What better advice was available for his purpose? In the winter months be busied himself in getting supplies of fuel for London's domestic fires, when coal shortages followed the cutting-off of communications with Newcastle.[59] His connections in London and the country made him a suitable person to serve the Parliament in this way.

By the autumn of 1644 he was able to return to Providence with the desired charter. The tide of power had turned in England. Williams rode home to New England on the resultant wave. He was hardly greeted with delight at Boston; but this time he could pass through without danger. He came armed with a letter of commendation bearing the signatures of leading peers in the Council of State and of radical members of parliament. The new-found strength of this group proved an unanswerable plea for safe conduct.[60] Boston's well-briefed elite knew that their own two representatives,[61] Thomas Weld and Hugh Peter, had been unsuccessful in their attempt to gain authority for Massachusetts over Providence and its adjacent lands. Williams had frustrated them cleverly by a well-timed exploitation of the changing English balance of power.

In the years that followed, the various pioneers of new settlements at Portsmouth, Warwick, and Newport fell out with Williams on numerous issues. Williams thought of himself as the founder of Providence Plantations and originator of the system whereby the first subsequent arrivals and those who came later received land, under his personal entitlement from Indian grants.[62] His patriarchal stance led him into misunderstandings and disputes with William Arnold and his son Benedict, in the Pawtuxet area—and into more prolonged and serious bickering with the quarrelsome William Harris.

Many of the settlers were Baptists; not at this period immersionists,[63] but believers in adult baptism by pouring. Williams joined them temporarily by undergoing baptism by affusion in early 1638 at Providence, but did not remain a member of their church. He came to doubt the validity of what had been done. There was a streak of high churchman in him; he was vexed by the problems of legitimate succession and duly empowered officiants. Roger Williams turned Seeker; he walked alone, looking for the coming of "new apostles" as effectual and unmistakably endowed as St. Paul. Williams first doubted the Church of England and rejected it, then the Presbyterian, Congregational, Baptist, and Quaker doctrines. These parties touched his life at sore points, in chronological order. Each in turn was linked with successive phases of political influence in Old and then in New England. He detested each in turn—and came to be detested in their eyes. When the Quakers came to Rhode Island in the mid-1650's Harris took up with their cause, with the result that political and property matters at Pawtuxet and in the vicinity became inextricable from religion. The Quakers, like the Baptists before them, attacked Roger Williams as a lone wolf and a proud spirit. As he advanced in age he became more and more testy. He regarded all these important little men as land-hungry and self-satisfied—another contemptible establishment in the making. Williams fixed his attention on Christ's deliberate choice of voluntary destitution and self-denial. His attitude can be construed as cranky protest or as *imitatio Christi*. Both elements are there. The constant irritability spoils the discipleship. The discipleship redeems the irritation.

No longer in the conventional sense a clergyman—he rejected the title because it suggested the unholy alliance of Church and state—Williams became a modest Providence landowner. He went on preaching to the Indians and to his fellow colonists who would listen. But after his first English journey in 1643 and 1644 he said the ministry of the Word should be free, not for hire.[64] In his writings he appealed to the evidence that the earliest apostles worked with their own hands to gain their living. He himself took to trade. With the senior John Winthrop he had acquired two small islands in the Narragansett Bay—Patience and Prudence.[65] He set up a trading post at Cocumscoussoc, near the present town of Wickford, and ran goats on a small island there, just off shore. He traded useful items with the Indians of the hinterland, but never enriched himself by selling alcohol and firearms as others did.[66] He could visit Providence in his small boat and easily go across in good weather to the towns of Portsmouth and Newport on the main island.

In 1646 the stormy ideas and personality of Samuel Gorton[67] invaded the Rhode Island scene. He had already unsettled Boston, where he claimed to be a loyal son of the Church of England, by his heterodox view of the person of Christ, his disparagement of sacraments and covenanted church fellowships, and his vehement contempt for magistrates.[68] He came to Providence, where Williams found his notions an embarrassment. The Baptists at Newport and Portsmouth were also shaken by his presence. He eventually left to settle the town and district of Warwick. Such arrivals contributed to the prevalent evaluation of the religious life of Rhode Island when looked at from over the fences of Massachusetts, Plymouth, and the Connecticut valley. From their tidy gardens the place seemed full of spreading weeds and stinking rubbish.

How could unity be forged out of this diversified society? The terms of the charter Williams had brought gave a basis for union to the four towns of Providence, Portsmouth, Newport, and Warwick. Generally speaking the auspices were not favourable. Only John Clarke,[69] the Baptist leader in Newport, was a faithful friend. William Coddington of Portsmouth, a bold and assertive man, was not easily won for the idea. He was inclined to pursue his own aim of dominating Rhode Island by making a unilateral submission to Massachusetts.[70] Gorton, in Warwick, actually tried, by going to London, to attach the Narragansett shore to Charles I.[71] Williams, in a term of office as chief magistrate, from the time of his return from London, fought all these divisive trends. On May 19, 1647, representatives of all four towns assented to the charter. Rhode Island had received the framework of its subsequent statehood.[72]

As Cromwell rose to power, and with the execution of Charles I in 1649, the young colony had to consider what new form of patronage would be appropriate at home. William Coddington, sensing opportunity, went to England and courted the attention of the opportunist political Independent, Sir Arthur Haselrig. He succeeded in getting himself appointed life governor[73] over the island of Aquidneck, now Rhode Island. The silent *coup d'état* upset the leaders of the Providence and Newport communities. The town of Warwick was threatened with incorporation into the Plymouth colony. At Pawtuxet, under William Arnold, there were fresh moves in the direction of a submission being made to Massachusetts, and for a time it seemed the union of the four towns might disintegrate.

In this uncertain time the property owners of Providence, Warwick, and the island of Aquidneck acted jointly to send two men, Roger Williams and John Clarke,[74] to England, in November 1651, to seek confirmation of their charter. Their choice of John Clarke proved to be politic. He and two of his friends, Obadiah Holmes and John Crandall, both Baptists, had visited another aged Baptist, William Witter, near the Massachusetts town of Lynn in July 1651.[75] During the visit they had openly maintained the Baptist position and were brought before the Boston court and sentenced to whipping. John Clarke penned the story of their sentences and punishments in a book called *Ill Newes from New-England*,[76] rounding off his tale with a lengthy polemic in favour of separating the spiritual and secular powers. Now that tolerationists were influential at court in Cromwell's England, the persecution seemed a heaven-sent bargaining counter in the quest for a new charter. The testy nineteenth-century Congregational historian, Henry Martyn Dexter, even claimed that the three Rhode Islanders left Newport "to obtain a little persecution in Massachusetts,"[77] but the evidence hardly justifies this suspicion.

Clarke wrote his *Ill Newes* rapidly. It came out in England in 1652. The title page declared that "while Old England is becoming new, New-England is become Old." The tone and content were calculated to appeal to the Baptists and Fifth-Monarchy Men,[78] militant visionaries who became stronger in the successive parliaments and the Council of State under the Protectorate. The concluding part of Clarke's tract takes a clear Baptist position and is fervently millenarian. He could count on a good hearing.

Roger Willams, on the other hand, did not linger after the

spring of 1654. By then his patron, Sir Harry Vane, who had
been still influential when he and Clarke arrived, had fallen
from grace and office. Williams was no orthodox Baptist; nor,
by this time, did he expect the millennium in the same way
as the more high-flown "saints." He knew Baptists and millenarians were well settled in power in both England and
Ireland. The diplomatic work, under the circumstances, could
be better handled by Clarke. Williams could go back to America
to restore his dwindling fortunes for he had sold his trading
post to pay for the voyage.[79] He was eager for reunion with his
wife, who faced spiritual loneliness, and he was concerned for
the welfare of their six children.

Williams wrote his *Experiments of Spiritual Life and Health*[80]
in order to help his wife in her spiritual trials. Here we find
the best clue to Roger Williams's inner life. Like all his
writings, it needs to be read and understood in the knowledge
that its author tried to fix his inward gaze on Christ, and
Christ alone, as guide. The *Experiments* is not another Puritan
manual of dutiful piety. Its subject is not the state of the
soul, but Jesus.

While in England he made two other contributions to the
debate about toleration and liberty of religious conscience and
practice—his *Fourth Paper, Presented by Major Butler*[81] and
The Bloody Tenent Yet More Bloody.[82] The second of these
replied largely and with considerable tedium to John Cotton,
who had replied to the earlier *Bloudy Tenent* by writing *The
Bloudy Tenent, Washed, And made white in the bloud of the
Lambe* (1647). These and the other writings of his second
visit to England reflect his inside knowledge of men and events
and his conversations with Vane, Cromwell, and John Milton—
then Latin Secretary of State.[83] The letters he addressed to
Mistress Anne Sadleir,[84] the daughter of his mentor, Sir Edward
Coke, were less deft, but their survival is a happy chance that
brings us closer to Williams as he was—loyal, loving, too
honest to be tactful.

Clarke did not follow Williams back to Rhode Island until

1663. He stayed on through all the switches in government under the late Protectorate. Finally he was successful in gaining the support of Charles II, when he returned to the throne and evidently was disposed to grant the largesse of toleration to Rhode Island, if only to pique Massachusetts. Clarke brought back a remarkable document, giving dissenters in the Rhode Island colonies the freedoms they were denied in England by the returning parliament of the cavaliers.

In London Williams had been in touch with a small group of Calvinistic "Seekers." They were dissatisfied with all visible forms of reformation in the Church and looked for Christ to come and restore His true ministry and sacraments. Williams never used the noun "Seeker" to describe himself, but he repeatedly calls Christians to the duties of seeking and searching. The "moderate" Calvinist group of Seekers with which he was associated were not prepared to accept the name except as a convenient tag attached by others to their movement. Even so, we can identify their ideas and activity with some accuracy through two tracts published in the 1650's—*A Sober Word to a Serious People* and *Strength in Weakness*. The author was their "principal apologist," John Jackson, of whose life little is known. Williams's earlier identification with their rising movement in the 1640's is attested to by several of his contemporaries, including the acute Scots Presbyterian, Robert Baillie,[85] and Richard Baxter.

The Seekers of this persuasion preached and prayed, but lived without sacraments pending explicit guidance from Christ about how to celebrate baptism and the Lord's Supper. In 1654, before Roger Williams left to return to America, this wing of the Seekers began to be infiltrated by proselytising bands of Quakers, the so-called "northern people," who came as missionaries from Westmorland, Cumberland, Lancashire, and Yorkshire, proclaiming that Christ was born in them, that they had the Light and were the saints destined to bear rule in the Kingdom.[86]

From that time forward Williams had special personal rea-

sons for disliking Quakerism and by 1657 they had arrived
in Rhode Island. His own convictions led him to recognize
their right to propagate their doctrines within the civil community of the colony; but he was determined to fight them
with every legitimate form of public controversy.

Many years still intervened before he could cope with the
Quakers at close quarters. Meanwhile, beginning in September
1656, he accepted a three-year term of office as president of the
colony and was again involved in internal politics. By contrast
with his high diplomatic mission at the metropolis of Europe
he found himself facing the squabbles and backbiting of a
few hundred frontier families in four rough-hewn towns hemmed
in by brush and seashore.

Coddington had submitted again to Rhode Island in March
of 1656. His patrons among the English grandees of the Independent party had been eclipsed. But in the Pawtuxet strip of
land William Arnold and his followers continued obdurate
against the personal influence of Williams. Many issues were
involved in the conflict. Sometimes they crystallised in litigation,
as in the odd affair of Richard Chasmore, who was required
by Williams to present himself to the Providence court on a
charge of bestiality.[87] We can sense Williams's sympathies turning
back, in matters of legal and political order, towards the standards of the notable common lawyers he had known in his youth.
In his struggles with the dissentients at Pawtuxet, with certain
Providence families, with William Harris and the Quakers,
his deeper loyalties tended to return toward old friends in
England and Massachusetts. He had more in common with
the solidity and clarity of those "old Orthodox men," whose
central Calvinist beliefs were like his own. Their great tradition
contrasted more than favourably with self-important small fry
of Rhode Island. He had fought English magistrates over the
cause of "conscience"; but he shared their religious values and
their respect for the ancient precedents of the Common Law.
Williams had staged a revolt of faith. In the order of politics
he was no anarchist. He was more than happy to defend the

rights of educated oligarchies against social and economic egalitarians—thrusting nobodies.

In 1658, William Arnold also made submission again to the government of Rhode Island. Five years later John Clarke triumphantly brought back a new charter. Roger Williams was then about sixty. He seemed to himself to have lived out the significant part of his days. Baptists, then Quakers, came to dominate the local scene. He found himself feeling like a relic of another day—an old man with a chip on his shoulder and fixed ideas in his head. The money he spent on his English journey was not reimbursed. Though he had sold his trading house at Wickford Point, at least once a month he travelled back there to preach to Indians and settlers. He also preached at his Providence house. But in 1660 he told the younger Winthrop, who was then governor in Connecticut: "Your candle and mine draws towards its end."[88]

In reality he then still had twenty-three years to live. Tiresome inactivity lay ahead, with occasional travel between the settlements, correspondence with the younger Winthrop and with some of his old friends. He was still at odds with William Harris over tracts of land he thought to have been annexed illegally from Indians.[89] We tend to judge these years by surviving letters, which suggest a life of varied business and social intercourse. For most of the time it was probably not so. Williams needed money;[90] he needed paper;[91] he craved books and the latest news from England. By the twentieth century Williams has become a folk hero. Yet for almost two centuries after his death and before his rediscovery by liberals, he was either misrepresented as a Baptist or more justifiably remembered in local Quaker circles as a learned but boring old gentleman who lived in the past and had been rude to their missionaries.

Rhode Island adherents of that new and dynamic sect could not forgive him for making common cause against them, intellectually, with the Massachusetts clergy. The Quakers had been harshly persecuted in the Bay.[92] George Fox himself visited Providence in 1672. Roger Williams challenged him to public debate. The challenge apparently did not reach him. Anyone who enjoys clashes between explosive personalities and can savour theological venom may regret that these two exceptional men never met. The gauntlet was picked up by three of Fox's disciples—John Stubbs, John Burnyeat, and William Edmundson. The seventy-year-old Williams met them in discussion at Newport, then at Providence. Hostile Quakers and their sympathisers were prominent in the audiences. The prolix book that came out of these queer disputations, *George Fox Digg'd out of His Burrowes*,[93] recorded the clash in wearisome detail, seasoned by literary insult. However, the book does not ramble, as has sometimes been alleged. It keeps severely to the structure set out in advance by its author and covers a range of theological matters with considerable controversial skill. Its pattern and development cannot be grasped without reference to a book it attacks unmercifully, and, if logic means anything, with good reason. This was a book called *The Great Mistery of the Great Whore*,[94] by George Fox and Edward Burrough, a tendentious and canting collection of Quaker rejoinders to many of the Quakers' critics. It is necessary to plough through all this stuff in order to make a balanced estimate of the Rhode Island debates. As a final extended flourish, George Fox counterattacked Williams in a book that has become a rarity—*A New England Fire-Brand Quenched*.[95]

Not that Williams was quenchable. . . . Many an otherwise idle hour between 1672 and 1676 went into the writing of his account of his battle with the Quakers. He was back fighting, in a new field. At last he could align himself publicly with such respected Calvinist scholars as John Owen[96] and Richard Baxter.[97] He respectfully addressed the book to them both and to their fellow "orthodox" theologians. He wrote a further flowery and honorific prefatory letter to King Charles II. In his argument with the Quakers he indignantly repudiated the charge that he was ever a convinced republican or had advocated the execution of Charles I.[98] The cruelest touch for Baptists and Quakers in Rhode Island followed the applause the book received from leading clergy and magistrates at Boston, where it was printed without charge to Williams by the good offices of the governor.[99]

In 1675 and 1676 New England Indians, led by the tragic sachem Philip from the region round Plymouth, staged their desperate revolt called King Philip's War. Williams was in touch with Philip and other Indian leaders until fighting broke out.[100] His letters to Boston show the weariness and sense of the inevitable he felt at the prospect of the coming disaster. The English were his countrymen. He could see the situation through their eyes. Treaties had been broken. Treachery was treachery. But Williams also knew the Indians were far from comprehending these European logical modes of thought and legal traditions.[101] On their side they felt eaten up by the rage and panic of being consistently misunderstood—and exploited by unscrupulous individual settlers. When war broke out Williams assisted the army of the united colonies. He served in the fighting as a captain of the Providence militia.

In December 1675, a force of a thousand men from Boston engaged the Indians in their fort in a swamp west of Kingston in the Narragansett country. The fort fell and about a thousand Indians and two hundred and fifty English died. Rhode Island forces did not participate, but other Indians took and burned the towns of Warwick and Providence in 1676. The house of Roger Williams was burned,[102] with his books and papers.

For the last seven years of his life he depended on his son. He was physically weak, yet mentally active. The Massachusetts authorities gave him permission to come back into their territory so long as he did not spread his peculiar opinions. Characteristically, he declined to use the liberty offered. He worked to put in order for the press some of his sermons to the colonists —they have apparently been lost, though some headings in manuscript form survive.[103] He was still short of paper and money. He was deputed by the town of Providence to put its dilapidated civil records in order after King Philip's War.[104] He wrote of himself, as late as 1679, as being "now near to fourscore years of age, yet (by God's mercy) of sound understanding and memory."[105] But by 1682, writing to Governor Bradstreet at Boston about the possible publication of his discourses to the English colonists of the Narragansetts, he said he was "old and weak and bruised (with rupture and colic) and lameness on both my feet."[106] In the same letter he referred, as he had so often done before, to the news from old England. "But all these are but sublunaries, temporaries and trivials," he added. "Eternity (O eternity!) is our business; to which end I am most unworthy to be your willing and faithful servant, Roger Williams."[107]

He died on some unrecorded date between January 18 and March 15, 1683.

3

Early Influences: The Separatist Fringe

WHEN ROGER WILLIAMS left Massachusetts for the life of the wilderness in 1636, he had become what his detractors called a "rigid Separatist."[1] Their recollection of him when he had been with them in England had been of a captious member of their Puritan brotherhood, but although there had been whispers of his discontent with a nonseparating position, it does not seem they expected, in 1629 or 1630, that he would run back into the arms of the disruptive and socially inconspicuous Separatists. After his transition to New England he moved, nevertheless, in that direction. His respect for some of the Separatist martyrs and exiles of the closing years of Queen Elizabeth can be documented. The remnant of their community in London made common cause, in some measure, in 1616, with Henry Jacob, the founder of a nonseparating covenanted Congregation in Southwark, on the south bank of the Thames.[2] Splits and debates rent the group, partly over the lawfulness of hearing preachers in the parishes of the Church of England; partly over infant baptism, when John Smith, the father of the English General Baptist movement "rebaptised" himself and others, leaving controversial writings on the subject after his death in 1612.[3]

Close study of Roger Williams's works shows that he was aware, like most orthodox Puritan "old Nonconformists," of the teachings of the Separatist fringe and of their rebuttal by more conservative Puritans, who refused to follow them in denying the power of the monarch in ordering the affairs of the Church. History written about the religious developments in England between 1590 and 1640, especially in the nineteenth century, depicted Anglican, Presbyterian, Independent, and Baptist communities as already in existence. In fact the lines did not yet run in this way. What came to be parties were only opinions, within a "solidary Puritanism," determined by lay and clerical resistance to the encroachment of the crown and the bishops on the "reformed" Church of England and the Common Law courts.[4] When James I came to the throne in 1603, the presumed year of Williams's birth, the Millenary Petition was presented to the new king as a general expression of the doctrinal position and social demands of these Puritan "old Nonconformists," as they came to be called. They were united by resistance and negation. Their conflicting parties were to become differentiated out only with the victory of their common cause in the Long Parliament, after 1640.[5]

The "Old Puritans' " negative attitude to those who dominated Church and civil government, their "betters," was not so strong, however, as their recoil from the name of the notorious Robert Browne.[6] That Elizabethan individualist, who had denied the power of the crown in the government of the Church, had gone to the further length of gathering conventicles "of the worthiest, were they never so few,"[7] without waiting for the permission of the state. Browne's real sin in the eyes of the old Puritans was that he tore the robe of Christendom. They did not use those exact words, but their own aim was to achieve control of the state in order to make a further religious reformation possible by using its machinery. Browne's direct action seemed to them to have been treason, not only to the Queen, but also to their own respectable and patient effort. None of them wanted to be called a Brownist. The name had the sting of guilt by association. They were equally averse to having their movement in any way mentioned alongside the name of Henry Barrow,[8] who was executed in London in 1593, as was his friend John Greenwood. Barrow's style of attack had been even more disrespectful than Browne's. Besides, before his conversion, he had been a "tosspot" and a patron of fancy ladies. Barrow had spurned Browne's name before his execution, on the ground that Browne had come back to the Church of England and recanted. The old Nonconformists, the great middle-of-the-road Puritans of the type of Perkins, Deering, Sibbes, Gooch, and Ames,[9] had refused to be called Brownists. Browne had, they believed, undermined the very idea that there should be a Church of England. Roger Williams, by 1631, had come to have the gravest doubts about the idea of a national Church.

Williams's psychological progress, through youth to social success, was a prelude to his later defiant acceptance of the obloquy of those Separatist Netherlands exiles and English extremists, whose social reputation was at best, poor. In tracing what happened to him, some exploration of the wider background of the period 1603–1640 will be required in relation to his own development and promise.

Williams, a Londoner and the son of a merchant tailor, all his life felt close to his birthplace—the greatest city and port of Europe. Men in trade remained his friends and allies. When he was a boy the roads from towns like Norwich and Bristol brought businessmen into his family circle. The depression in the cloth trade during the first half of the seventeenth century[10] may have affected his father's trade. One of his brothers became a "Turkey merchant."[11] The opening up of Mediterranean markets was connected with the stopping of profitable outlets on the continent during the Thirty Years War, 1618–1648. Frustration and anti-Romanism flowed together, with an undercurrent of thwarted enterprise. As plunder of Spanish fleets under Elizabeth gave way to American colonisation,[12] men of Williams's class also became anxious over the eventual disposition of the wealth of the Church at home.[13] The conscientious activity of archbishops like Bancroft[14] and Laud[15] struck them as being the raising of the head of the wounded Roman dragon in England; they contemplated bitterly what might happen to business if alienated revenues of the Church were permanently redirected by the activity of a conscientious episcopate,[16] out of the control of lay patrons.

On his mother's side Williams descended[17] from the Pemberton family of St. Albans in Hertfordshire. His uncle and godfather, Roger Pemberton, was a landowner. At one time he was High Sheriff of his county. Sir James Pemberton, another uncle, became Lord Mayor of London in 1611. He was a goldsmith. The goldsmiths were predecessors of the London bankers. Finance and trade were there on both sides of the Williams family. The landed gentry stood in the background of his boyhood through his godfather (after whom he was probably named). It is fanciful to think that Williams was a poor London boy who made good. From his youth he is more likely to have been aware of his "middle station" in English life. The religious and political power game—being played all over the country by merchants, gentry and lawyers was probably raging in the background of his boyhood. With such connections it is harder to represent the young Williams as sympathetic with the policies of Archbishop Bancroft, or an uncomplaining supporter of moderate ceremonies and the surplice in Church.[18]

The first extant letter Roger Williams wrote after his arrival in the New World suggested strongly that his Puritanism and individualism had been part of his makeup from about the age of nine. In this letter,[19] written from Plymouth, he discussed with Governor John Winthrop of Boston a point in church order. This concerned the age when it was fitting for a man to assume office in a church as a ruling elder. The question belonged to internal debate among Calvinists, who were aware of Calvin's fourfold division of the ministry into Pastors, Teachers, Elders, and Deacons laid down for the church of Geneva:

Among other pleas for a young counsellor (which I fear will be too light in the balance of the Holy One) you argue from twenty-five in a Church Elder. 'Tis a riddle as yet to me whether you mean any elder in these New English churches; or (which I believe not) old English—disorderly functions, from whence our Jehovah of armies more and more redeemed his Israel—; or the Levites, who served from twenty-five to fifty, (*Numbers 8.24*); or myself, but a child in everything (though in Christ called and persecuted even in and out of my father's house these twenty years). I am no Elder in any church, no more nor so much as your worthy self, nor even shall be, if the Lord please to grant my desires that I may intend what I long after, the natives' souls; and yet, if I at present were, I should be, in the days of my vanity, nearer upward of thirty than twenty-five.

Williams was reminding his correspondent that Winthrop had argued for admittance to the eldership at twenty-five in discussions on this subject at Boston. He said he did not know whether the argument was based on the current practice in New England or in old. He expressed hope that in old England the Church was being gradually liberated from the shackles of old precedent by the progress of further reformation, so that entry to the eldership at twenty-five did not have binding force. Then he came to a possible argument from the Book of Leviticus—the position of the Levite in the Mosaic arrangements for temple officers. Finally Williams asked whether Winthrop had in mind his own suitability for such an office. He disavowed his own capacity, taking the word elder literally to mean what it said. He called himself still "a child." Then followed the enigmatic reference to his own childhood, which has usually been treated out of context. "In Christ called," means that he had been given faith to trust that God had chosen him for salvation. But what is meant by "persecuted in and out of my father's house"? Throughout his writings Williams regarded voluntarily accepted suffering as a genuine sign of God's choice or election. He often said that since Christ was persecuted, his followers would necessarily be persecuted if they were to become witnesses. He was a literalist. He knew

that the Greek word for a witness was literally "martyr." In
some way, since his intense boyhood religious experience, he
appears to have suffered for his faith. Possibly, in such a household, his parents and family shared his faith. When he left
home to go to school at Charterhouse and to study at Cambridge,
the same difficulties may have attended him. Even on the less
likely supposition that his father ran him out of the house
for holding views contrary to the father's own, the analysis
holds; he seems, in some way, to have withstood opposition and
hardship for what he believed. The linkage of the idea of witness
and suffering with Williams's desire not to be an office holder
in a local congregation, but to be an apostle, a missionary, a
man sent to gain "the natives' souls"[20] testified, when the letter
was written, at New Plymouth in about 1632, to the underlying
continuity between his experiences in early youth and his desire to be a witness. Roger Williams saw his vocation as a mobile
preacher rather than supervisor of a stationary Christian community. The Williams of youth looked forward to the Williams
of maturity, the person and example of Christ being his guide.

Some have thought that because biblical and theological
considerations ruled his decisions in this way, Williams was
after all no lawyer, no politician. Vocationally speaking, he may
not have been either, but he became a shrewd legal tactician
and political infighter. Given his family background and path
of advancement, his early years in London seem to account
for his familiarity with the life of young men who came up
from the towns and shires to learn the law at the Inns of Court,
the "third university" of England.[21] The outrageous element in
his later controversial style recalls the heavy blows given and
received in courtroom exchanges. Ironic thrusts penetrate the
logic and the scripture texts.

The religious experience of his boyhood can hardly be understood apart from that pragmatic world. The twentieth century
thinks of piety as compartmentalised away from practical life.
For Williams it was all in one piece. Another revealing passage
concerning his boyhood faith makes the point. It forms part of

his address "To the People called Quakers," prefacing *George Fox digg'd out of his Burrowes*[22]:

> The truth is (as Edmund Burroughs and others of you say of your-selves), from my childhood (now above three score years) the Father of lights and mercies touched my soul with a love to himself, to his only-begotten, the true Lord Jesus, to his Holy Scriptures, &c. His infinite wisdom hath given me to see the city, court and country, the schools and universities of my native country, to converse with some Turks, Jews, papists, and all sorts of Protestants, and by books to know the affairs and religions of all countries, &c.

(The use of the breathless "&c." is a badge of Williams's style.) Much of the quotation is Calvinist Puritanism blended with summarised autobiography. "Truth" for the early Quakers meant authentic religious knowledge, inward revelation from God. Yet the stress in Williams's testimony was not on what had happened to him, but on the One who did it. He had been objectively "touched" from beyond himself by the majestic Calvinist God. Even love of God was infused from outside by God himself, to whom that love returned. The "true Lord Jesus" was so described because the Quakers, according to Williams, had discovered a false Christ, an inward, subjective, not an outward, objective Saviour. With a rapid backward look, the old man summarised his past, given to him by predestination from the all seeing wisdom orthodox Calvinists believed to govern every event and survey all creation and every life unceasingly. London; the contacts with the royal court of King James I when Williams worked with the Lord Chief Justice, Edward Coke, in the court of Star Chamber; these were first recalled. The "country" was the world of his uncle and of his own many contacts with the gentry. He saw himself at Charterhouse and Cambridge, among scholars and learned godly preachers. What travels or what meetings in London may be indicated by the mention of Turks, Jews, and Papists, we have no way of telling, but we can well believe his sociable nature and family contacts brought him into touch with the many types of Protestants he mentions in his books. His wide reading,

known from allusions in his books, makes his claim to acquaintance with geography and comparative religion quite credible.
The variegated career of Roger Williams was, in his own mind,
wrought in one piece—with the Eternal Son of God, Christ, as
the artificer who did the work.

When he says God gave him "a love to his Holy Scriptures"
we reach the heart of Williams's life and thought. He several
times declared that the sword of steel issued from the smith's
and the cutler's shop, but that the sword of the Lord Jesus
issued out of his mouth.[23] The Geneva Bible from which he
generally quoted, or rather the original languages that lay
behind it, he regarded as the last testament of the Lord Jesus,
indications for the carrying out of His will in the world after
He had left it and before His return.[24] Every part of the Bible
to Williams was the Word, issuing out of the mouth of the
Lord Jesus, only now in written form. "That word literal is
sweet," he wrote to the younger Winthrop in 1651, "as it is the
field where the mystical word or treasure, Christ Jesus, lies
hid."[25] Antithesis between the literal and the mystical must
not suggest to us that Williams was a mystic in the technical
or Catholic sense of that word. He simply indicated that grasping
the mysterious meaning of the Bible is no easy matter. Perry
Miller believed that he had found the clue to Williams's thought
in a habit of allegorising away the more knotty parts
of the Old Testament, treating the old Israel as a "type," or
foreshadowing of the new Israel, the Christian Church.[26] He
did this, of course, but his adversary John Cotton did the same.
Calvin, their common teacher, had thought in this way about
the termination of the old dispensation by the new and the
gathering up of some of the old order into the new. The old
was thus a "shadow," or prefiguring, of the fulfilment in Christ.
Indeed, in the New Testament itself, the argument is implicit in
the thought of the apostle Paul (in letters he wrote to Corinth
and the Galatian churches; *I Corinthians 10*; *Galatians 4.21–31*).
The Gospel according to St. Matthew, in its total structure,
and in the contrast between Moses and Christ in the sermon
on the Mount, attempts to show that the old covenant, or

testament, has been annulled, and that in Jesus a certain
completion, preparatory to the end of the world, has displaced
the partial prototypes of Old Testament religion. The Old
Testament has a hidden meaning, therefore, but it is made
explicit in Jesus. The main charter for this kind of biblical
interpretation is a New Testament writing Williams used repeatedly—the Letter to the Hebrews. Here, in the Christian
Bible itself, was a book that took up the "Platonic" method
of the rabbis in the Hellenistic synagogues and announced
that the end of the world was dawning and that the old law, the
sacred Torah of the Jewish covenant, contained only "a shadow
of the good things to come, not the very image of the things"
(*Hebrews 10.1*). The question for Williams and Cotton, as for
Calvin before them, was not whether a typological principle of
interpretation should be used. That it should was clear in
the Bible itself. They had simply to decide how to use it.
Hence, for them all, the literal word, pointing as it did to the
first coming of Christ and to the second rôle they expected he
would assume in the end of the world, contained a mystical
treasure that had to be dug out. Typological method was no
personal fad of Williams. On the other hand, his denial that
the sword of steel should be used to defend and uphold the
Church (Christ's realm) entailed a breach with the assumptions of mediaeval Europe and with the actual practice of
Calvinist, Lutheran, and Zwinglian Protestantism. Williams
argued that

Moses in the Old Testament was Christ's servant, yet Moses, being but
a servant, dispensed his power by carnal rites and ceremonies, laws,
rewards and punishments, in that holy nation, and that one land of
Canaan. But the Lord Jesus, the Son and Lord Himself, was come, to
bring the truth, and life, and substance of all those shadows, to break
down the partition wall between Jew and Gentile, and to establish the
Christian worship and kingdom in all nations of the world. Mr. Cotton
will never prove from any of the books and institutions of the New
Testament that unto those spiritual remedies applied by Jesus Christ
against spiritual maladies He added the help of the carnal sword.[27]

The appeal was to the New Testament itself to establish the principle involved (*Hebrews 3.5–6, Ephesians 2.13–18*). Williams went on to say:

If it appear (as evidently it doth) that this king (Jesus the King of Israel), wears his sword (the antitype of the Kings of Israel their swords) in his mouth, being a sharp two-edged sword, then the answer is as clear as the Sun, that scatters the clouds and darkness of the night.

Again Williams appealed to the Letter to the Hebrews (4.12). He was answering Cotton's claim that Christ "never abrogated the carnal sword in the New, which he appointed in the Old Testament," and he followed up with the reminder that

Master Cotton knows the profession of the Lord Jesus, *John 18,* that his kingdom was not earthly, and therefore his sword cannot be earthly; Master Cotton knows that Christ Jesus commanded a sword to be put up when it was drawn in the cause of Christ, and added a dreadful threatening, that all that take the sword (that is the carnal sword) for his cause, shall perish by it.

The idea that the Word of God is a "sharp two-edged sword" was drawn from the Book of Revelation (2.12) as well as the Letter to the Hebrews. We should think of Williams with his Bible open before him when he wrote. What he said cannot be understood without uncovering many such specific passages of both Old and New Testaments, which were constantly recombined and paraphrased to make his points. His prose was so saturated in this kind of allusion that it discourages those who are not thoroughgoing biblicists. The Letter to the Hebrews, among all the biblical books helps us best to trace the way he thought; but it is not enough to know that his method is "typological"; we have to follow Williams's ideas by referring back to the particular passages of the Bible he used and by trying to interpret their meaning on his terms.

The last book in the Bible, the Revelation of St. John the Seer, opens a way to understanding the element of openness, of hope and expectancy, that led Roger Williams to New England and eventually to Rhode Island. He did not go there to become the pioneer of a new political order, though that was a byproduct of his exile. He had in mind that he should, as he put it, "seek Jesus who was nailed to the gallows."[28] His reading of John's Apocalypse, of the book of Daniel, and (more oddly) the Song of Solomon, led him to share in the widespread anticipation that Christ would soon return to reign on earth. John's Revelation was probably written against the background of persecution of the early church in the Roman empire in the last decade of the first century. But it speaks of martyrdom, rejection, and persecution as necessary preludes to Christ's final liberation of those who live and suffer for Him, and those who have already died in His cause. The wars of religion in Europe and the persecutions and sufferings of the Reformation's martyrs had been described anew in the sixteenth century in this apocalyptic setting by John Foxe's *Acts and Monuments*, a book that was, for men like Williams, staple reading alongside the Bible itself. They had been brought up on its pages. The dilemma for them was to try to read the signs of the personal return of the ascended Christ in the confused struggles between Protestant and Catholic nations at the end of the sixteenth and the beginning of the seventeenth centuries.[29]

Speculation about the meaning of the parts of the Book of Revelation that refer to a thousand-year reign of Christ with his saints on earth[30] had been transmitted from Germany and the low countries by awareness of Martin Luther's hopes for the defeat of the Turk and the fall of the papacy. Luther branded the pope as antichrist, seeing in him the power of Satan, acting in the name of Jesus. The compilers of the *Magdeburg Centuries*, a sixteenth-century Lutheran record of the history of the Church, had viewed the future as a millennial kingdom. The Englishman John Bale,[31] as early as 1650, had used the closing verses of the thirteenth chapter of The Book of Revelation as a prediction of the suffering of the faithful churches, seen as a woman and her offspring, persecuted in the wilderness by a great dragon. Bale had been influenced by English translations of the German Anabaptist millenarian, Melchior Hofmann, who had made the same identification.

Foxe, by implication, had gone further and suggested in the

later editions of his huge work that the scene of Christ's
coming reign would in the first place be among his Englishmen.
In England, which had, so the British mediaeval chronicles
said, been the first foreign recipient of the good news of Christ's
first coming, the rule of the heavenly Christ with His saints
would be established when the Roman dragon had been cast
down, and England's purging away of the dregs of popery had
been thoroughly carried out. Fox urged Queen Elizabeth as
diplomatically as possible, to go forward with reformation for
the sake of hastening the desired end. The nonfulfilment of the
hopes he entertained led other Englishmen in the reigns of
James I and Charles I to seek the reasons for the delay.[32]

Two Cambridge teachers, Thomas Brightman[33] and Joseph
Mead,[34] kept speculation alive by preparing elaborate systems
of prediction and fulfilment based on Daniel, Revelation, and
the Song of Solomon (or Canticles). Their influence on a
generation of godly preachers in the parishes of England helps
to account for intense interest in the millennium, that comes to
the surface in sermons and tracts of the 1640's and 1650's; but
a parallel stream of millennial enthusiasm, in a somewhat different form and closer to what we find in Roger Williams,
may be traced among the Separatist minority. Some of the
distinguishing elements in it are found in the touching letter
which Williams wrote to the elder Winthrop, probably in
August 1636, soon after his banishment. Winthrop had asked
him six questions about his faith. These were fortunately included with the replies and give a particularly interesting summary of where the defector from Massachusetts stood. When
Winthrop asked him what he had gained by his "new-found
practices" he responded that he was trying to imitate Christ
for the sake of witnessing to His future coming:

> I confess my gains, cast up in man's exchange, are loss of friends,
> esteem, maintenance, &c.; but what was gain in that respect I desire to
> count loss for the excellency of the knowledge of Christ Jesus my Lord,
> &c. To His all-glorious name I know that I have gained the honour of
> one of His poor witnesses, though in sackcloth.
>
> To your beloved selves, and others of God's people yet asleep, this

witness, in the Lord's season at your waking, shall be prosperous, and the seed sown shall arise to the greater purity of the Kingdom and ordinances of the Prince of the kings of the earth.[35]

In two short paragraphs here Williams indirectly quoted both St. Paul (*Philippians 3.7–8*), and (*Revelation* [of John] *11.3*). He then invoked the image of the Church as a company of sleepy and inattentive virgins, who would be insufficiently prepared for the advent of the bridegroom, Christ (*Matthew 25.1–13*). After further explanations, full of allusions to the Book of Revelation, he answered Winthrop's inquiry "Are you not grieved that you have grieved so many?"

I must (and O that I had not cause) grieve, because so many of Zion's daughters see not and grieve not for their souls' defilements, and that so few bear John company in weeping after the unfolding of the seals, which only weepers are acquainted with.[36]

To many modern eyes such statements may look almost incomprehensible; but Winthrop knew what Williams meant. Jesus had told the women of Jerusalem that they wept at His crucifixion, but that they would rejoice when He returned to vindicate His cause, in the coming of the Kingdom of God in power. John, the author of the Apocalypse, had wept because he could not open the seven seals of a book that contained the symbolic keys to the mystery of the fall of the persecuting power and the coming of the Messiah as final judge and king (*Revelation 5.4–5*). Williams warned Winthrop that the New England churches were still at rest in a measure of prosperity and ease. He was sure they had not yet come out of the "Babylonish captivity" of the Church of England, the successor to the "Babylon" of the Church of Rome. Appealing to the Old Testament captivity of the people of Israel in Babylon, Williams named the penitential Psalms and other Psalms expressing the theme of triumph after suffering, as inspirations of his own separation in search of God's fully purged and restored Church:

Though you have come so far, yet you never came out of the wilderness to this day. Then, I beseech you, remember that yourselves, and so also many thousands of God's people, must yet mournfully read the

seventy-fourth, seventy-ninth, eightieth and eighty-ninth psalms, the
Lamentations, *Daniel 11*, and *Revelation 11, 12, 13*. And this, sir, I
beseech you do more seriously than ever, and abstract yourself with a
holy violence from the dung heap of this earth, the credit and comfort
of it, and cry to Heaven to remove the stumbling blocks, such idols,
after which sometimes the Lord will give his own Israel an answer.

Read in one way this is just a long sequence of texts; in another it is obedience to a vision. Asked about his own "spirit"
or attitude, and his aim, Williams went on:

> Concerning my spirit, as I said before, I could declaim against it, but
> whether the spirit of Christ Jesus, for whose visible kingdom and
> ordinances I witness, &c, or the spirit of Antichrist *(I John 4)* against
> whom only I contest, do drive me, let the Father of Spirits be pleased to
> search, and (worthy sir) be you also pleased by the word to search: and
> I hope you will find that as you say you do, I also seek Jesus who was
> nailed to the gallows, I ask the way to lost Zion, I witness what I
> believe I see patiently (the Lord assisting) in sackcloth, I long for the
> bright appearance of the Lord Jesus to consume the man of sin: I long
> for the appearance of the Lamb's wife also, New Jerusalem. . . .[38]

The verbs "search" and "seek" were already by 1636 highly
significant for Williams. He used them for the rest of his
life, together with the noun "search." He came to be described
as following "that sort of sect which we term Seekers."[39] The
leading English Puritan, Richard Baxter, could even refer to
him by 1656 as "the father of the Seekers in London,"[40] with
what degree of justice has to be determined. At the time of
his banishment he cannot have seemed to himself to have been
starting some new sect. His so-called "seekerism" sprang from
the mixture of willing suffering and millennial hope we find
among certain Separatists, with whom he had been in contact
through their writings and representatives, possibly even throughout his growth from boyhood to manhood.

Many Separatist groups in exile in the Netherlands in the
late sixteenth and early seventeenth centuries shared the
prevalent interpretation of the Song of Solomon as a picture of
the Church wandering in the wilderness, a conception Williams
often used. The book of Canticles was included in both the

Jewish and Christian Bibles as an allegory of the relationship between the Messiah and his people. It is an erotic cycle of poems, deliberately thus given a hidden meaning for the sake of apologetic and devout meditation. In the ancient world, and probably until the eighteenth century, the sexual element in the book was usually frankly faced. The original meaning was accepted, then elevated into a simile of superior religious rapture. This use of the Song was common during the middle ages and was adopted intact at the Reformation. Then in England early in the seventeenth century expositors began to read the book "prophetically." They treated it not only as a similitude of the relationship of Christ and his virgin bride, the Church, but as a recapitulation of the Church's entire history. The attempt to explain it in this way, and to expound its successive chapters parallel to supposed equivalents in Daniel, Revelation, and even the Letters to the Seven Churches of Asia Minor, near the beginning of John's Apocalypse, is a curiosity of scriptural exposition. Thomas Brightman treated the book by this principle in his *Propheticall Exposition of the whole Booke of the Canticles*,[41] written at some time before his death in 1607, but not published widely until his complete works were issued in 1644. "This Prophesie," Brightman wrote, "agreeth well neere in all things with that of Saint John in the Revelation. They foreshew the same events in the like times."[42] The fashion of exposition spread. In 1617, Richard Bernard, the rector of Batcombe in Somerset (in all probability to be identified with Williams's father-in-law to be) published his *Key of Knowledge for the Opening of the Secret Mysteries of St. Johns Mysticall Revelation*, in which he acknowledged his debt to Brightman's commentary on the same book but differed from him about details. At the end of his book Bernard asked that his interpretation be used to guide men to "hearken to the unerring voyce of Christ and his Church" and quoted the first and seventh verses of the fourth chapter of Canticles:

Christ. Behold thou art faire (my love) behold, thou art faire, there is no spot in thee.[43]

The underlying agreement of Revelation with the Song of Solomon was implied in much that Roger Williams drew from the second of these two biblical books. Particularly, he kept returning to the thought that the Church is like a bride who expects to be reunited with her lover in a restored paradise, when Christ calls her out of dispersion and sorrow in the wilderness to union with Himself. But in all his writings he was reserved about making this figure of speech into a detailed prediction of the events of his own times. He took the posture of the unsatisfied seeker. He could not call himself a finder. The wilderness of the Narragansetts country all about him, with its unexplored hinterland, affected his imagination, but a natural humility held him back from the pinpointing of predictions in the Canticles and the apocalypses of Daniel and St. John. His conviction that the Christian Church was a small flock, gathered out of all the nations by the Great Shepherd made him more reticent than other millenarian inquirers about the destiny of the English people in ushering in a happy ending of history. When striving to fathom what he thought to be the mysteries of the apocalyptic books he often used the words "probably" or "general."

Against these blessed followers of the Lamb must (probably) the rage of this bloody Beast rise high in that his great slaughter of them, and triumph three days and an half over them *(Revelation 11)* and this not long before his own eternal downfall.

Many have been the interpretations of that prophecy, and some late applications of the witnesses, and time, to particular persons and times of late. But (with all due respect to the apprehensions of any studious of the truth of Jesus) I conceive the matter is of a more general consideration.[44]

The words belong to a publication of 1652, but the sentiment was there long before. Williams's sympathies lay with the poor, oppressed Netherlands exiles and the minority Separatist "little flocks" in England, rather than with the more notable academic interpreters of the evidences for the arrival of the millennium. He saw these separated brethren, wandering in a wilderness seeking their release, but not knowing when or how it would arrive. It seemed to him that their posture was closer to Christ's sufferings and was more likely to be rewarded with His blessing, in the form of a Church renewed, when the time came for them to be delivered.

Even before he came to New England Roger Williams had scruples about the willingness of his Puritan friends in Essex and the rest of East Anglia to use the parts of the Prayer Book that seemed to them acceptable. In July 1629, when he was chaplain in the Masham household, Williams appears to have been among those who gathered to discuss the colonising plans of the Massachusetts Bay Company.[45] The meeting occurred at Sempringham, the country seat of the Earl of Lincoln and a rallying point for supporters of the venture. He described later how he had pursued the matter on horseback with John Cotton and Thomas Hooker. Cotton later became a minister of Boston in New England, but was then still at St. Botolph's in Boston, Lincolnshire. Thomas Hooker,[46] later to become successively a minister at Newton (Cambridge) in Massachusetts and at Hartford, was then, like Williams, in Essex. The passage recalling the occasion in Williams's *Bloody Tenent Yet More Bloody* is set immediately after Williams had denied Cotton's argument in his *Bloudy Tenent, Washed*, that the act of ordination was not essential to a true calling of a Christian minister of word and sacraments:

> I answer: ordination, or laying on of hands, compriseth the whole ministry (*Hebrews 6*), wherein if election or ordination be false, I see not how the ministry is true, any more than a marriage can be true where either consent, or solemnity by a true power, is wanting.[47]

A guarantee of succession in the ministry, in other words, mattered to Williams. He returned many times to this text, *Hebrews 6.2*. He did not find a true "apostolic succession" in the Church of England, which he accused of "a false and invented way of prayer by the Latin or English Mass-book."[48] Williams, even in 1629, wanted full separation from the worship of the Church

of England, because he thought its ministers were no ministers,
but ministers of Antichrist, while its worship was not simply
defective, but "false."[49]

   . . . Possibly Master Cotton may call to mind that the discusser
[Williams], riding with himself and one other of precious memory
(Master Hooker) to and from Sempringham, presented his arguments
from Scripture why he durst not join with them in their use of Common
Prayer; and all the answer that yet can be remembered the discusser
received from Master Cotton was that he selected the good and best
prayers in his use of that Book, as the author of the Council of Trent
was used to do in his using of the Mass Book.

The author of the Council of Trent was a Roman Catholic
historian, Sarpi, the kind who takes his own path when he
thinks "nihil obstat."[50] Such indefinite picking and choosing
was not for Williams. He considered unhallowed trafficking with
"Babylon" was as bad as belonging to it body and soul.

    From Cotton, in another place,[51] we learn that Williams was
friendly with a man named Sabine Staresmore, who became
a Separatist exile in the Netherlands after 1616, apparently after
controversies he had in London in the bosom of Henry Jacob's
Independent, or nonseparating Congregation, founded in Southwark in that year.[52] The nature of the differences is not entirely
clear from a book by one Richard Maunsel, *The Unlawfulness
of Reading in Prayer,* which has "a defence of the same Reasons"
by Staresmore. Conjecture is that Staresmore, who may have
come from a Leicestershire family,[53] participated in the unsettled negotiations between Jacob's congregation and the
remnants of the "ancient" church of Barrow and Greenwood,
which had survived in London after the death of its martyrs
in 1593 and the exile of other notable Separatist leaders in
Middleburg, Amsterdam, and Leyden. Staresmore arrived in
Amsterdam and made contact with Henry Ainsworth, the
Separatist scholar and spokesman. This was before Ainsworth's
death in 1622. Whatever his views may have been while in
London, he acted in Amsterdam together with Ainsworth[54]

and with Ainsworth's successor John Canne, who was the
apologist of "ancient Separatism," meaning the principles of
church government upheld by Barrow and Ainsworth. It is
doubtful whether Staresmore ever held office as pastor or teacher.
But in Amsterdam he seems to have become reconciled to
Canne's ministry, thereafter returning to London. The evidence
suggests that he was an in-between person, with loyalties in
both nonseparating Congregational groups and the old Separatist
remnant congregations in both England and Holland. Before
he went abroad he suffered imprisonment in London in 1618,
as we learn from Governor Bradford's *History of Plymouth
Plantation* and a letter of Staresmore reprinted there.[55] The fact
that he is quoted at length by Bradford as a man of merit
testifies to his integrity and suggests he may have shared his
concern, about whether to separate or not to separate, with
the remnants of the Leyden Church remaining in the Netherlands under their pastor, John Robinson, after the sailing of
the *Mayflower* in 1620.

The problem for Robinson was readjustment of his conscience
at a time when the group that emigrated to the New World
in 1620 sought and obtained the silent connivance of the
English authorities for their going. His position, acknowledging
that there was a true Church of Christ in the parishes of the
Church of England and that it was permissible to worship and
hear preaching within them, brought him back "one half
of the way"[56] and made the New Plymouth settlement of the
Pilgrim Fathers into "semi-Separatists," who by 1620 were more
in sympathy with Boston than with the true Separatist line
running through Barrow and Greenwood to Francis Johnson's
Amsterdam church, and to Henry Ainsworth. But New Plymouth
had in common with these more rigid Separatists the experience
of exile and hardship. Their struggle with the bishops and
the Crown, when they were driven into the Netherlands from
their own country about Norwich, gave them feelings of compassionate friendship toward their more radical fellow-Calvinists
in London. Staresmore exemplified the tension. We do not

know when or where Williams came into touch with him, but
the association could go back into the confused history of the
London "conventicles" before 1620. Once the issue between
Separatist and non-Separatist comes to the surface in Williams's
writings, it is obvious that he has lived, halting between the
alternatives, but without taking a final stand, for a long time.

It is sometimes forgotten that the first controversial exchange
between John Cotton and Roger Williams took place as the result
of Williams's having shared with others the text of a letter Cotton
wrote him about his Separatism, at the time of his banishment
from Massachusetts. The letter somehow was printed. When
publishing his *Bloudy Tenent of Persecution* Williams issued
Mr. Cottons Letter Examined and Answered.[57] Cotton, in turn,
responded in *A Reply to Mr. Williams his Examination; And
Answer of the Letters sent to him by John Cotton.* Cotton was
surprised and offended that his first letter to Williams had
been printed, as it had been private. He recalled that he had
engaged in correspondence about it with Sabine Staresmore, who
had read it. This is how Cotton describes the publications:

> How it came to be put in print, I cannot imagine. Sure I am it was
> without my privity, and when I heard of it, it was to me unwelcome
> news, as knowing the truth and weight of Pliny's speech, *Aliud est
> scribere uni, aliud omnibus* [It is one thing to write to one man; another
> to write to everybody]. There be [some] who think it was published by
> Mr. Williams himself, or by some of his friends, who had the copy from
> him; which latter might be the more probable, because himself denieth
> the publishing of it. And it sticketh in my mind that I received, many
> years ago, a refutation of it (in a brotherly and ingenuous way) from a
> stranger to me, but one (as I hear) well affected to him—Mr. Sabine
> Staresmore; to whom I had long ago returned an answer, but that he
> did not direct me where my letter might find him. But I do not suspect
> Mr. Staresmore, nor Mr. Williams himself to have published it; but
> rather some other (unadvised) Christian, who (having gotten a copy of
> the letter), took more liberty than God alloweth to draw forth a private
> admonition to public notice in a disorderly way.[58]

Thus Cotton's first communication to Williams had been an
attempt to negate Williams's Separatist position. Cotton called

his letter from Staresmore a "refutation" of Cotton's attack on Williams. It follows that Staresmore was on the side of the Separatists against the nonseparating position of Henry Jacob and the Massachusetts Congregationalists, at least by the time he wrote to Cotton, which must have been soon after 1636. Cotton said it was "many yeares ago" when he wrote the above-quoted memory of it in 1647. Staresmore's importance in any attempt to reconstruct Williams's awareness of the Separatist fringe is that he was a living bond with Separatist groups mentioned elsewhere in the writings of Williams, even though we come to know of Williams's association with Staresmore only through an aside from Cotton. The famous Boston preacher evidently took it for granted that his informed readers would know that the position of the "rigid" Separatists had been a live option, a kind of suppressed possibility, for Williams for a long time.

Nowadays, for purposes of convenient analysis, we compartmentalise and classify the Puritan communities of the 1620's. Cotton and Williams, who lived through those years, could see only a nation-wide movement of Englishmen bent on resistance to kings, prelates, monopolists, and court spongers, in the name of reformation. Many roads were tried within the composite brotherhood, to avoid full conformity—from lecturing and domestic chaplaincies, through colonisation, to voluntary exile and total separation.[59] The last of these was embraced by a number of able thinkers and men of action. Some, like Cotton, were shocked by it, as having a flavour of anarchy; others, like Williams, were drawn to it. The communication, friendly and unfriendly, between Separatists and non-Separatists can be deduced from much that was written on both sides at the time.

What did Roger Williams himself say about the Separatists? He accused John Cotton of condemning "the witnesses of Jesus (the Separate Churches in London, and elsewhere)."[60] Cotton had replied "that neither Christ nor his Apostles after him, nor Prophets before him ever delivered that way."[61] The Boston preacher said he could not pray for such people and he blamed them "that being desirous of Reformation, they stumble not only at the inventions of men, but for their sakes at the Ordinances of the Lord, because they separate not only from the Parishes, but from the Church at Plymouth, and of that whereof Mr. Lathrop was Pastor." (Lathrop[62] had been the successor of Henry Jacob and had migrated, for a time, into Massachusetts, where he became pastor at Scituate). Cotton had further regretted that Williams's separation might "help erring, though zealous souls against the mighty Ordinances of the Lord."[63] Williams countered by giving a number of reasons for his own adherence to the Separatists and by asking "how can Mr. Cotton be offended that I should help (as he calls them) any zealous souls, not *against* the mighty Ordinances of the Lord Jesus, but to seek after the Lord Jesus without halting?"[64]

The expressions used imply that Cotton regarded Williams's choice of separation as subversive—a denial of his own true and clear Congregational way, and a dangerous leftward deviation from the "semi-Separatist" temporary protests of Henry Jacob's and John Robinson's groups in London, the Netherlands, and New England.

To this earlier testimony Williams later added a revealing aside, in 1652, in his address to the general courts of New England preceding his *Bloody Tenent Yet More Bloody*. Here, as in most of what he said about his Separatist beliefs, he again used the idea that there was a "liberty of searching" in the voluntary groups, divorced as they were from state oversight. Separatism was congenial to him because it provided the atmosphere in which he could pursue three unattainables that determined the pattern of his life's obedience—the form of the true Church, the promise of Christ's return, and suffering with Christ (which was, for him, central and held the other two together):

It hath been the common way of the Father of lights to enclose the light of His holy truths in dark and obscure, yea, and ordinarily in forbidden books, persons, and meetings, by Satan styled conventicles.[65]

And he proceeded:

> There is one commodity for the sake of which most of God's children
> in New England have run their mighty hazards, a commodity marvel-
> lously scarce in former times (though in some late years, by God's most
> gracious and mighty hand, more plentiful in our native country): it is a
> liberty of searching after God's most holy mind and pleasure.[66]

It is fortunate for us that Williams's *Examination* of Cotton's
letter on his banishment survived. By the late 1640's and the
1650's it might not have been good diplomacy for Williams to
publish the names of the Separatists he admired. By then
he had to preserve good relations with all who would help
Rhode Island, including more conservative non-Separatist Independents. As it is, we have here a discussion between the two
men which is of great interest for understanding the relationship between the minority Separatist congregations and the
future Independents, who afterwards took John Cotton's "middle
way,"[67] between separation, and conformity to the Elizabethan
settlement of the Church of England. Williams, in his *Examination*, first dropped the names into the debate when dealing with
John Cotton's claim that the Puritans had suffered in England
when Separatist conventicles had been "winked at." Williams
claimed that the reverse was true:

> Now for their sufferings: as the Puritans have not comparably suffered,
> (as but seldom congregating in separate assemblies from the common)
> so have not any of them suffered unto death for the way of non-
> conformity to ceremonies, &c. Indeed, the worthy witness Mr. Udall was
> near unto death for his witness against bishops and ceremonies; but Mr.
> Penry, Mr. Barrow, Mr. Greenwood, followed the Lord Jesus with their
> gibbets on their shoulders, and were hanged with Him and for Him, in
> the way of separation. Many more have been condemned to die,
> banished, and choked in prisons; I could produce [evidence] upon
> occasion . . .

Williams was familiar with the trials of the non-Separatist,
John Udall,[68] but his closer sympathy was for the Separatist
martyrs, whose witness had been death, in the steps of Christ.

To godly preachers working among the gentry, favourable
mention of the names of these three turbulent and allegedly
seditious people amounted to treason.

Williams went on at once to argue that separation was the
logical result of Puritanism. He cited a contemporary successor of
the old "conventiclers," the ever-busy John Canne,[69] of London
and Amsterdam, sometime printer, sometime distiller, unmoving
Separatist and fervent millenarian, the author of *A Necessitie
of Separation from the Church of England proved by the Nonconformists' Principles*.[70] Canne's book had been published in
1634. Williams was aware of it by 1644. Cotton confessed, "I
have not seen his book."[71] Williams, who had, said:

> I believe that there hardly hath ever been a conscientious Separatist
> who was not first a Puritan; for (as Mr. Canne hath unanswerably
> proved) the grounds and principles of the Puritans against bishops and
> ceremonies, and profaneness of people professing Christ and the
> necessity of Christ's flock and discipline, must necessarily, if truly
> followed, lead on to and enforce a separation from such ways, worships,
> and worshippers, to seek out the true way of God's worship according to
> Christ Jesus.[72]

There was a social dimension to Williams's reasons for following
the Separatists. It is recognizable often in his prolonged controversies with Cotton, who represented the security of a lawyer-
gentry-merchant establishment. Williams believed ministers like
Cotton should have forsaken their positions of respect and
honour among their wealthy patrons, the merchants and gentry,
in order to embrace the lot of the despised. Although he was
no leveller, Roger Williams may be accused by his critics of
a form of inverted snobbery. John Wesley, a century later,
had to swallow his pride before taking to the highways with
the sweaty multitude and consenting "to become more vile."
Williams, unlike Wesley, seemed sometimes to pursue hardship
like a masochist. But the reason he gave was that the way of
the Cross was the only true *imitatio Christi*.

> Most of God's servants who, out of sight of the ignorance, unbelief,
> and profaneness of the body of the national Church, have separated

and durst not have longer fellowship with it; I say most of them have been poor and low, and not such gainful customers to the bishops, their courts, and officers.

That worthy instrument of Christ's praise, Mr. Ainsworth, during some time (and some time of his great labours in Holland) lived upon ninepence per week, with roots boiled, &c.; whereas, on the other side [nonseparating Puritans], such of God's servants as have been non-conformists have had fair estates, been great persons, have had rich livings and benefices, of which the bishops and theirs (like greedy wolves) have made the more desirable prey.[73]

The "old Separatists" were thus men of greater worth for Roger Williams than the less radical Puritans, the forerunners of the Independents and Presbyterians. Cotton replied to him by asserting that the sufferings of the Puritans—he was indignant at Williams's use of the opprobrious term—were at least equal. He took the opportunity to doubt whether John Penry died confident in his position and to insinuate that the poverty of Ainsworth could have been due to the meanness of his flock. He had a good word for John Greenwood as "a more tender, and conscientious spirit" (but said Barrow had kept him rigid, intractable). Cotton considered Barrow an impossible person. He invoked the precious memory of "godly Mr. Dod," pithy preacher and hero of all Puritans, to make his point:

This I can say, from the testimony of holy and blessed Mr. Dod, who, speaking of this Barrow, God is not wont (saith he) to make choice of men infamous for gross vices before their calling, to make them any notable instruments of reformation after their calling. Mr. Barrow, whilst he lived in court, was wont to be a great gamester, and dicer, and often getting much by play, would boast, *Vivo de die, in spem noctis,* nothing ashamed to boast of his hopes of his night's lodgings in the bosoms of his courtesans. As his spirit was high and rough before his reformation, so was it after, even to his death. When he stood under the gibbet, he lift[ed] up his eyes, and, "Lord", saith he, "if I be de-ceived, Thou hast deceived me." And so, being stopped by the hand of God, he was not able to proceed to speak anything to purpose more, either to the glory of God or to the edification of the people.[74]

Barrow's thought, almost certainly conveyed to Williams through his writings, can be made out beneath the surface of Roger

Williams's own. The two men had much in common. Each abandoned hopes of advancement for relative obscurity. Each was a difficult character, determined to win all or nothing. They both indulged in what Williams late in life called "sharp Scripture language,"[75] a euphemism for abuse of their opponents. Barrow's favourite target, the Antichrist at work in the prelates' Church, became a controlling metaphor in the thought of Williams. When he came to write the *Bloody Tenent Yet More Bloody* (after 1650) he did not want to run into strife by mentioning Barrow by name and quoting his books, so he told Cotton:

> Concerning the Church of England, whether a daughter or no of the great whore of Rome, it is not here seasonable to repeat what the witnesses of Christ to bonds, banishments, and death (whom Mr. Cotton here calls the rigid separation) have alleged in this case.[76]

By his frequent reference to Rome as the whore, and to the Church of England as partaking in defilement and representing the whore's "uncleanness," Williams was like yet another obstinate Separatist prisoner. This was John Wilkinson, "another ancient stout Separatist"[77] who wrote *An Exposition of the 13. Chapter of the Revelation*, published in 1619 after his death. He was a Barrowist, an eager interpreter of the Book of Revelation as referring to the "Antichristian Clergie" of England. The Church of England's hierarchy was called by Wilkinson "an ougly compounded and deformed monster."[78] This Barrowist description equated the clergy with the "image of the beast" (*Revelation 13.15–18*). Earlier in his small book, Wilkinson had contrasted the socially eminent clergy with God's true followers (obviously referring to flocks like his own, at Colchester, where he had been imprisoned for Separatist activity):

> They [the grander clergy] are not of the number of God's elect and chosen in Christ, and given unto Him for His portion and heritage, whose condition is to be hated, despised, persecuted, and afflicted in the world for righteousness' sake; in whom the Lamb, Christ Jesus, as in His

members, hath been slain since the beginning of the world; which condition, those which cannot brook and endure, but count it a pleasure to live deliciously for a season, and take delight to enjoy the pleasures of sin, may, thereby, be discerned not to have their names written in the Book of Life.[79]

The quotation is steeped in a mythology of exile, suffering, and deliverance, drawn from several different places in the Bible; its interest in relation to Williams is the congruity of its ideas with his. Others who knew John Wilkinson remarked on another point; he and his disciples came to believe that there was no true and valid succession of ministry left in the world and that Jesus Christ would have to come with requisite power and authority to raise up "new apostles" and restore the Church to its intended full purity. When we explore the "Seekerism" of Williams, these views of Wilkinson will be seen to take their place in a line of thought that runs from the Rhine Valley and the Netherlands in the mid-sixteenth century to the sixth decade of the seventeenth century in England. Sometimes they were joined with heterodox doctrines of the person of Christ, but in Wilkinson and Williams they are found alongside otherwise orthodox Calvinism.

John Wilkinson's other tiny book, now rare, *The Sealed Fountain*,[80] is a Calvinist defence of infant baptism against the Arminianism and antipaedobaptism of the early English General Baptist, John Murton. Wilkinson wrote this tract from his Colchester prison to Murton, then in Newgate prison, London.[81]

By the time he published the *Bloudy Tenent* in 1644 Williams had also come to respect Murton, whose *Objections: Answered*[82] had much in common with the *Humble Supplication*, the tract on liberty of conscience, written with milk and smuggled out of gaol, and referred to by Williams as a valuable item in his fight for "soul liberty":

The author of these arguments against persecution, as I have been informed, being committed by some then in power close prisoner to

Newgate for the witness of some truths of Jesus, and having not the use of pen and ink, wrote these arguments in milk, in sheets of paper brought to him by the woman, his keeper, from a friend in London, as the stopples of his milk bottle.

In such paper, written with milk, nothing will appear, but the way of reading it by fire being known to this friend who received the papers, he transcribed and kept together the papers. . . .[83]

But Murton and the author of the *Humble Supplication* were early General Baptists. Murton believed Christ intended to die for *all* men; Williams believed that he died to win the chosen only. His views on the atonement between God and man were thus Arminian and opposed to Williams's Calvinism. More than that, Murton rejected the Seeker claim that there were no valid apostolic men left in the world to be true ministers; he held that the command to baptise was still binding, without waiting for authorised new apostles to undertake the task. How could Williams refer to Murton, and to the group of Netherlands early Baptist pioneers with such approval as he did? He even spoke warmly of John Smith, the gifted Arminian leader of the exiled Netherlands Baptists who broke with the Amsterdam Barrowists. The ever-watchful Calvinist John Cotton referred to Smith's deathbed testimony in biting terms:

Sad and woeful is the memory of Mr. Smith's strong consolation on his deathbed, which is set as a seal to his gross and damnable Arminianism and enthusiasm, delivered in the Confession of his faith. . . .[84]

But Williams was more tender;

as to that concerneth Mr. Smith, although I knew him not, and have heard of many points in which my conscience tells me it pleased the Lord to leave him to himself; yet I have also heard by some (whose testimony Mr. Cotton will not easily refuse) that he was a man fearing God; and I am sure Mr. Cotton hath made some use of those principles and arguments on which Mr. Smith and others went concerning the constitution of the Christian Church.[85]

The psychological byplay here was subtle. It is as though Williams had a witty eye on Smith, Cotton, and himself. Smith was Arminian and worse; very well then; Williams, too, disagreed with him. Yet Cotton and Williams both knew that the men of New Plymouth, and their former pastor, John Robinson of Leyden, had expressed their love for Smith's person, whatever his opinions. All of them knew that the idea of a locally covenanted and gathered people formed part of the program of Plymouth, of Boston, and of the early Baptists. The method Williams used was not smearing by association; it was a reminder of things held in common, with an implied plea for more generosity toward brothers who were thought to err. Williams's Calvinist common ground with Cotton was always there. They both knew it. Cotton wanted the civil magistrates to require that common ground, and more, as a minimum religion to safeguard the *true* religion of the elect. Williams fought for a legally sanctioned right to separate and be tolerated. His own Separatism led him to demand genuine pluralism, religious liberty for all, Christian or non-Christian. In doing so he became prophetic of the future. It is not hard to think of Williams being in accord with several elements in John Smith's *Last Booke,* in which he said:

I am not of the number of those men which assume unto themselves such plenary knowledge and assurance of their ways, and of the perfection and sufficiency thereof, as that they peremptorily censure all men except those of their own understanding, and require that all men upon pain of damnation become subject and captivate in their judgment and walking to their line and level. . . .[86]

John Smith's name raises a further probability. This is that the Reverend Richard Bernard, Smith's most troublesome English detractor, was the father-in-law of Roger Williams.[87] Mary Barnard, the woman Williams married in the parish church of High Laver, near Otes, in December 1629, was in service as a lady-in-waiting to the stepdaughter of Sir William Masham, Joan (Jug) Altham. Jane Whalley, another lady resident at Otes, and a niece of Lady Barrington, had been the earlier object of Williams's frustrated love, when Lady Barrington disapproved of his suit. This Jane Whalley was the daughter of Richard Whalley, a leading Nottinghamshire gentleman, who had presented Richard Bernard to the living of Worksop, Nottinghamshire, in 1601. Bernard (or Barnard) had a daughter named Mary. A Masachiel Barnard is known to have migrated to Massachusetts, and there is a reference to a Mr. Bernard there as being the brother of Williams's wife. The presumptive evidence that Richard Bernard's daughter became the wife of Roger Williams is therefore strong, though not quite conclusive.

Bernard had been at Christ's College, Cambridge, at about the same time John Smith was studying there. The two men were intimate friends, and when Bernard first went to Worksop he became caught up in Separatist activity in the region. John Robinson, William Brewster, Richard Clyfton, Henry Ainsworth, and William Bradford lived nearby. They had formed their own congregations, gathered and disciplined companies "of the worthiest" though they did not go as far as Barrow in open venom against the bishops. John Smith, at nearby Gainsborough in Lincolnshire, was one of the ardent supporters of the way, though not yet a Baptist. He was young and magnetic. Bernard, at first, yielded to the Separatist enthusiasm.[88] He gathered a more tightly disciplined "church within a church" as the core of his parish.

In 1606 Bernard faced a crisis, involving his career and status. His metropolitan, the Archbishop of York, Matthew Hutton, died and was succeeded by Toby Matthew, who proved less indulgent toward the more radical Puritans. Bernard had to decide whether he would continue in his parish or take the decisive step and join the Separatists in persecution and exile. He chose security and became involved during the next few years in a literary controversy with Smith and Robinson. He defended the Church of England as genuinely apostolic and cast himself firmly in the moderate Anglican Puritan mould. He accepted the articles and Prayer Book, but tended to let ceremonies go by default. Two of Bernard's books illustrate what happened to him. In 1608 he published *Christian Ad-*

vertisements and Counsels of Peace,[89] embodying "dissuasions from the Separatists Schisme, commonly called Brownisme." This was a long refutation (of two hundred pages) of the errors of Barrow, Greenwood, Browne, the brothers Johnson, Smith, and their friends. It revealed Bernard as a learned, slightly fussy and ambitious ecclesiastic, anxious to please by literary labours dedicated to his lay patrons. There are signs that some of the gentry regarded him as an enthusiast, but a bore.[90] In 1610 he issued *Plaine Evidences*,[91] which affirmed that "the Church of England is Apostolicall, and the Separation Schismaticall." The book was directed "Against Mr. Ainsworth the Separatist, and Mr. Smith the Se-Baptist: Both of them severally opposing the Booke called the Separatists Schisme." Bernard dedicated it, in rather fulsome Latin, to Toby Matthew, his archbishop and to the memory of Archbishop Grindal, one of Toby's predecessors in the see of York. Grindal's moderate Puritanism had earned him the disfavour of Queen Elizabeth and, after he had been promoted to Canterbury, lonely sequestration in his blind old age.[92] The book itself is an answer of some 340 pages to arguments used by Ainsworth and Smith in their replies to Bernard's earlier dissuasive against Barrow and Greenwood.

If Bernard was Roger Williams's father-in-law he may have been an additional source of information about Smith, who bitterly attacked Bernard's defection from the Separatist camp, but before his own death expressed regret for having been so caustic.[93] Bernard was another, alongside the men of New Plymouth, "whose testimony Mr. Cotton would not easily refuse." Was a natural dissenter like Williams, in identifying himself with the Separatist fringe in 1629, reacting against the respectable conformism of his own father-in-law, as well as the conventional "culture religion" of the Puritan squires among whom he was living?

John Smith's transition, in the Netherlands, out of Barrowism into Arminian views on the subject of predestination might have been calculated to alienate a life-long Calvinist like Williams. But the founder of Rhode Island learned to live with many differing "consciences," as antinomians, Gortonists, and varieties of Arminians—"doleful generalists"[94] he called them—descended on the colony and took up residence. The Rhode Island of the late 1630's became a microcosm, a preview of the sectarian pluralism that would flourish in England of the early 1650's; and in other respects the prolonged "search" of Roger Williams for the form of the true Church led him to value the Baptists and their witness.

Smith had been deeply concerned about the recovery of the right external form of the ordinance of baptism. Williams shared the concern; he was for a few months in 1639 a "rebaptised" cofounder of a Calvinistic Baptist Church at Providence.[95] John Clarke, like Williams a Calvinist, helped to make the Baptists a force in Providence and Newport, so that by 1649 Williams could write to John Winthrop, Junior, about his relationship with the Baptists in warm but reserved terms. In what he said he did not suggest that immersion, the outward form, counted for much. His own temporary membership with the Baptists had been after baptism by pouring or sprinkling. He was prepared, in 1649, to accept "dipping" (as a soundly-based novelty); but his real reservations lay in "high church" scruples over the authority of the officiant, and the relationship of any "new" baptism to his belief that Christ would return and restore the Church's sacraments in pristine purity. Williams wondered whether there must not be more martyrdoms and a fresh resurgence of the Church of Rome before all this took place:

> At Seekonk a great many have lately concurred with Mr. John Clarke and our Providence men about the point of a new Baptism, and the manner by dipping: and Mr. John Clarke hath been there lately (and Mr. Lucar) and hath dipped them. I believe their practice comes nearer the first practice of our great Founder, Christ Jesus, than other practices of religion do, and yet I have not satisfaction, neither in the authority by which it is done, nor in the manner; nor in the prophecies concerning the rising of Christ's Kingdom after the desolations by Rome, &c.[96]

Some perplexity about legitimate succession of ministers was also felt by both Roger Williams and John Smith. Smith's

English followers eventually found the problem so vexatious that they established relations in the Netherlands with the Rijnburgers or Collegiants, who sought an authenticated and orderly "apostolic" baptism.[97] Roger Williams's knowledge of the Dutch language may have gone back to the days of his early childhood in London, where he lived in Smithfield near Dutch families who worshipped as a church in the London parish of Austin Friars.[98] Did Williams learn to read and write Dutch in his father's business? Did he ever visit the Netherlands in his earlier years? Were there any contacts between him and the Collegiants, whose type of theological inquiry was similar to that of the later English Seekers? What Dutch books other than a New Testament did he possess and read? What Collegiant and early seeker ideas were current among Dutchmen in southeast England during his boyhood? How did the Barrowist, John Wilkinson, absorb these influences? Were there, among London merchants in the Netherlands and North African trades, some whose lives conveyed to the young Williams the radical doctrines he embraced so firmly after 1629? These questions may never be answered with certainty, but they are inevitably raised when Williams is described by his contemporaries as a "Seeker." His seeker posture was not assumed independently of his early exposure to the Separatist fringe, but arose out of it. The latent strength of this continuing body of Separatist opinion in England between 1603 and 1640 has often been underestimated.[99] For people temperamentally like Williams it was fascinating because it upset the Puritan court and country "bluebloods."

Whatever Separatist ingredients there may be in the mature Williams, he may not be dismissed, however, as simply a dissident soul in protest, a "come outer." The Bible and the figure of "the true Lord Jesus" dictated his doctrine and his life. He genuinely believed in a kind of aristocracy of the crucified. His positive allegiance was made plain in the words[100] he addressed to readers of his *Bloody Tenent Yet More Bloody* in 1652:

I believe and profess that such persons, such churches, are got nearest to Christ Jesus, on whose forehead are written these blessed characters of the true Lord Jesus: first, content with a poor and low condition in worldly things; second, an holy cleansing from the filthiness of false worships and worldly conversations; third, an humble and constant endeavour to attain (in their simplicity and purity) to the ordinances and appointments of Christ Jesus; fourth, are so far from smiting, killing, and wounding the opposites of their profession and worship, that they resolve themselves patiently to bear and carry the cross and gallows of their Lord and Master, and patiently to suffer with Him. In the number of such, his poor servants, who as unfeignedly desire—notwithstanding any plea against persecutors and persecution—I say as unfeignedly desire, to suffer as cheerfully with Christ Jesus as gloriously to reign with Him, desires to be,

Thine unfeigned, though unworthiest of all the followers of Jesus,

ROGER WILLIAMS

4

Pathway to Power: Education

K INGSHIP AND LORDSHIP recur almost obsessively in the writings of Roger Williams as ideas that have to be understood in Christian terms and transformed. Williams's defence of religious liberty has led people to look everywhere for this as his central theme, but when the toleration controversy of the 1640's and 1650's is set within the development of his life and thought as a whole, his defence of liberty of conscience assumes its place as an aspect of his biblical understanding of authority—divine and human. His personal development was, at first, an ascent from comparative obscurity in the life of a London merchant's family to a point where he could contemplate gaining prizes of advancement and fame in both Church and State. Having come within sight of this goal, he turned his back on it and "counted it loss." The experience of St. Paul, whose own moment of power had been given him when he had led in Jewish persecution of the young Christian Church, affected Williams's view of his own life. Paul's road of ambition and promotion had at first involved stamping out the young Christian movement and securing the unity of Judaism. Williams, who desired above all things to be an "apostle," had Paul's about-face in mind when in 1630 he renounced preferment and eminence to go to the New World and accept identification with the Separatists.

A statement of St. Paul in his letter to the Philippians keeps reappearing in the letters and tracts of Roger Williams. Its language had come to exemplify his own decision. Paul had traced his impeccable qualifications and record as a leader in the élite Pharisee group of Judaism. He then declared:

> What things were gain to me, these I have counted loss for Christ. Yes, truly, and I count all things to be loss for the excellency of the knowledge of Christ Jesus my Lord: for whom I suffered the loss of all things, and count them but dung, that I may gain Christ. *(Philippians 3.7–9)*.

Williams many times called the advancement and pleasure of the Church and court a "dunghill."[1] "I have not been altogether a stranger to the Learning of the Egyptians," he said, in issuing his *Hireling Ministry None of Christs* in 1652, "and I have trod the hopefulest paths to worldly preferments, which for Christ's sake I have forsaken."[2] The echo of Paul is unmistakable; the reference is autobiographical.

For Williams advancement had come through the encouragement of his distinguished sponsor, Sir Edward Coke, who enabled him to go to Charterhouse School in London and afterwards to Cambridge. Much labour can be spent on reconstructing Williams's life at school and the university by describing normal student life and reading at Charterhouse and at Pembroke College.[3] But Williams was not a normal boy. He had individual qualities of pugnacity and dissent that make conventional teachers despair. He shared the pugnacity with Coke.[4] The Lord Chief Justice may have warmed to it, while recognising that it needed taming and shaping if it was ever to be dedicated to the future service of the throne, law, and Church of the English people.

When Williams came under the notice of Coke and began by serving him as a shorthand writer, the great judge, against his will, had been driven by King James I into a position where he tried to resist the monarch's encroachments on the traditional prerogatives of the Common Law courts.[5] As Attorney for Queen Elizabeth and Chief Justice of the Common Pleas, Coke had acquired a detailed knowledge of Common Law precedent that has seldom been rivalled. His learning and practical sagacity were embodied in the books he wrote in his enforced retirement. James I and Charles I, with their absolutist pretensions and assurance of divine right, feared Coke's learning and the powerful support he could rally among common lawyers and merchants.[6]

As early as 1608, when he was still Chief Justice of the Common Pleas, Coke had become the enemy of Bancroft's policy when that Archbishop tried to claim jurisdiction for the ecclesiastical court of High Commission in financial cases involving lay patronage.[7] Coke repeatedly issued "prohibitions," to restrain appeals, in matters involving land or money, from the Common Law courts to the courts of the Church, thus infuriating both Bancroft and the King. To relieve the situation James engineered the "promotion" of Coke from his presiding role on the Common Law bench to the doubtful honour of Lord Chief Justice,[8] in which office the King hoped to tame him. Here Coke had to preside over the royal court of the Star Chamber, where the King, in theory, could himself sit because of the royal prerogative. Against all precedent James I did so on a famous day, June 20, 1616.[9] It was in the Star Chamber that Williams served the great judge. Perhaps it was on this occasion, and at other times in the course of Coke's official duties, that Roger Williams met King James and formed an opinion of him as a man. Like Sir Edward Coke, Williams never questioned the divine sanction of the crown or the subject's duty of fealty to the King as supreme magistrate; but with Coke he held that the King's power was defined by the laws and therefore he was within the law, not above it. Williams's memory of the struggles between the eminent judge and the King would have been still vivid when he wrote, in 1670, his long and revealing letter to Major Mason,[10] an old friend, who fought as captain in the Pequot War of 1636 and lived to become a leader of the Connecticut colonists. Speaking of King Charles II, Williams wrote:

Sir, the King's Majesty, though his father's and his own conscience favoured Lord Bishops, which their father and grandfather King James, whom I have spoke with, sore against his will, also did; yet all the world may see, by his Majesty's declarations and engagements before his return, and his declarations and parliament speeches since, and many suitable actings, how the Father of spirits hath mightily impressed and touched his royal spirit, though the Bishops much disturbed him, with deep inclination of favour and gentleness, to different consciences and apprehensions as to the invisible King and way of his worship.[11]

The words "sore against his will" cannot mean that King James favoured Lord Bishops reluctantly, since it was the King's conscience, according to Williams, that led him into the policy. They can hardly mean that Williams somehow nailed the King and held him unwillingly to listen. They seem to mean that when Williams had the chance to speak with James I he took a line that opposed the King's policy, which would have been in character for Williams, both as Coke's servant and in his own right.

Coke, for his part, favoured bishops, but he did not favour "Lord Bishops" in the derogatory sense Williams employs. Coke received them as spiritual lords in the Church, but he was at one with the anticlerical lawyers and merchants in opposing what they regarded as encroachment on the ancient legal and property rights of the laity, particularly if the bishops acted as royal creatures and asserted the rights of the Church against the Common Law in the name of the Crown. It would be in character, too, for James I to indulge in bluff and unrehearsed cross-questioning on such issues with a boy who was Coke's minion.

How did Roger Williams first come to be employed by Coke? We have no precise information, though there was an early story in Rhode Island[12] that he was observed taking sermons in shorthand in the parish of St. Sepulchre where Coke worshipped when in London. One of Coke's recent biographers emphasises that he was a Protestant and a good Church of England man, but not a Puritan.[13] The description needs qualifying. Coke was one of the great men of the realm, and he circulated among great lords and higher clergy. But the depth of his affection was with the host of country justices among whom he had moved in his legal career. He had little patience with two kinds of men on the make—the fawning type of bishop who had risen from low place to royal favour, and the more numerous parish clergy, styled Puritan, who attacked the Church's Prayer Book liturgy and had their own designs on future power. To say that he was not a Puritan means that he was as "anticlerical" toward them as toward others. On the other hand, his lawyer friends, mostly Puritan allies and sympathisers, were lay defenders, with Coke, of the "good old cause" of a Protestant state religion "by the laws established" and according to the standards of the "best reformed churches."[14]

Sir Edward provided entrée for Roger Williams into that lawyers' world where much of his political work would be done on his return to England in 1640, after the assertion of the lawyers' power in parliament. His success in gaining a charter for Rhode Island came primarily through friendship with such laity, many of whom had been inspired, partly by Coke, to treat the "high court" of parliament as the best field for battle against James I in 1621 and Charles I in 1628. The Petition of Right and Coke's classic speeches in its defence during the stormy sessions of the 1628 parliament[15] suggest elements in Roger Williams's later teaching about the proper autonomy, under God and the law, of the civil or lay domain. When his own turn came to take a share in denying the Stuarts' crown rights in the doctrine and property of the Church, his best friends were not Puritan clergy, but city fathers and country lawyers. His taste of what responsible power meant came as a result of associations with laity he met after his years at Charterhouse and Pembroke College, Cambridge. He warmed to the laity, as he never did to the clergy, because they were in their own way assured and realistic people, whereas the Puritan clergy tended to be sycophantic toward their lay patrons and dependent upon their favours to gain a share in the ease and status Williams considered incompatible with the Christian's true example, the Cross.

The affection between Coke and the younger Williams was reflected in a series of strange letters[16] Williams addressed, thirty-five years afterwards, in 1652, to Mistress Anne Sadleir, Coke's daughter by his first and happier marriage. She had married Sir Ralph Sadleir, grandson and heir of one of the richest men in England.[17] Williams could not resist the urge to reestablish contact with Mrs. Sadleir, as one member of Coke's family he had known. His debt was too great to lie unhonoured. In the course of the correspondence he initiated, which became more peppery on both sides as it proceeded, the depth of the relationship between sponsor and protégé becomes apparent, together with the pain felt on Williams's side at the rupture implied in his choice of Separatism. As soon as he began to address Mrs. Sadleir, Williams's epistolary manner reverted to the somewhat exaggerated courtesy he used in addressing gentry and members of their families. Everything became at once more studied and balanced. His approach to Mrs. Sadleir may be contrasted with the familiar voice he had employed in a letter written at about the same time to his friend Gregory Dexter, a Londoner who had been his printer and had then joined him in Providence: "My love to your cousin Clemence, and all desire love, especially our godly friends."[18] To Mrs. Sadleir he wrote from his London lodgings with a different voice:

The never-dying honour and respect which I owe to that dear and honourable root and his branches, and, amongst the rest, to your much honoured self, have emboldened me, once more, to enquire after your dear husband's and your life, and health, and welfare. . . . I am . . . bold to crave your favourable consideration, and pardon, and acceptance, of these my humble respects and remembrances. . . .[19]

Williams explained that he was enclosing a copy of his *Experiments of Spiritual Life and Health*, the meditations on interior discipline he had written for his wife during an illness of hers. "I could have dressed forth the matter," he explained, in a kind of apology for plainness of style, "like some sermons which, formerly, I used to pen. But the Father of lights hath long since shown me the vanity and soul-deceit of such points and flourishes."[20] That may have been the case, but it was necessary for Williams to account for the disparity between the "flourishes" of his letter to his patron's daughter and the bare and simple manner of the enclosure. He pointed out that he had forsaken the ornaments and graces of his education for stern reasons:

> I desire to know nothing, to profess nothing, but the Son of God, the King of souls and consciences. . . . How much more should we rejoice in the wounds of such as we hope love us in Christ Jesus, than in the deceitful kisses of soul-deceiving and soul-killing friends.[21]

This was certainly buying trouble from a lady who had married a royalist and had reacted to the civil war by entrenching herself in the more conservative side of her beloved father's political and ecclesiastical judgments and prejudices. But Williams continued:

> My much honoured friend, that man of honour, and wisdom, and piety, your dear father, was often pleased to call me his son; and truly it was as bitter as death to me when Bishop Laud pursued me out of this land, and my conscience was persuaded against the national Church and ceremonies, and bishops, beyond the conscience of your dear Father. I say it was as bitter as death to me, when I rode Windsor way, to take ship at Bristow, and saw Stoke House, where the blessed man was; and I then durst not acquaint him with my conscience, and my flight. But how many thousand times since have I had honourable and precious remembrance of his person, and the life, the writings, the speeches, and the examples of that glorious light. And I may truly say that beside my natural inclination to study and activity, his example, instruction, and encouragement, have spurred me on to a more than ordinary, industrious, and patient course in my whole course hitherto.[22]

The words used were carefully weighed; they give insight into the relationship between the younger Williams and Coke. The old man's own son, "fighting Clem,"[23] inherited his passionate nature, but hardly the qualities Williams indicated he had learned as a "son" under Coke's guidance. The understanding between the elder Coke and Williams seems to have been close, so that his decision to separate and go to America was like the "death" a son feels when he rejects the beliefs of a father and departs. When he mentioned Laud, Roger Williams had in mind more than a simple breach between himself on the one side and Coke on the other. He could not stop at Coke's great house at Stoke Poges in his journey to the coast from Otes. There was more than one reason for his not daring to halt. Sir Edward was himself rusticated there.[24] The Lord Chief Justice had clashed with the will of the king and the policy of the most favoured bishops. He was living quietly but under surveillance. Coke's respect for the throne and the bishops was mixed with defiance of the royal policy in the Church. Had he not framed the Petition of Right in the parliament of 1628? Had he not suffered in the tower for upholding the law in the teeth of his royal master and the bishops? Even his writings, in which he defined the royal prerogative, the *Institutes* and *Reports*, would be confiscated at Stoke by royal agents before he died in 1634.[25] In 1630 he was under the shadow of this displeasure. Williams knew that. His own religious "conscience" was not identical with the conscience of Coke; but each man had his quarrel with the Stuart policy in matters of Church and State. For Williams to have called at Stoke would have been dangerous for both men, quite aside from any regret and rage the old man might have expressed at Williams's threatened reversion to the conventicles.

The last part of Williams's already quoted remarks to Mrs. Sadleir shows how he felt toward his protector and confirms that he learned much by way of political guile and practical wisdom from the years he spent as Coke's hopeful "son," his pensioner at Charterhouse and Cambridge. The personal influence he felt came first in his tribute, but with it went recognition of Coke's life, his struggle to defend the laws of England against personal royal prerogative. By the time he wrote to Mrs. Sadleir, Williams had read Coke's books, at least in part. They had been rescued from oblivion and published posthumously, by order of the Long Parliament on May 12, 1641.[26] Coke's speeches from the bench and his power over the parliaments that Williams had eagerly observed in 1628 and 1629 were still in his mind; he recalled the dogged industry of the great man, an example to himself to improve the long hours with writing, journeys, and political manoeuvre. "As your honorable father was wont to say," he told Mrs. Sadleir, "he that shall harrow what I have sown, must rise early."[27] The self-confidence of Coke comes through.

Mistress Sadleir was riled. She had been turned against all Puritans by the execution of Charles I and the trauma of the Civil War. Her reply was curt. She suggested Williams read the *Eikon Basilike,* compiled in the form of soliloquies and attributed to the executed king; Hooker's *Ecclesiastical Polity*; Lancelot Andrewes' sermons; Jeremy Taylor; and Jackson on the creed—all books dear to royalists. She told Williams what he knew: "some of these my dear father was a great admirer of, and would often call them the glorious lights of the Church of England."[28] Mrs. Sadleir returned Williams's piece unread, with cool courtesy. She signed herself "Your friend in the old way, Anne Sadleir."[29]

Williams was not done. He had the knack of getting himself into deeper water by persisting when not wanted. With a second letter he sent a copy of his *Bloody Tenent Yet More Bloody.* His diplomatic sense seemed to fail him when he had to deal with upper class ladies. He had trouble of the same sort in 1629, with Lady Barrington, at Otes, in Essex. Mrs. Sadleir sent him a further reply, polite but sharp. This provoked his much longer letter, containing two religious admonitions set out in numbered points. In effect Williams told her to read the Bible more carefully. He included unflattering insinuations about her devout Anglicanism and her wealth:

As to the religion and the worship of God, the common religion of the whole world, and the nations of it, it is but customary and traditional, from father to son, from which (old ways, &c), traditions, Christ Jesus, delivers his, not with gold and silver, but with his precious blood. *(I Peter 1. 18, 19)*[30]

Other sections of the letter hinted that Mrs. Sadleir might not be regenerate, and in a postscript Williams twisted his rather crude knife in the wound by recommending his "old friend" to read

Jeremy Taylor's *Liberty of Prophesying*, one of the few cogent
pleas for liberty of conscience that came from the side of the
bishops. This was too much even for the politeness of Anne
Sadleir. She told Williams roundly what many had wanted to say
to him: "It seems you have a face of brass, so that you cannot
blush."[31] She had been irritated by what he had said about the
royal family in his last letter; particularly about Charles I. "As
for the King," he had written, "I knew his person, vicious, a
swearer from his youth, and an oppressor and persecutor of good
men (to say nothing of his own father) . . . Against his and his
blasphemous father's cruelties, your own dear father, and many
precious men, shall rise up shortly and cry for vengeance."[32]
Quite apart from the questioning of *The King's Book*, Mrs.
Sadleir could hardly have failed to know that Coke had rather
low opinions (in private) about the personalities of the first two
Stuarts, whereas she (and no doubt her eminent husband) by that
time shared the horror of regicide and the admiration of
Charles's courage that had swept their party. She gave as good as
Williams in reply:

> For the foul and false aspersions you have cast upon that King, of
> ever-blessed memory, Charles, the martyr, I protest I trembled when I
> read them, and none but such a villain as yourself would have wrote
> them.[33]

Continuing the process of mutual recommendation of books she
suggested Williams get a copy of Clement Walker's scurrilous
and juicy *History of Independency* and lashed out at Williams's
friend, the poet John Milton, over his tract on divorce:

> For Milton's book, that you desire I should read, if I be not mistaken,
> that is that has wrote a book of the lawfulness of divorce; and, if
> report says true, he had, at that time, two or three wives living. This,
> perhaps, were good doctrine in New England; but it is most abominable
> in Old England. For his book that he wrote against the late King that
> you would have me read, you should have taken notice of God's judg-
> ment upon him, who stroke him with blindness, and, as I have heard,
> he was fain to have the help of one Andrew Marvell, or else he could
> not have finished that most accursed libel.[34]

Mrs. Sadleir had read Taylor's book on liberty of conscience and did not like it. "I say, it and you would make a good fire," she continued (not being able to discern she was speaking of a future bishop). However, she set right her outburst by her evaluation of Laud, which followed immediately:

I believe, howsoever he be slighted, he will rise a saint, when many seeming ones, such as you are, will rise devils.[35]

At the end of the correspondence, the lady turned again to remember the side of Coke that Williams had rejected:

I cannot conclude without putting you in mind how dear a lover and great an admirer my father was of the liturgy of the church of England, and would often say, no reform[ed] church had the like. He was constant to it, both in his life and at his death. I mean to walk in his steps; and, truly, when I consider who were the composers of it, and how they sealed the truth of it with their blood, I cannot but wonder why it should now of late be thus condemned. By what I have now writ, you know how I stand affected. I will walk as directly to heaven as I can, in which place, if you will turn from being a rebel, and fear God and obey the king, there is hope I may meet you there; howsoever, trouble me no more with your letters, for they are very troublesome to her that wishes you in the place from whence you came.[36]

The double meaning in this parting sentiment was sealed for posterity by a note Anne Sadleir wrote on the letters when she put them all away:

This Roger Williams, when he was a youth, would, in a shorthand, take sermons and speeches in the Star Chamber and present them to my dear father. He, seeing so hopeful a youth, took such liking to him that he sent him in to Sutton's Hospital [Charterhouse] and he was the second that was placed there; full little did he think that he would have proved such a rebel to God, the king, and his country. I leave his letters, that, if ever he has the face to return into his native country, Tyburn may give him welcome.[37]

Her idea was obviously to hold the documents with thoughts that Williams might be executed in some future restoration of the royal line. We thus owe the preservation of the correspondence, which tells us much about Williams's links with Coke, to the malevolence of an understandably exasperated woman.

Any attempt to go over the tracks of Roger Williams at school and Cambridge tells us little of his teachers and experiences. Charterhouse, or Sutton's Hospital,[38] was a recent foundation in which Coke was deeply interested. His financial sponsorship of a London boy meant that he hoped Roger Williams would receive thorough training in classical languages, self-expression and the social finesse needed for later high office. There are many instances in the seventeenth century in England of opportunities in education leading people of modest birth to prestige. The career of Archbishop Laud is one of these.[39] The King's Council, with its surrounding legal advisers and diplomats was still then the centre of effective power in the realm. Well-educated clergy and nimble-witted administrators could move swiftly into office if they had the necessary training in school and at one of the universities. The career of Doctor John Preston during the reign of James I gives us an example of what could be done at court by Puritan clergy who moved easily among the gentry and could catch the eye of the King and his advisers.[40] During the period before 1640 polish and preferment were natural roads to the court, where the power of Church and State met in the monarchy. England, as much as any other European country, accepted the assumption behind the Peace of Augsburg, concluded in 1555— *cuius regio eius religio*; the religion of the ruler is the religion of the subject; the national ruler is supreme, under God, in the visible Church.

In accepting the aid Coke offered him, Roger Williams must surely have known throughout his schooldays that he was being trained, on such assumptions, to accept the pattern as then found in England. Changes in liturgy, canon law, and diocesan structure there might be, if the Puritan cause prevailed; but there would not be any disturbance of the belief that the monarch was the nursing father of the Church and its titular supreme governor. The crown was sovereign over all jurisdictions, political and ecclesiastical, and seemed likely to remain so, whatever outward changes might be achieved in the external forms of the Church's life. If Roger Williams in boyhood and youth was subject to the influence of the Separatist fringe, he probably had to insulate himself against that influence in accepting his patron's path to influence and advantage. The traces of his experience during the years of preparation, between 1617 and 1628, are present in many of his meditations on the attempts of the clergy to stake out their "seats and saddles of their great and settled maintenance"[41] in the high places of the land. He knew what those ambitions were and how they were covered over by rationalised "pure motives" and desires to serve. He had known it all himself, so that his reflection had a quality of retrospective self-understanding and regret for a world that was later renounced:

> Since I know what it is to study, to preach, to be an elder, to be applauded; and yet also what it is to tug at the oar, to dig with the spade and plough, and to labour and travel day and night amongst English, amongst barbarians, why should I not be humbly bold to give my witness faithfully, to give my counsel effectually, and to persuade with some truly pious and conscientious spirits, rather than to turn to law, to physic, to soldiery, to educating of children, to digging—and yet not cease from prophesying—rather than to live under the slavery, yea and the censure (from Christ and His saints, and others also) of a mercenary and hireling ministry?[42]

"Prophesying" meant faithful preaching, which to him no longer depended on professional clergy; but the transition Williams made through school to Cambridge and his chaplaincy at Otes was not despised when he paid tribute to the intellectual equipment he had been given. He never attacked sound learning or good manners. Social distinctions, and property were also accepted from his boyhood and not abandoned. "Every one that hath friends," he said, in 1652, "may be preferred to fellowships in colleges, to the superstitious degrees and titles of Divinity (as they call it) and by these stairs ascend up the Gospel preferments of rich and honourable benefices." But he continued at once:

> Far be it from me to derogate from that honourable civility of training up of youth in languages, and other humane learning, whether in the City of London, or other towns and cities.[43]

In the margin of the book, at the same point, he inserted the observation that "Institution of youth in humane learning, withal instructing them with the knowledge & fear of the Lord" was "most Christian and honourable."

Memories of his London schooling were not frequent in Roger Williams's later writings. Charterhouse, in any case, was a stepping-stone to a greater world of scholars and clergy. The eyes of the boy would have been fixed on all that, as he became familiar with "grammar rules"[44] of Latin and Greek and moved through logic and rhetoric, toward the art of formal disputation, or dialectic, which was still used in the universities. He became adept at it. Roger Williams was an educated man; not a great scholar with a mastery of many ancient books, but a skilful debater, who knew how to analyse and divide up propositions, to weigh, refute, concede, and develop arguments. On the whole he kept free of the pedantic catalogues and minute considerations in which Puritan scholastics like William Perkins of Cambridge used to delight. That was because he invariably addressed himself to a single practical issue. His weapons were timely pamphlets or letters, not systematic discourses. They may have been blunt but they were effective, because they did not dwell on small issues but drove to the point in hand. On the foundations he laid at Charterhouse he extended his later knowledge of languages. Quite casually, in a letter to the younger Winthrop from London in 1652, he described his meetings with John Milton and others and his work as a language teacher:

> It pleased the Lord to call me for some time, and with some persons, to practice the Hebrew, the Greek, Latin, French, and Dutch. The Secretary of the Council, (Mr. Milton) for my Dutch I read him, read me many more languages. Grammar rules begin to be esteemed a tyranny. I taught two young gentlemen, a Parliament man's sons, as we teach our children English, by words, phrases, and constant talk, &c.[45]

The practical bent of Williams's mind is seen in his first book, the *Key into the Language of America*.[46] The *Key* was published long before John Eliot's Indian Bible. Williams was the first to present the "strange speech"[47] of the American Indians to an English public. He was an accurate observer and applied his grammatical sense to the analysis of parts of speech. His modesty about his ability in the language of New England's natives notwithstanding,[48] he considered his grasp sufficient for compiling a provisional dictionary or grammar, but this, he said, he "purposely avoided, as not so accommodate to the benefit of all, as I hope this form is."

A dialogue also I had thoughts of, but avoided for brevity's sake; and yet—with no small pains—I have so framed every chapter, and the matter of it, as I may call it an implicit dialogue.

It is framed chiefly after the Narragansett dialect, because most spoken in the country, and yet, with attending to the variation of peoples and dialects, it will be of great use in all parts of the country.

Whatever your occasions be, either of travel, discourse, trading, &c., turn to the Table, which will direct you to the proper chapter.

Because the life of all language is in the pronunciation I have been at the pains and charges to cause the accents, tones, or sounds to be affixed.[49]

Brevity, usefulness in travel and trade, pronunciation; these were the governing considerations. Williams's practical streak appears often in later life. His decisions to separate and emigrate were not purely theological. His family background was practical. The time he spent at Charterhouse and Cambridge gave him a prolonged taste of academic and clerical life. His choice of the practical laity as friends and correspondents, as fellow-workers and fellow-colonists, expressed his preference for action over thought. Pure scholars and professional clergy annoyed his restless spirit. He was intelligent, but in a functional way. The precedents, compromises, and adjustments of the English law appealed to his type of mind far more than the privileges of professional intellectuals. His motives were mixed. He rejected scholarly and clerical preferment for two reasons—it was a satanic temptation, and he disliked it. Theology was interwoven with temperamental revulsion.

Remarks Williams made about the two great universities of

England and the very title "scholar" illustrate the point. Among the implied objects of his biting words in *The Hireling Ministry None of Christs*[50] in 1652 were Independent ministers who had accepted high posts at Oxford and Cambridge under Oliver Cromwell, men like John Owen[51] and Thomas Goodwin:[52]

> We may . . . see our great mistakes, both of ourselves and our fore-fathers, as to the pretended seed-plots and seminaries for the ministry, the universities of Europe, and the universities of this nation. For although I heartily acknowledge that among all the outward gifts of God, humane learning and the knowledge of languages and good arts are excellent, and excel other outward gifts as far as light excels darkness, and therefore that schools of humane learning ought to be maintained in a due way, and cherished; yet notwithstanding, *in ordine ad ministerium,* as to the ministry of Jesus Christ (any one of those ministries, *Ephesians 4* and *I Corinthians 12*), upon a due survey of all their institutions and continual practices, compared with the last will and testament of Jesus Christ, they will be found to be none of Christ's, and that in many respects.[53]

In what followed Williams criticized the arrogation of the title "scholar" by clergy and males. The clergy of Oxford and Cambridge were unfavourably contrasted, as disciples (or scholars, learners) with the humble seamstress, Dorcas, whose story had been told in the ninth chapter of the Book of Acts:

> As to the name "scholar"; although as to humane learning many ways lawful, yet as it is appropriated to such as practise the ministry—have been at the universities, as they say—it is a sacrilegious and thievish title, robbing all believers and saints, who are frequently, in the Testament of Christ, styled disciples or scholars of Christ Jesus. . . . And this title is so much theirs that both men and women, believing, were called scholars (*Acts 9*): "There was a certain disciple, or scholar, called Dorcas."[54]

Williams went on to characterise the preciosity of students and teachers at universities. His contempt was so strong that there is reason to think he was reminiscing with distaste. His years at Pembroke College, in the mid-1620's, were marked by political

agitation in London and by combined action against the King
and the bishops all over the country. When Williams later became domestic chaplain at Otes he was effervescing with enthusiasm for the Puritan "plots" in parliament. He journeyed to
London and became a reporter of events in the parliament of
1629 for members of Sir William Masham's eager household.[55]
Interests like this hardly spring up unheralded; Roger Williams
had chafed at the bit at Cambridge. His career there had been
brief, and though he graduated, he had probably seen enough
of the place for his own taste. It was an establishment. He took
what he could get—and proceeded thereafter to bite the hand that
fed him; he attacked the university teachers for

their monkish and idle course of life, partly so genteel and stately,
partly so vain and superstitious, that to wet a finger in any pains or
labour, it is a disgraceful and an unworthy act. But the Church is built
upon the foundation of the apostles and prophets, who were labourers,
fishermen, tent-makers; Jesus Christ, although the Prince of Life, yet a
poor carpenter, the chief corner stone. And I cannot but conceive that,
although it should not please the most holy and jealous God to stir up
this renowned state, and their renowned Cromwell (the second) to deal
with our refined monasteries as that blessed Cromwell (the first) did
with the more gross and palpably superstitious in Henry VIII's days:
yet in His time the Lord Jesus, whose is all power in heaven and earth,
will spew these seminaries of hirelings and mystical merchants out of
His mouth, as He hath done their fathers, the superstitious and bloody
bishops, before them.[56]

"Mystical merchants" was an unkind expression, referring to
those described in the 18th Chapter of the Revelation as having
"waxed fat" by the power of the luxury of the wanton whore,
Babylon the Great, meaning, for a Puritan, the vestiges of
mediaeval "popery."

Williams reacted with equal vehemence to the ancient customs
and ceremonies of the universities, fulminating against

their popish and vaunting titles, so strange from the New Testament
and language of Christ Jesus, or any word or title that came forth of His
blessed mouth: Bachelors of Divinity (or godliness), Doctor of Divinity;

so clearly and expressly opposite to the command of the Lord Jesus: "Call no man father, doctor," &c., that is by way of eminency in spiritual and heavenly regards, "Rabbi, Rabbi; Doctor, Doctor," &c.

Roger Williams went on to say that he omitted,

(because possibly for shame left off in these days) their childish ceremonies, used even by the most holy and conscientious, in their superstitious commencings and creatings, &c., their holy gowns (black and red), holy cassocks, holy caps, holy scarfs, holy rings, yea and holy boots also, &c.; all as far from the purity and simplicity of the Son of God . . . as the honest attire of some sober and chaste matron from the wanton and flaunting vanities of some painted harlot.[57]

Despite this, Williams could use the ornate rhetoric of the schools if it suited him. He did it—perhaps inconsistently—to ingratiate himself with upper class personages or with the parliament or the Council of the realm.[58] He was aware of his own prolixity and admitted he had used stylish flourishes and classical turns of speech in his earlier preaching. At Cambridge he would have been exposed to the controversy going on at the time within the Puritan fold, between the adherents of Latin elegance, tropes and allusions, and the severe pruning and "plain style" advocated by Puritan teachers like William Perkins or William Ames and "painful preachers" like Arthur Hildersham and John Dod.[59] They purged their writing and speaking of "conceits" in order to communicate with the down-to-earth laity through what they called "homely similitudes."[60] They also resorted to a simplified logical method learned from the Frenchman Ramus.[61] This was intended to cut through the logic-chopping of the late mediaeval schools to reality. The tension between the two styles: on the one hand, the older courtly manner, which had prevailed under Elizabeth and was to continue in the preaching of the Anglican Caroline divines, and on the other, the plain speech of the Puritans, was at work in Williams. It accompanied an inner struggle and choice. Should he write as he had been encouraged to write at Charterhouse? Was there not something to be said for classical elegance and "metaphysical" depth? Or must the skill acquired be abandoned, the way of expression purged? Had not

Sir Edward Coke liked, on occasion, to talk with a more "elevated" voice and make his point among the great?

Something of the same struggle can be sensed in the contrast between the earlier and later style of John Cotton, who became Roger Williams's adversary. Cotton, the son of a modest Derby lawyer,[62] had been sponsored at Cambridge earlier than Williams and had made an eminent clerical career. He became the Fellow of a College and later successful incumbent of a wealthy church at the English Boston. His Puritan "conversion" led to a gradual purgation of style similar to Williams's own. There the parallel stops; because Cotton was, and always remained, in some ways an academic. His language became more sinewy, dryer; but the earthy metaphors and moments of fused passion were rarer than in Williams. Williams reverted to the speech of the Londoner. Cotton reverted to something closer to good lawyers' prose. Both bore the scars of inward wrestling associated with their years at Cambridge, when they had to choose whether to converse with the Church and the court, or with the "practical" lay patrons of the Puritan clergy.

In Williams the choice was never finally made. He lived in an ambivalent way. Given leisure and stimulus he might have made a great writer. He was well aware of his "boldness and prolixity."[63] He could refer to Latin in genuine Barrowist rage as "the whore's tongue of Italy,"[64] but he used it himself when his inspiration ran away and his contemplation of the heights and depths of man's estate took hold on his mind: "It was a motto in one of the late Parliaments: cornets under a shower of blood 'Transibit,' "[65] he told John Winthrop, Junior, in 1660. Classical power of expression and a nostalgia for heraldry were still affecting his imagination; so he could quote Martial,[66] and could indulge in manly exhortations to the younger Winthrop that must have recalled their common ground in learning "good letters" when they were youths:

While we are here, noble Sir, let us *Viriliter hoc agere, rem agere humanam, divinam, Christianam,* which I believe is all of a most public genius.[67]

This was moving; but sometimes Williams's vacillation between the ornate and homely was not so edifying. When he addressed the parliament he could grow baroque:

> You cannot (ever renowned Patriots) but like some grave Commanders of Fleets and Armies, who have brought their Ships and followers through tempestuous storms and bloody fights, to joyful Rest and Harbours! You cannot but look back with Admirings, with Praisings, with Resolvings to cast your Crowns, and Heads, and Hearts, and Hands, (for the remaining Minutes of the short Candle of your life) at his Feet, in whose most High and most gracious Hands have all your Breaths and wayes been.[68]

By contrast, when he attacked his old Providence enemy William Harris he could be offensively plain:

> W. Harris, who, being an impudent morris-dancer in Kent . . . under a cloak of separation, got in with myself, till his self-ends and restless strife, and at last his atheistical denying of heaven and hell, made honest souls to fly from him. Now he courts the Baptists; then he kicks them off and flatters the Foxians; then the drunkards (which he calls all that are not of the former two amongst us); then knowing the prejudices of the other Colonies against us, he dares to abuse his Majesty and Council, to bring New England upon us. . . .[69]

By the time those words were written he was an old man; he had almost given up being obsequious to anyone; but it took him a long time to resolve the temptation to indulge in rhetoric for the sake of showing off. There are times, though, when we are grateful for the hint of formal pageantry that lingered in his style; at his best he reminds us of the simple splendour of the Venerable Bede or Chaucer:

> How thankful unto God, unto man, should we poor strangers be, for the least crumb, or drop, or rag, vouchsafed unto us, when we remember we are but strangers in an inn, but passengers in a ship; and though we dream of long summer days, yet our very life and being is but a swift, short passage from the bank of time to the other side, or bank, of a doleful eternity?[70]

After he fled Massachusetts Roger Williams knew long periods of hunger for books and writing materials in his chosen wilderness. He could be terse about schools, universities, and the goal of fame they sought, yet at the same time he would plead for more paper,[71] eagerly inquire for Carpenter's *Universal Geography*,[72] allude to the naturalist Gesner,[73] follow the pamphlet warfare in London with avidity.[74] His rejection of his own intellectual preparation did not mean a total reaction against learning; only a denial that learning should be a prerogative of clerics and their royal road to the wrong kind of power. In criticising the universities he looked forward to their desacralising. They had, in his mind, become redoubts for forces of lordly ambition masquerading in the garments of divinity. Williams had come to loathe the royal mystique behind the "state Church" system. He questioned radically the Stuart claim, namely, in his own words,

that civil magistracy is not merely a civil thing, in the very nature and essential qualities and beings thereof; but rather some *divinum quid,* and that kings and queens and magistrates are gods, not only by way of allusion and consimilitude, . . . but really they are sacred (or holy) persons, their majesties sacred, their crowns sacred, and their very kingdoms and empires sacred. Hence that most horrid, blasphemous character on the forehead of the Whore and of the Beast, *Sacrum Romanum Imperium,* that Sacred, or Holy, Roman Empire.[75]

The course of his formal education had been, for Williams, an attraction into the sphere where sacral kingship still determined the attitudes of court laity and court clergy alike. Even Cromwell accepted the title Lord, and almost accepted the title King, within the atmosphere created, from mediaeval times onward, about the throne of the greatest in the land. In his *Bloody Tenent Yet More Bloody* Williams often referred obliquely to the ambition of the clergy, which had once been his own temptation. John Cotton, his opponent in the controversy about "persecution," was an appropriate person to nudge, because Cotton had renounced security in order to emigrate, but in Williams's view had again succumbed to temptation, when he stood on the side of the colonial gentry of the new Boston, a fresh set of magistrates invested with the old theocratic aura. Williams also thought Cotton had preferred conformity to hardship in dealing with the case of Anne Hutchinson, the antinomian leader. Though not quite fair to Cotton, Williams pressed him at such sensitive points. Both antagonists knew what was implied concerning power and ease, as contrasted with the Cross.

In a wistful aside, part of his description of his own labours in compiling *The Bloody Tenent Yet More Bloody*, Roger Williams said he too, "tis true . . . might have run the road of preferment, as well in Old as New England, and have had the leisure and time of such who eat and drink with the drunken, and smite with the fist of wickedness their fellow servants."[76] The Old Testament reference to *Isaiah 58.4* would not have been missed by Cotton, nor the implication that he was one of Williams's smiters.

"The truth is," Williams wrote,

> the great gods of this world are god-belly, god-peace, god-wealth, god-honour, god-pleasure, &c. These gods must not be blasphemed, that is evil spoken of, no, not provoked, &c. The servants of the living God, being true to their Lord and Master, have opposed his glory, greatness, honour, &c., to these gods and to such religions, worships and services as commonly are made but as a mask or veil, or covering of these gods.[77]

Commenting on John Cotton's pleas for the legitimacy of disbanding conventicles, Williams pointedly struck at Cotton's education and attitudes:

> How grievous is this language of Master Cotton, as if he had been nourished in the chapels and cloisters of persecuting prelates, and priests, the Scribes and Pharisees? As if he never had heard of Jesus Christ in truth and meekness. . . .[78]

It had come to seem to the exile that

> rarely this world admitteth or not long continueth a true servant of God in any place of trust and credit, except some extraordinary hand of God over-power, or else his servants by some base stairs of flattery or worldly compliance, ascend the chair of civil power.[79]

Williams had observed how ministers could "make magistrates stairs and stirrups, for themselves (the clergy) to mount up in the seats of their great and settled maintenance."[80]

Mr. Cotton, he dared to affirm, as he looked at his adversary's situation in New England, sat "in as soft and rich a saddle as any throughout the whole country, through the greatness and richness of the merchandise of the town of Boston, above other parts of the land."[81]

Using a simile drawn from the "white," the bull's-eye at the centre of archery targets, Williams stated his contrast with devastating effect:

The clergy (sacrilegiously so called) in all ages since the apostasy [the falling away of the Church from a presumed New Testament purity] have, like some proud and dainty servants, disdained to serve a poor despised Christ, a carpenter, one that came at last to the gallows, &c. And therefore have they ever framed to themselves rich and lordly, pompous and princely, temporal and worldly Christs, instead of the true Lord Jesus Christ, the spiritual King of His saints and people. And however it suits well the common end to retain the name of Christ (as the Lord Jesus prophesied many false Christs should arise, and many should come in His name, &c.) yet most sure it will be found that a temporal crown and dignity, sword and authority, wealth and prosperity, is the white that most of those called scholars, ministers, bishops, aim and level at. . . .[82]

During the years of his adoption as a "son" by Sir Edward Coke, Williams had himself known what it felt like to drive toward that target; but when he came to live among the gentry, his aim changed.

5

Personal Crisis: The Gentry

T HE RECORDS OF THE University of Cambridge show that Roger
Williams was entered there at Easter 1625 as a "pensioner," or
supported scholar. He graduated Bachelor of Arts early in 1627,[1]
thereby earning the title of a "gentleman," which was bestowed
on graduates of Oxford and Cambridge in their own right. Upon
graduation he was obliged to sign a form of assent to a set of
three articles required of those entering holy orders. These had
been laid down in 1583 by Archbishop Whitgift and were intended to bring anti-Prayer Book Puritans into line.[2] The text of
the articles, which were embodied in Archbishop Bancroft's
Canons of 1604, provided for assent to the royal supremacy, the
consonance of the Prayer Book with the word of God, and the
acceptance of the Thirty-Nine Articles. When looked at carefully
and taken tongue-in-cheek, the articles could be, and were, signed
by many convinced Puritans who opposed both the Elizabethan
ceremonies and the rule of the prelates. The act of conforming
meant wriggling into the fold; but wriggle they did.

It has been assumed that because Roger Williams subscribed
he must have been a compliant Prayer Book Anglican, at least of
the loyal sort to which his patron Coke belonged. But this does

not necessarily follow. The first article simply said "that her majesty, under God, hath, and ought to have, the sovereignty and rule over all manner of persons born within her realms, dominions, and countries of what estate, either ecclesiastical or temporal, soever they be." It went on to reject the authority of foreign powers in England, thus covering the case of the Roman Catholic recusants. Whitgift seems to have specified royal supremacy over persons of the ecclesiastical estate, rather than over ecclesiastical causes, probably so as not to alienate the civil and common lawyers who were such powerful lay patrons. When Williams took the articles he could assent to the proposition that King James was supreme in the realm over his person, if not his spiritual conscience.

The second article declared "that the Book of Common Prayer, and of ordering bishops, priests, and deacons, containeth nothing in it contrary to the word of God, and that the same may lawfully be used, and that he himself will use the form of the said book prescribed in public prayer and administration of the sacraments, and none other." This was more difficult, though it could be argued that the doctrine of the Prayer Book was sound and the ceremonies not "contrary" to the divine command, but not in accord with it either, simply "dregs of popery," of no great moment and gradually being eliminated as the Book was being disregarded by many celebrants at the points where they desired omissions in practice. People like Roger Williams often knew they could obtain licences as godly preachers from sympathetic bishops and be permitted to serve as supported lecturers or chaplains in ample households. They would then not be directly involved in "public prayer and administration of the sacraments" in any parish church, so the second article would not apply.

The Thirty-Nine Articles were then, as they are now, construed in many senses and could be held as provisionally agreeable to the word (or will and command) of God, pending further reformation. After signing his certificate at Cambridge, Williams could present himself to any bishop for a quiet ordination ceremony (or be tolerated unordained), after which he could preach, teach, and care for souls even though not introduced to a parish, at the request of a suitably influential lay patron. Under some such formula he was serving at Sir William Masham's manor house of Otes, in Essex, by 1629.

Between 1625 and 1633, a group of Puritan laity from the London vicinity and from the West Country, combined to raise funds with the aim of acquiring church livings and lands sufficient for the endowment of "godly preachers," an unattached "church within the Church" designed to further Puritan doctrines and aims.[3] Inevitably they clashed with the determined William Laud, who correctly identified their objective and had the enterprise dissolved. The "lay feoffees for the purchase of impropriations" as they were called "were later to be accused of favouring dative, removable men, whose allowance by the ordinary was unnecessary," while an analysis of their membership shows they were interested in colonisation as a Puritan refuge and strongly suggests that they represented "a much larger group of Puritans in and about London."

There is no evidence that at Otes Williams came under the scheme, but he could well have been one of the "dative removable men"[4] who felt the pressure of Laud's policy in 1630 and were obliged either to present themselves to the ordinary (meaning a bishop who would insist on presentation to a parish) or to slip quickly out of the country and join the ranks of some 20,000 Englishmen who emigrated to America between 1628 and 1640.[5] Both possibilities—a parish ministry and emigration to New England—are indicated in his letters to Lady Joan Barrington, the mother-in-law of Sir William Masham, his employer:

It is well known (though I would gladly conceal myself) how a gracious God and tender conscience (as Balak said to Balaam) hath kept me back from honour and preferment. Besides many former offers and that late New England call, I have since had two several livings proffered to me, each of them a hundred pounds per annum; but as things yet stand among us I see not how any means and I shall meet that way. Nor do I seek, nor shall I be drawn on any terms to part (even to my last parting) from Otes, so long as any competency can be raised or liberty afforded.[6]

Williams's statements support the assumption that he became a household chaplain, a tame cleric among the gentry on account of his being a rebel and an objector when he left Cambridge, so that he had to find Puritan lay protection. He suggested to Lady Barrington that his reasons for not accepting a parish were well known. The reference he made to Balak and Balaam was no casual aside. Balak was the king of Moab, referred to in *Numbers* 22, who had tried to hire a prophet named Balaam to put a curse on the divinely chosen people of Israel then invading his kingly territory. The refusal of Williams to denounce radical Puritanism and conform is implied by an examination of what Balak said when he offered Balaam a rôle as "court prophet":

And the princes of Moab rose up, and they went unto Balak, and said, Balaam refuses to come with us. And Balak sent yet again princes, more, and honourable than they. And they came to Balaam, and said to him, Thus saith Balak the son of Zippor, let nothing, I pray thee, hinder thee from coming unto me: For I will promote thee unto very great honour, and whatsoever thou sayest unto me I will do: come therefore, I pray thee, curse me this people. And Balaam answered and said unto the servants of Balak, If Balak would give me his house full of silver and gold, I cannot go beyond the word of the Lord my God, to do less or more *(Numbers 22.14–18)*.

Williams's talents were undoubted. He had received offers of good livings in the Church in England and an invitation, probably through the organisation of the New England Company[7] in 1628. He may have declined this because he knew his views on complete separation from the parishes of the Church of England in its preaching and Prayer Book services went beyond the position of the sponsors of the New England scheme. The phrase "as things yet stand among us" echoed another in the same letter, "as things stand now in England" and referred to the impossibility of his accepting a parish while the Prayer Book and ceremonies, with the policy of the bishops and the King, remained. Otes was the ideal refuge for him until things changed in the Church or he died, but his words proved that he was aware of the possible drying up of financial support for such appointments and the threat of being evicted by episcopal action. His situation at Otes was precarious throughout. He was aware of it. So was Lady Barrington. In the letter he was proposing marriage to her niece and hinting that she might be interested (as a rich widow) in endowing the match in a manner befitting a gentleman. Her response to the hint was negative. Assent would surely be like tying her niece, with appropriate insurance, to the tail of a wayward kite. Roger Williams might blow in any direction, if and when the wind grew higher.

Williams found himself, therefore, in the position of many an English bachelor cleric in the seventeenth and eighteenth centuries. His code as gentleman required that he should not soil his hands with the toil of the laity. He was in his late twenties and eligible on account of his gifts and graces. Much of his time had to be spent praying, expounding the scriptures and advising conventionally pious women on the state of their souls, a notoriously dangerous calling when plied among the young, unmarried, and impressionable. In Williams's case the proximity of London meant he could succumb at times to the lure of the great city's political and ecclesiastical arenas. He was used as a companion and message-bearer in this way by the laity who were involved in parliamentary or legal business.[8] At the same time, he was not really one of them. As a clergyman (a name he later frequently deprecated) he was not even accepted by the more notable advanced Puritan preachers as enjoying exactly their status. The eminence and authority of John Cotton, Hugh Peter[9] (virtual chaplain to the lay feoffees), and others like them, must have galled his spirit. Their consciences were at ease in their livings and great places; his could not be reconciled to accept the partial conformity they took for granted. He was a "godly preacher" at this stage, but not more. Everybody knew what a tempest slumbered inside him; but at Otes he could truthfully say to Lady Barrington:

I have learned another lesson; to still my soul as a weaned child and give offence to none. I have learned to keep my study and pray to the God of heaven (as oft as I do pray) for the everlasting peace and welfare of your kind ladyship, whose soul and comfort is in the number of my greatest cares.[10]

The condition of resignation did not last. Such a suppression of his impulsive self helped to lead to the coming explosion. But the sentiment was genuine for the time being.

The crisis came in early 1629, when disappointment in love led Roger Williams to formulate a tactless critique of formal country-house Puritanism in the second of his two letters addressed to Lady Barrington about his love for her niece, Jane Whalley. The first letter gives the background. It is fortunate that it has survived in the archives of the Barrington family, because it confirms the picture of Roger Williams derived from study of his later writings and provides us with a psychological motive that is intertwined with his choice of the wilderness and with his open identification with the theology and practice of the Separatists. The rejection of his suit was in itself a rebuke to his new-found status as gentleman. The distinguished lady who gave him no for an answer became in his mind a symbol of the intermixture of haughty status and Puritan piety he ever afterward condemned as painted show and unregenerate pride. Lady Barrington had become a widow in the preceding year, 1628.[11] Part of Williams's duty at Otes was to "comfort" her, using that word in its older sense of strengthening by spiritual means. He knew what a formidable person she was; the very representative of that great network of squires, justices, merchants, adventurers, who by their intermarriages and commercial schemes, as well as their unity in religion, formed the opposition to the Stuart royal claims.[12] By the marriage of her daughter to Sir William Masham, the Essex alliance now called "the classic Hampden-Barrington connection"[13] had been further strengthened. She was an aunt of Oliver Cromwell. The Earl of Warwick, Oliver St. John the lawyer and politician, John Pym, John Hampden, were a few of those who moved in the circle of East Anglian grandees with which she was familiar through birth and experience. Her late husband, Sir Francis Barrington of Hatfield Broad Oak, had been richer than the Masham family. Her niece, Jane Whalley, with whom Williams fell in love, was the daughter of Richard Whalley, a prominent Nottinghamshire gentleman known for his patronage of Puritan clergy. She and Williams were thrown together and may have shown it before he set matters in order by writing his first letter to Lady Barrington, whose niece was also her ward. What he said, as he wrote on an unknown date before May 2, 1629, is put with the courtly religiosity expected of a doting domestic chaplain; he was badly in love; he addressed the letter,[14] in absence, "to his honorable good ladie, Ye Lady Barrington at Hatfield Priorie":

Madam

Your ladyship may wonder at this unwonted absence! And also ask what means this paper deputy! Give me leave, dear Madam, to say, with David to his brothers in the field, "Is there not a cause?" A just, happily, and known cause, I am sure, to your ladyship (who as an angel of God discerneth wisely), a known and open cause.

Williams was in an exalted state. His love had been returned by Miss Whalley and it appears they had been hatching this hopeful approach to her aunt while Williams had been neglecting his ministry to the widow in mourning for the sake of paying less-than-secret attentions to the niece.

Many and often speeches have long fluttered or flown abroad concerning your Ladyship's near kinswoman and my unworthy self.

Lady Barrington was then informed that he was now stepping into the open to seek a match that lay above his station and means:

The nearness of her blood to your ladyship and godly flourishing branches hath forced me to confess her portion, in that regard, to be beyond compare invaluable.

Many years later Roger Williams would use the same conventional metaphor of root and branches, when he wrote to the "much honoured" Mrs. Sadleir, the daughter of Sir Edward Coke,[15] but now he went on to mention another obstacle to the match, Miss Whalley's alleged attitude, "much accused for passionate & hastie, rash & unconstant," a character not born out by her later career as the wife of a not-very-remarkable New England minister, William Hooke, recalled as a chaplain to Cromwell in

1656.[16] Exposure to Williams could easily have earned her the reputation he mentioned, though just for the time being. Then, in an honest acknowledgment he faced up to the fact that it was "some indecorum for her to condescend to my low ebb," but offset the obstacle by telling Lady Barrington that Jane Whalley's real and prospective wealth did not amount to much. "That portion it hath pleased God to allot her (as I heare) is not for present & happily as things stand now in England shall never be by us enjoyed." The enigmatic sentence seems to imply that Jane Whalley will inherit the title to a living in the Church of England which Williams, and therefore his hoped-for bride would feel they must renounce for conscientious reasons. The implication that, if she married him, Jane Whalley would stay "happily" poor must have been especially distasteful to Lady Barrington. Williams continued to pile on this built-in dissuasive without appearing to know it:

> I shall impart the utmost to your ladyship, more punctually [exactly] than ever yet to any. Beside this means [his own support at Otes] I now from hence enjoy little there is yet I can call mine. After the death of an aged loving mother, amongst some other children I may expect (though for the present she be close and will not promise) some twenty pounds or twenty marks per annum. At hand, undisposed of, I have some seven score pieces and a little (yet costly) study of books. Thus possessing all things I have nothing, yet more than God owes me, or than my blessed Saviour had Himself.

This noble offer of holy poverty was followed up immediately by what appears to be a threat of seizing an alternative offer of somebody else's daughter if Lady Barrington failed to close with the bargain:

> Poor yet as I am, I have some few offers at present, one put into my hand, person and present portion worthy. Yet stand they still at door, and shall until the fairest end the Lord shall please to give to this shall come to light.

The prodding finger of Miss Whalley may be seen behind Williams's proposal:

I have been told to open to your ladyship the whole anatomy of this business. To wrong your precious name and answer her kind love with want would be like gall to all the honey of my life and mar my marriage joys. The kind affection of your dear ladyship and worthy niece is of better merit and desert.

All of which looks suspiciously like a lovers' conspiracy to extract a wedding portion out of a canny old lady, who turned it down.

A prophetic woe, uttered by Williams against Lady Barrington, then became the substance of his second letter,[17] for which the domestic chaplain chose some of the most tactless barbs in his armoury. To learn from other items in the Barrington family letters that she was offended comes as no surprise. The "still soule" of the "weaned childe" reverted, in this further letter of May 2, 1629, to fierce squalling. The introduction, with its seaman's metaphor, was in the manner of the true Williams. He must have been told by Lady Barrington not to show his face in her house again, but he adjusted to the new situation and proceeded to tell Lady Barrington (his calling, surely?) that she was in danger of becoming reprobate and eternally lost because of her hypocrisy and pride:

Madam,

I am forced, with the seaman, for want of a full gale to make use of a side wind and salute your ladyship by another, being for a time shut out myself. I doubt not but your good wisdom and love have fairly interpreted my carriage in the late treaty, and also trust, quieted and stilled the loving affections of your worthy niece. We hope to live together in the heavens, though the Lord have denied that union on earth. Dear Madam, let me beg your Christian pardon if I shall acquaint your ladyship with a business of more weight and consequence, and much nearer concerning yourself . . .

The next step was to quote the prophet Jeremiah and set himself for the prophet's task of upsetting the great and noble people who were at ease in Zion:

What I shall now express to your ladyship hath long lain like fire in my bones (*Jeremiah 20.9*). *I said I should not make mention of his name* [i.e. God's name] *in this kind to you, but his word was in my heart as a burning fire shut up in my bones and I could not stay.*

Williams could not have reflected long on the incongruity of this outburst with his previous letter and fawning suit for the hand of Jane Whalley. He set to, recalling her family cares and her bereavement of the preceding year as "loud alarms to awake you." Telling her "the Lord hath a quarrel against you" he said: "Encouragement to be naked and plain your ladyship was pleased to give me at Otes." He then availed himself of the invitation to practise godly frankness:

> If ever (dear Madam) when there is but the breadth of a few grey hairs between you and your everlasting home, let me deal uprightly with you. I know not one professor [believer] amongst all I know whose truth and faithfulness to Jesus Christ is more suspected, doubted, feared, by all or most of those that know the Lord.

As a next move Williams appealed to the fears felt by numbers of his fellow ministers for Lady Barrington's eternal salvation. The witnesses apart from himself, however, remained anonymous and the implication of clerical tattle about her state of soul must have been insufferable:

> It hath almost astonished me (and I trust will deeply affect your ladyship) that not only inferior Christians but ministers, eagle-eyed, faithful, and observant to your ladyship, after so many years of God's patience towards you, so long profession, such helps, means incomparable, should yet be driven to sigh, to say little, to suspend their judgments, to hope, but fear and doubt.

Lady Barrington was informed that there were fears the world had choked the seed of the Gospel in her; that she seemed distant, "strange," when others were active in religious pursuits; that her spiritual growth seemed to have stopped, "young plants of yesterday giving fairer testimonies of greater fruitfulness." The last observation could easily have carried a veiled comparison between the cool widow and her ardent niece.

Next Williams rather unctuously invited Lady Barrington to use *Psalm 51.11* and *71.9* in her prayers. If she bothered to look them up she would have found they were both about the danger of being rejected by God, the second including the request: "Cast me not off in old age." But the sharpest blows were toward the end of the letter; they were included in six numbered points, reflecting on the wholesome truth that God does not take social rank into account in deciding who will be predestined to salvation and damnation. The first point quotes the Book of Job directly, the second reminds her of Christ's words that her soul might be required of her that very night, the third proves that God has the whip hand even over titled persons, the fourth pictures Lady Barrington and her family in the flames of the hereafter, the fifth cites the prophet Ezekiel's regretful observation that "she hath wearied herself with toil: yet her great rust goeth not forth out of her; her rust goeth not forth by fire (*24.12*)," the sixth hopes for the softening of the lady's hard heart in time to guarantee her safety:

1. First, *Job 34.19: He with whom we deal accepteth not the persons of princes, nor regardeth the rich more than the poor, for they are the work of his hands.*

2. When birth [is] greater, maintenance more ample, time longer and means of grace more plentiful, then a great account of the Lord is expected. (*Luke 12*).

3. The Lord will do what he will with his own. He owes you no mercy. (*Exodus 33.19*). *I will be gracious to whom I will be gracious and I will show mercy to whom I will show mercy.*

4. Call to mind what a cut, what a gnawing worm it will be (the Lord, the Lord forbid it) if ever you cast up your eye towards heaven and see so many blessed branches in the bosom of Christ and your stock rejected.

5. Slight not, I beseech you, all these late loud alarms and sharp files with which the Lord hath striven to burnish you (*Ezekiel 24*).

6. Remember, I beseech you, your candle is twinkling and glass near run. The Lord only knows how few minutes are left behind (*Psalm 95.10*): *Forty years was I grieved, then I swore in my wrath they should never enter into my rest.* No heart but a trembling heart can get assurance the Lord hath not sworn; to that heart he hath sworn to be gracious. . . .

Lady Barrington's displeasure was not enough to have Roger Williams dismissed from the Masham household. During the next seven months he pressed another suit for marriage successfully. Perhaps Mary Barnard, lady-in-waiting and companion of Joan (Jug) Altham, was the person referred to as "offered" in his first letter to Lady Barrington. Jug Altham was the daughter of Lady Masham by her first marriage.[18] A maid-in-waiting to such a person in a great house was frequently a poor clergyman's daughter.[19] Her station in life, by virtue of her clerical father's rank as gentleman, was the same as that of her mistress, but she took service because her means were less and she needed the money. The case[20] for thinking that Mary Barnard was the daughter of the Rev. Richard Bernard (frequently spelt as Barnard in his lifetime) of the parishes of Worksop, Nottinghamshire, and Batcombe, Somerset, is strong for several reasons. Richard Bernard's patron in the living of Worksop, to which he was presented in 1601, was Sir Richard Whalley, the brother-in-law of Lady Masham. In 1613 he was presented to the parish of Batcombe, in country close to the Rev. John White,[21]—the "patriarch" of Dorset, and collaborator, with the Masham and Barrington families in the various schemes of colonisation in New England. Within White's circle Bernard was regarded as a good man, a sound Puritan, but not stable in his judgments.[22] The setting of common interest and family acquaintance reinforces the identification of Williams's bride with Richard Bernard's daughter. The will of Richard Bernard has not been discovered, so final confirmation of Mary Barnard's identity is lacking, but a certain Masachiel Bernard who went to New England in 1635 seems to be referred to by Roger Williams's enemy William Harris as "the brother of Mr. Williams his wife,"[23] though Harris included no initial or first name in his reference. Masachiel Bernard was a tailor from Batcombe, which perhaps brings identification a little closer.

A person like Mary Barnard would have brought income and background more suitable than Jane Whalley to a match with Williams. Her father would at that time have been eager for it. Williams was a Cambridge man, like himself, with similar beliefs, as far as he could make out. He was able enough to be well regarded by the Mashams and their friends. Reports about him, through clergy and laity coming and going between London, Essex, and the West Country must have given a picture of a zealous Puritan, hostile to ceremonies, but in the mainstream of the movement, where Bernard himself had come to stand, after a brief earlier flirtation, at Worksop, with Separatism.

Of Mary Barnard herself we know little. She was six years Williams's junior. She bore him six children[24] and he spoke of her with affection in several of his extant writings. She seems to have been respected (and somewhat pitied) by New Englanders who watched her patience during her husband's career. It would not be normal for a "second-best" match of this kind to be the product of romance. More probably it was a suitable contract that made each party content in the beginning and developed into enduring love. The best reminder of that love and its grounding in faith is Williams's *Experiments of Spiritual Life and Health*,[25] addressed in 1651 to his wife during a serious illness when he was travelling among the Indians. This tender book, a revelation of his inwardness, shows something of the quality of the relationship between husband and wife—fidelity based on the belief that life here was best when lived as preparation for eternity.

> Yea, how busy, how diligent, how solicitous should we be (like strangers upon a strange coast waiting for a wind or passage) to get dispatched what we have to do before we hear that final call, "Away, away, let us be gone from hence . . ."[26]

he wrote to his "dearest Love and Companion in this Vale of Tears." The little book is a good example of the Puritan's detachment from life, which was the secret of his active involvement in every part of it.

After his collision with Lady Barrington and his marriage with Mary Barnard, Roger Williams responded to the crisis in his life by strongly asserting his own identity. His precocious talents had ripened, but to what end? The direct road to fame pointed out and prepared by Sir Edward Coke now lay closed because of what he believed (and what King Charles's bishops shortly ensured) about high office in the Church. William Laud had been named to the See of London on July 1, 1628.[27] But was there an alternative way for him? If he had married above his station in a prominent family of gentry he might have been among the distinguished group of Puritan ministers who chose exile in the Netherlands, formed their "Congregational Classis"[28] there, and returned to England as right-hand men of the Independent political party during the Civil War, after 1643. Such were Thomas Goodwin, Philip Nye, Jeremiah Burroughes, Sydrach Simpson, and William Bridge, the publishers of the *Apologeticall Narration* and the architects of the successful Congregational plan that split the Westminster Assembly of Divines.[29] Not all the five apologists were Netherlands exiles, but all were hand-in-glove with militant gentry and merchants. They were also close to the group of ministers who eventually chose the way of John Cotton, Richard Hooker,[30] John Eliot,[31] and Hugh Peter[32]—chaplains to another wing of the many-sided lay conspiracy against the Stuart policy in Church and State. This group chose emigration to New England, for the sake of proving that a decentralised state-church Congregational polity would work. Their hope was that their transatlantic experiment would become the prototype of the England of tomorrow. Their promised land worked along the same lines as the system devised by the Congregational classis in the Dutch Netherlands; they rejected a national covenant and pioneered a polity of freely contracting or covenanted local congregations, kept pure in their church order and doctrine by the watchful oversight of Calvinist magistrates and ministers working in partnership for what they believed to be the good of the entire community.[33]

Neither of these groups, the official ministry of Netherlands or of New England, would be for Williams. His affair of the heart at Otes gave a bitter taste to all things clerical—dependence on the money of the gentry, their favour, and their financial and political ups and downs. His hour of ambition led to double frustration—he had to postpone enjoyment of Jane Whalley until heaven; and also, he now felt, the company of the noble and

mighty. The second followed in his mind from the first while he
was in this emotional state; but he had at hand the best of
precedents, Jesus Christ, who had been rich in heaven but became poor among the despised. As he swallowed the disappointment of losing Jane Whalley and embraced Mary Barnard,
Williams resolved to renounce the satanic temptations of power
that Christ had withstood and to find his identity in becoming
a prophet instead of a cleric, an apostle instead of a mere pastor,
a witness against Christendom in all its settled forms instead of
one of Christendom's compliant spiritual valets. In practical
terms this meant accepting as examples Barrow, Greenwood,
Ainsworth, John Smith, and the imprisoned "mechanick preachers" of the "poorer sort" in London and in Colchester, rather than
the well-placed and satisfactorily rewarded university graduates
who had become his friends at Cambridge and at Otes.

Roger Williams interpreted the meaning of his rebuff from
Scripture as a divine summons to turn his back on human power
and receive the transmuted power that he located always afterwards in the bearing of the Cross. A follower of Jesus Christ, as
he was to remind John Cotton, on excellent scriptural authority,

maketh (as I may say) Christ's cross the first figure in his alphabet,
taking up his cross and gallows (in most ordinary persecution), which,
with self-denial, are the assured terms his servants must resolve to look
for.[34]

Setting a distance between himself and his former friends did
not mean for Williams a rupture of relationships. When he spoke
warmly of the graces and godly wisdom of many of them he was
quite sincere. He always retained his bond with them on the
point of the eternal and inscrutable decree of "the Father of
Lights," who would undoubtedly bring some of them to everlasting salvation. He did not question their grasp on truth at that
point.

Nor did he fundamentally shift the ground of his controversy
with them. He began by criticising their conception of power and
their claim to be the possessors of the definitive truth about God's

will for Church and State. His quarrel was not then, nor later, about the problem of religious liberty for its own sake; much less civil liberty. Rather, when he looked at Christ, he saw a person in a minority of one, who testified against the high priests, Herodians, Romans, Pharisees, and Sadducees. Christ was poor and persecuted. He did not lay down a new law and defend it by state power. He had a conscience other than that held to be rightly informed among the powerful and great. Williams said many times that it was "the coming of his Son the Lord Jesus"[35] that made clear the divine will, which was that consciences, though erring, should be free and uncoerced. His recognition of this was not a codification of his reading of the Bible. He derived it from the person of Christ and said that the idea of conflict of doctrines, short of violent and disorderly conduct, was inseparable from the meaning of the story of Christ and of the experience of the apostle Paul face-to-face with hostile establishments in a pagan Roman Empire.[36]

His brothers among the future Independent clergy believed they had the truth and that error had no right to propagate itself. Williams believed they were in error themselves about the problem of power and that they had failed to grasp the meaning of the Christian revelation as a negation of conventionally understood power. He did not himself despair of knowing the truth. He thought he had a firm grip on the central doctrines of Christianity. But he was still waiting for further revelation from God to show him the truth about the right form of the visible Church and to give men the power to be genuine apostles again. The settled and respectable Puritan clergy were not, to him, apostolic men. By definition an apostle was a man who was sent out to make a Church among unbelievers, through the power of God. All those admirable chaplains, lecturers, godly vicars, and fellows of colleges, his peers and elders, were pastors, shepherds of static flocks rather than builders with God of a Church made of "living stones"[37] from all nations under heaven. There was a great distance between them and the New Testament. He was ready to admit the same about himself. But his calling was to stand out, away from the conventional temple; to preach, wait, and pray sorrowfully for the further revelation of God's anticipated final kingdom. Sometimes, founding his conception of his task on the "two witnesses prophesying in sackcloth,"[38] who precede the time of the end in the Book of Revelation, he thought of himself as a prophet to both churches and states. Between 1629 and 1636, he thought he might have found the visible remnant that would be used to restore the Church to obedience,[39] for it seemed to him that the Separatists and Baptists were close to the desired biblical forms of worship and church discipline. But his confidence in them waned. He came in the end to stand by himself. He had found his identity in being himself and saying what he conceived he was bidden by God to say.

In the light of his position it is easy to understand what he thought of the leading ministers in Massachusetts, New Plymouth, and Connecticut. Samuel Skelton, Thomas Hooker,[40] Samuel Stone,[41] John Cotton, John Davenport,[42] Hugh Peter, John Eliot, Thomas Shephard[43]—all were great names to him; many he loved; all he honoured "for their persons"; but they had elected to remain among the upper classes and not to soil their hands with toil. He had gone irrevocably with despised heretics, small farmers, traders, herders, tinkers, tailors, brewers, and printers. A man who has made this choice considers his former well-heeled associates high and dry; they wonder whether he is out of his mind.[44]

Williams's abrupt departure for New England gave his more conformable friends in old England little opportunity to evaluate him in his guise as prophet until he returned to upset their plans with the *Bloudy Tenent* in 1643. Those who went to New England were severely plagued by his Separatist doctrine and his outrageous social behaviour. They included the Earl of Lincoln's former steward, Thomas Dudley,[45] who emigrated from Northampton, was many times Massachusetts governor and often mentioned in Williams's correspondence with the elder Winthrop. Dudley had been a member of John Cotton's congregation in the old Boston. The views he held on Roger Williams's betrayal of his class and calling may be deduced from the verse alleged to have been found in his pocket after he died. The item was quoted by Cotton Mather, John Cotton's grandson, with clear approval:

> Let men of God, in courts and churches, watch
> O'er such as do a toleration hatch,
> Lest that ill egg bring forth a cockatrice
> To poison all with heresy and vice.
> If men be left, and otherwise combine,
> My epitaph's, *I died no Libertine.*[46]

Others more or less in sympathy with this "honoured" Protestant old soldier, were his son-in-law Simon Bradstreet, and the two Boston worthies from old England's Boston, Thomas Leverett and Richard Bellingham, all appearing in the pages of Williams's surviving correspondence. They and others formed a corporation as close in New England as they had been in the old. Their sentiments are embodied in the officially sanctioned histories of the Massachusetts colony, commencing with the jejune but entertaining account by the militia captain Edward Johnson, entitled *The Wonder-Working Providence of Zion's Saviour in New-England* and published in 1654.

In 1669 Nathaniel Morton, secretary to the Plymouth administration, published a more sober early record covering Williams and his delinquency. There is not much judgment of the character of the heretic, but the fact that he *was* one, according to Plymouth and the Bay, is underlined. Williams read Morton's *Memorial* in the year of its publication. He wryly informed the younger Winthrop in Connecticut:

> Sir, since I saw you I have read Morton's Memorial, and rejoice at the encomiums upon your father and other precious worthies, though I be a reprobate, *contempta vitior alga* [More vicious than spurned dross].

Another Plymouth record, of earlier date, was not published until the nineteenth century, but gives a much more compassionate estimate. The entry belonged to the reminiscences of

William Bradford, *Of Plymouth Plantation,* and embodies the
spirit of the distinguished Pilgrim governor, who was a true son
of their Leyden pastor, John Robinson:

> Mr. Roger Williams (a man godly and zealous, having many precious
> parts, but very unsettled in judgments) came over first to the Massa-
> chusetts, but upon some discontent left that place, and came hither,
> (where he was friendly entertained, according to their poor ability),
> and exercised his gifts amongst them, and after some time was admitted
> a member of the church, and his teaching well approved; for the
> benefit of which I still bless God, and am thankful to him, even for his
> sharpest admonitions and reproofs, so far as they agreed with truth.[47]

Following a regretful allusion to the career of Williams at Salem
and his later troubles, Bradford continued:

> But he is to be pitied, and prayed for, and so I shall leave the matter,
> and desire the Lord to show him his errors, and reduce him into the way
> of truth, and give him a settled judgment and constancy in the same;
> for I hope he belongs to the Lord, and that He will show him mercy.[48]

When William Hubbard came to write his *General History of
New England,* covering the years to 1680, he drew heavily on
Morton, but editorialised on Williams in a way that reflected the
mind of the leading magistrates and ministers of Boston. Hubbard was minister at New Ipswich, Massachusetts, and in the
first graduating class at Harvard in 1642. The Massachusetts
General Court gave him fifty pounds in 1682, a few months before Williams died, in gratitude for his history.[49] Hubbard neatly
placed the members of the gentlemanly oligarchy, his patrons,
the group whose ways and values Williams left:

> It must not be denied that they were the offspring of the old Non-
> conformists, who yet always walked in a distinct path from the rigid
> Separatists, nor did they ever disown the Church of England to be a
> true church, as retaining the essentials of faith and order. And although
> they could not persuade themselves to live contentedly under the wing
> of episcopal government, yet their offence was rather at the ceremonies
> than the discipline and government thereof.[50]

When he came to Williams and his colleague, Skelton, at Salem,
Hubbard began to spice his narrative with aspersions:

The ministers about Boston now being increased to a convenient
number, . . . did use to meet once a fortnight at one of their houses
in course, where some question of moment was debated. Mr. Skelton,
pastor of Salem, and Mr. Williams (as yet not ordained any officer
there), out of a rigid separation jealousy, took exception at it, prognosti-
cating that it might in time bring forth a presbytery, or superintendency,
to the prejudice of the churches' liberties, (a spirit of separation had, it
seems so early fly-blown their understandings), from whom issued the
fiery flying serpents, that were, not long after, so ready to annoy, and
with bitter invectives sting every magistrate and minister, that did not
approve of their sentiments; the venom of which spirit had soon after infected so many of that church and people of Salem, as will appear. . . .[51]

Hubbard devoted a chapter to the "disturbance, both civil and
ecclesiastical, in the Massachusetts, occasioned by Mr. Roger
Williams, in the year 1634."[52] He lamented that

he was one of whom it may be affirmed by all that knew him, that he
had a zeal, and great pity it was that it could not be added, according
to knowledge; for then by the one and by the other, he might have been
of great use in the church of God, wherever his lot had been cast. But
for want of the latter, the more judicious sort of Christians, in Old and
New England, looked upon him as a man of a very self-conceited,
unquiet, turbulent, and uncharitable spirit.[53]

Lady Barrington, and many other "judicious sort of Christians"
would have applauded Hubbard's description, no less than the
reminder that "they were wont to say in Essex, where he lived,
that he was divinely mad; as if his too much zeal, as Festus said
of Paul's too much learning, had made him beside himself."[54] At
least Williams would have been comforted by the implied equa-
tions between himself and St. Paul on the one side, with the
gentry and the Roman provincial governor Festus on the other
(Acts 26.24), which can only be regarded as an ineptitude in
Hubbard as "court historian."

The flower of this tradition in the early estimation of Roger
Williams was reached, however, in the Reverend Dr. Cotton
Mather's *Magnalia Christi Americana* or, *The Ecclesiastical
History of New England, from its first planting in the year 1620,*

unto the Year of our Lord, 1698, first published in London in 1702. When he came to Williams, the grandson of John Cotton pulled out several stops and replayed a tune he seems to have heard often, from his youth upward, among his family and friends. He made Williams an example of "the Spirit of Rigid Separation in one remarkable Zealot, vexing the Churches of New-England."[55] There is a derogatory Latin flourish across the centre of the page:

Hic se aperit Diabolus! (Here, along came the Devil in person.) "I would chuse rather to leave a veil than a scar upon the memory of any person, that by his miscarriage hath made himself too memorable,"[56] wrote Mather. Whereupon he proceeded to scar Williams's memory:

> In the year 1654, a certain Windmill in the Low Countries, whirling round with extraordinary violence, by reason of a violent storm then blowing; the stone at length by its rapid motion became so intensely hot, as to fire the mill, from whence the flames, being dispersed by the high winds, did set a whole town on fire. But I can tell my reader, that about twenty years before this, there was a whole country in America like to be set on fire by the rapid motion of a windmill, in the head of one particular man.[57]

Out came the phrases—some Mather's own, others perhaps recollected from conversations over many years covering Williams's case. The miscreant was "a preacher that had less light than fire in him";[58] the misguided Salem church had been "affected with the fierceness of his talking in publick; and the starchtness of his living in private."[59] When he withdrew from the Salem congregation "he kept up a meeting in his own house, whereto resorted such as he had infected with his extravagancies."[60] After all the argument between Williams and the ministers of the Bay, Mather described a victorious debating point made against the offender by the learned Thomas Hooker, his former neighbour in Essex and later first minister at Hartford, Connecticut:

> Hereupon Mr. Williams chose to hold his peace, rather than make any answer: such the giddiness, the confusion, the autocatacritic of

that sectarian spirit. I have read of a gentleman who had an humour of making singular and fanciful expositions of scripture; but one Doctor Sim gave him a dose of physick, which when it had wrought, the gentleman became orthodox immediately, and expounded at the old rate no more. Pity this Dr. Sim had but undertaken the cure of our Mr. Williams.[61]

From the point of view of Cotton Mather and the excellent people whose memories he honoured in his orotund book "these things were, indeed, very disturbant and offensive."[62] But the *Magnalia* makes qualified recognition, in closing its account of Williams, of his acceptability as a colleague and friend both to New Englanders of the Winthrops' quality and to noble leaders in old England:

> Mr. Williams . . . was very instrumental in obtaining a charter for the government of Rhode-Island, which lay near and with his town of Providence, and was by the people sometimes chosen governour; but for the most part he led a more private life.
>
> It was more than forty years after his exile that he lived here, and in many things acquitted himself so laudably, that many judicious persons judged him to have had the root of the matter in him, during the long winter of this retirement. . . .
>
> There was always a good correspondence always held between him and many worthy and pious people in the colony, from whence he had been banish'd tho' his keeping still so many of his dangerous principles kept the government, unto whose favour some of the English nobility had by letters recommended him, from taking off the sentence of his banishment.[63]

Mather finally mentioned his services in combating the Quakers; he knew he spoke as the mouthpiece of the "judicious" and "worthy and pious persons" to whom he referred. Through him we gain a good, if somewhat embroidered, idea of what the colonising gentry tended to think of Williams.

Not all of them, however. Before going to New England Williams had known John Winthrop, the squire of Groton, Suffolk, not far from Otes. Here was a man who knew the various worlds of Roger Williams—London, the university, the law, the

country—but without conforming too slavishly to the ways of any
or all of them because his faith had been won out of personal
trouble and acted as a glass to put all else in focus for him. It has
been rightly pointed out that the elder Winthrop was a true
gentleman who was not much interested in keeping up with the
Joneses of his day.[64] Such a man, though he was a trusted magistrate and had assented to the act of banishment, Williams could
genuinely call friend. Winthrop's references, in his *Journal*,
to Williams's views, trial, and exile were accurate and fair.
Winthrop disapproved of much of what Williams said and did,
but he loved him. How deeply Williams returned the regard is
seen in the letters he wrote to the older man until Winthrop's
death in 1649. While still at Plymouth Williams had corresponded with Winthrop, and in 1637 had negotiated the cession
of a small island called Prudence, to the northwest of Rhode
Island itself, partly in his own name and partly for Winthrop.[65]
They ran pigs there, and there they might both have found
refuge if things had gone badly for the Massachusetts Bay as a
result of adverse political trends in England.[66] Williams had
acquired an adjacent small island called Patience.[67] Winthrop
acted as his agent in negotiating the settlement of outstanding
debts still owed to him by people in Boston. "I will ever mourn
(the Lord assisting), that I am no more (though I hope ever)
yours,"[68] Williams told Winthrop soon after his settlement at
Providence. In June 1645 he wrote:

> Sir, (excepting the matters of my soul and conscience to God, the
> Father of Spirits) you have not a truer friend and servant to your
> worthy person and yours, nor to the peace and welfare of the whole
> country, than the most despised and most unworthy Roger Williams.[69]

With the son, the younger John Winthrop,[70] so long the
leading man in the colony of Connecticut, Williams had even
more correspondence. They met more often and had liked each
other since their meetings before they crossed the Atlantic:

> Your loving lines in this cold, dead season, were as a cup of your
> Connecticut cider, which we are glad to hear abounds with you, or of

that western metheglin, which you and I have drunk at Bristol together
&c.[71]

When he wrote in those terms to John Winthrop, Junior, in
February 1660, he looked back to a day some thirty years before
when they took a glass of English mead in midwinter weather,
probably before Williams sailed for New England. The younger
Winthrop, almost Williams's exact contemporary, was a citizen of
the world. He had been at Trinity College in Dublin, had made
the grand tour in 1628, and after the Restoration was among the
supporters of science and industry who promoted the Royal
Society. "All countries," he said, had come to seem to him "like
so many inns, and I shall call that my country where I may
most glorify God, and enjoy the presence of my dearest friends."[72]
This man had his father's generosity of spirit and an even
greater breadth of outlook. He and his family were recalled
gratefully in a letter written in May 1664 by Williams:

Sir, I waited for a gale to return you many cordial thanks for your
many cordial expressions of ancient kindness to myself, and the public
peace and wellfare. . . . My humble desires are to contribute my poor
mite (as I have ever, and I hope ever shall) to preserve plantation and
public interest of the whole New England and not interest of this or
that town, colony, opinion, &c.[73]

Sir, when we that have been the eldest, and are rotting, (tomorrow
or next day) a generation will act, I fear, far unlike the first Winthrops
and their Models of Love: I fear that the common Trinity of the world,
(Profit, Preferment, Pleasure) will here be the *Tria omnia*, as in all
the world beside: that Prelacy and Papacy too will in this wilderness
predominate, that God Land will be (as now it is) as great a God with
us English as God Gold was with the Spaniards, &c.[74]

That old quarrel between Williams and the "judicious," the
"worthy" and "pious" gentry over their "common Trinity"[75] per-
sisted; now he saw the same idol pursued by his immediate
Rhode Island neighbours. The two Winthrops were gentlemen
of a different stamp, possessing much, but not tethered to any
of it. Their practical good sense and absence of pretence were

in contrast to much of what Williams saw in some social climbers and religious guides of the new Boston.

Another of the good kind was Edward Winslow, a leading man at New Plymouth at the time of Williams's "winter flight" and foundation of Providence. Winslow breathed much the same spirit of concern and brotherhood as Bradford. In his testimony of 1670 about the events of that winter Williams mentioned the names of Winthrop and Winslow in one of his most memorable pages:

> Mr. Winthrop privately wrote to me to steer my course to Narragansett Bay and Indians, for many high and heavenly public ends, encouraging me, from the freeness of the place from any English claims or patents. I took his prudent motion as a hint and voice from God, and waiving all other thoughts and motion, I steered my course from Salem (though in winter snow, which I feel yet) unto these parts, wherein I may say Peniel, that is, I have seen the face of God.[76]

The biblical reference is to the blessing of Jacob, when he was a threatened traveller who wrestled with God (*Genesis 32.30*). The sequel to Winthrop's confidential prompting follows:

> I first pitched, and began to build and plant at Seekonk, now Rehoboth, but I received a letter from my ancient friend, Mr. Winslow, then Governor of Plymouth, professing his own and others love and respect to me, yet lovingly advising me, since I was fallen into the edge of their bounds, and they were loath to displease the Bay, to remove but to the other side of the water, and then, he said, I had the country free before me, and might be as free as themselves, and we should be loving neighbours together. These were the joint understandings of these two eminently wise and Christian Governors and others, in their day, together with their counsel and advice as to the freedom and vacancy of this place, which in this respect, and many other Providences of the Most Holy and Only Wise, I called Providence.[77]

Later in the same letter Williams inserted the most intimate of his descriptions of Winslow's goodness:

> It pleased the Father of spirits to touch many hearts, dear to him, with some relentings; amongst which, that great and pious soul, Mr.

Winslow, melted, and kindly visited me, at Providence, and put a piece of gold into the hands of my wife, for our supply.[78]

Bradford, the Winthrops, and Winslow, with others like them, continued to receive from Williams the deference due to their eminent station. His letters to them were studded with expressions of honour and courtesy. Although he fraternised with common men, he never adopted the doctrines or attitudes of the English Levellers and Diggers. His revolt against the uppish gentry had nothing to do with social egalitarianism. He objected to their motive—secure status—and to their attempt to hallow it with a mantle of religiosity. He could honour those who had the status but who did not particularly care whether they had it or not. This he regarded as a participation in true royalty, which was also true humanity, and was defined by willingness to surrender power for the sake of God and man.

Williams's close friendship with the younger Sir Harry Vane may be explained originally in the same light. Vane's motive for emigration was like his own. Winthrop's *Journal* tells the story:

Henry Vane, comptroller of the king's house, who, being a young gentleman of excellent parts, and had been employed by his father (when he was ambassador) in foreign affairs; yet, being called to the obedience of the gospel, forsook the honours and preferments of the court, to enjoy the ordinances of Christ in their purity here. His father, being very averse to this way, (as no way savouring the power of religion), would hardly have consented to his coming hither, but that, acquainting the king with his son's disposition and desire, he commanded him to send him hither, and gave him license for three years' stay here.[79]

The date was 1635. Every word in Winthrop's account was used with his usual forethought. From the time of Vane's arrival he and Williams found common ground. One of them had been commanded out of England by the King. The other had been "pursued" out by Bishop William Laud. Each had been convulsed by a crisis that involved his identity, career, and deepest beliefs. Neither rejected power and rank as means to good human ends. Both sought a "heavenly" frame of mind, by seeking to follow Christ in his denial of self. The motives of the two men were confused, doubtless, because they could not recognise the part played in their drastic decisions by their parents, early influences, and upbringing; but the affinity they felt in Massachusetts continued through their middle years. Williams, for his part at least, came to see the meaning of his personal crisis in terms he set down clearly out of the Bible in 1652, when defending a tract called *Zeal Examined*,[80] which some suspect to have come from the hand of Vane himself:[81]

That charge from heaven *(James 2.1). My Brethren, have not the faith of our Lord Jesus with respect of persons* . . . seems, at first blush, to intrench upon civility and good manners, except it be granted, that in Christianity the greatest respect is not given to greatness of Place, Birth, Wealth, Authority, Braverie, &c. but to the greatness of Humility and Grace of Christ, according to that of the Lord Jesus *(Matthew 18). Whosoever shall humble himself as this little child, the same is the greatest in the Kingdom of Heaven.*[82]

6
Outside the Camp: Mission

ALMOST AS SOON as he reached America Roger Williams found his imagination affected by the forest horizons, marshes, and deserted coasts of New England. The wastes, threatening and impenetrable without a guide, confirmed what all good Calvinists knew from their apprehension of their lostness and their deliverance. The world, as pictured in many places in the Bible, is a terrifying "desert," in the strict sense of the word. Only a powerful and all-seeing Eye can find the lonely figure wandering in the forest maze and send a Rescuer, whose guarantee is that He will restore the wanderer, if he genuinely trusts, to a final paradise, an ordered garden of fraternal happiness and love. The paradise is the Church. The wilderness is the world.[1] But there is a greater danger than being in the wilderness, that is, to mistake one of the artificial paradises of merely formal religion, for the genuine Paradise that only Christ, by his personal presence and oversight, can reestablish and authenticate.

The symbolism thus established and confirmed in the mind of Williams became a background for his vocation and endeavour as an apostle. Williams took his place among the most remarkable thinkers about the Christian mission. He did not think of missionary enterprise as an attempt to subvert the Indian peoples from their culture to his own. In his thinking and activity as friend and preacher among the primitive Americans he tried to refrain from cultural imperialism and to permit the message he shared with the Indians to judge both English and Indian cultures impartially in its own light. He also strove to let the message he bore expose his own failures and weaknesses. A remarkable feature of his missionary career is the fact that he became realistically critical of the relatively small but pretentious "Christian world" and pointed out that it was altogether too overweening in its own claims to superiority and that God was as fond of the non-Christian people in the world as he was of the so-called Christians.

The prevailing image of missionary obedience in the thought of Williams is that of going out, being sent, being forlorn in the wilderness except for the help of the presence of the Son of God. He was not a complete individualist in his presentation of this vision. His belief was that the nature of the Church must participate in the nature of Christ when He was on earth, and that it will do so only by being an outcast, lost, and lonely "little flock." To be like this meant shedding the protective apparatus of Christendom, living with Christ in the world, however harsh, without the benefit of special protection from the alliance of Church and State, the implied sanctification of the armies and material enticements of the English colonising "power."

On the title page of *Christenings Make Not Christians*,[2] one of the most searching expositions of the biblical theology of mission in the English language, there is a line-block drawing set in a rectangle. This obscure emblem shows a tall woman, with uncovered breasts, striding through a wilderness, with a bow in one hand and an arrow in another. She wears what looks like an Indian headdress. Above her head to the right is a gleaming compound of the sun and the crescent moon. At her feet is a lamb. Hitherto the decoration seems to have been passed over as a printer's ornament, but it is, in fact, a com-

pressed representation of an aspect of Williams's theology of
mission. For him, as for many Bible students of the period (the
small book was issued in 1645) the true Church was described
in a horrific symbol from the twelfth chapter of the Book
of Revelation. A woman, the figure of the true Israel (construed
as the Christian Church) is in childbirth and brings forth Christ;

and her child was caught up unto God, and unto his throne. And
the woman fled into the wilderness, where she hath a place prepared of
God, that there they may nourish her a thousand two hundred and
threescore days *(Revelation 12.5–6)*.

It may seem strange that this should be the woman shown
on the title page of Roger Williams's book, because the figure
of the woman in the Book of Revelation has the sun and moon
under her *feet* when she is introduced at the beginning of the
vision; but to an initiated person of Williams's time the dis-
crepancy would not have been disturbing, because the woman
in the Book of Revelation was identified with the bride-to-be,
who is lost in the wilderness and looking for her lover, in
the Old Testament poem of the Song of Solomon:

> Who is she that looketh forth as the morning,
> Fair as the moon,
> Clear as the sun,
> Terrible as an army with banners? *(6.10)*

In case the picture should seem too martial, the woman has
at her feet the Lamb, which is the sign of the presence of
Christ, of His way of submission, as though to underline a
favourite point the author liked to make—that the weapons
of the Christian warfare are spiritual, persuasive, not coercive.[3]

The mission Williams believed he must undertake was not
his own; he held that it belonged to the true Church and could
not be undertaken by the "stay-at-home," settled ministry of
the New England towns. It required apostles, men sent out
from the settled places into the harsher environment. Not that
Williams thought the issue out in exactly such terms; his mind
was rather bound to the picture language of the New Testa-

ment. Like all who expected Christ to return in person, he was eager to know the meaning of the prediction that there will be "two witnesses" charged by God to "prophesy a thousand two hundred and threescore days, clothed in sackcloth" (*Revelation 11.3*). The period of time mentioned is the same as that for which the woman is described in Revelation as being in the wilderness—and prophesying, as the seventeenth century knew better than the twentieth, meant preaching under the guidance of the Spirit of God. To Williams therefore the duty of the true Christian was to go out into the wilderness of a world wider than the settled congregation, there to wait for the fulfilment of the expectation that when the task of witnessing was complete all would be set to rights, in both Church and world, by Christ who had the times and seasons in his hands and would terminate the period of wilderness wandering by restoring the Church as it ought to be (*Revelation 11.1–2*).

Under the rubric of the restoration of the Church it becomes easier to account for the close link in Williams's thought between his millennial hopes and his interest in the right form of baptism and of ordination to the ministry. If the Church is believed to be lost in a wilderness, the proper arrangements for these key ceremonies can hardly be made until the Church has been "found" again and everything adjusted in accordance with the will of the Church's Master and Lover. Baptism and ordination belong to the making of the marriage bed of the true Church according to the line of thought that Williams and others, including John Cotton, drew from their fantasy in reading the Song of Solomon. The whole world, including the so-called Christian world must therefore be guilty of varieties of spiritual fornication, committed, as Williams rather indelicately liked to explain at frequent intervals, by lying in "beds of false worship." That there must have been a true and acceptable way of baptising, celebrating the Lord's Supper, and ordaining ministers, Williams was willing to concede; in fact, it was a matter of great significance to him always. He often drew his certainty of this from referring to a passage in the Letter to the Hebrews:

Let us cease to speak of the first principles of Christ, and press on to perfection; not laying again a foundation of repentance from dead works, and of faith toward God, of the teaching of baptisms, and of laying on of hands, and of resurrection of the dead, and of eternal judgment *(Hebrews 6.1–2)*.[4]

If in New Testament times there was no need to speak of all that again, the foundation principles of matters like baptism and ordination must have been quite clear at that time; now, however, according to Williams they were not clear; and certainly the routine "christenings" of the Christians were not the same thing as New Testament baptism. He himself felt clear enough about the first two of the six foundation principles laid down in the text from Hebrews; he felt confident he could leave the last two in the hands of God; but what of the middle two? There lay his dilemma. Where was his authority as a true apostle? What sort of baptism should he use, even supposing the Indians repented and believed? He was involved in a kind of theologically motivated hesitancy about introducing even repentant and believing Indians into what he called "a church estate." He deliberately chose the subtitle "Of the Name Heathen" for his book *Christenings Make Not Christians* because he was afraid the vast majority of Europe's Christians were heathen, and their worship heathen, just as surely as the Indians. The argument for this underlies that terse little book, which came to the keen eye of the Presbyterian Robert Baillie soon after publication. Its existence could be gathered from Baillie's words before its recovery from oblivion by Dr. Dexter in 1881.[5] Said Baillie, speaking of the official New England Independent clergy:

Of all that ever crossed the American seas, they are noted as most neglectful of the work of conversion. I have read of none of them that seem to have minded this matter. Only Master Williams, in the time of his banishment from among them, did assay what could be done with these desolate souls, and by a little experience quickly did find a wonderful great facility to gain thousands of them to so much and more Christianity, both in profession and practice, than in the most of our people doth appear. But the unhappiness of these principles whereof we speak did keep him, as he professeth, from making use of that great oportunity and large door which the Lord there hath opened to all who will be zealous for propagating of the Gospel.[6]

Baillie's proofs of this, in the section of his book called *The Testimonies,* are in keeping with his usual careful attempt to convict people out of their own mouths. Though the text he quotes is not word for word out of Williams's book as we have it, the sense is precisely the same and the verbal correspondence is close. Here is Williams's own statement, which may be compared with Baillie's citations:

All nations now called Protestants were at first part of that whole earth, or main (anti-Christian) continent, that wondered after, worshipped, the Beast, &c.

This must then, with holy fear and trembling—because it concerns the Kingdom of God and salvation—be attended to: whether [they are] such a departure from the Beast and coming out from anti-Christian abominations, from [the Beast's] marks in a false conversion and a false constitution, or framing, of national churches, in false ministries and ministrations of Baptism, Supper of the Lord, Admonitions, excommunication . . . ; or whether . . . joined still unto [the Beast's] Christendom?

If now the bodies of Protestant Nations remain in an unrepentant, unregenerate, natural estate, and so consequently far from hearing the admonitions of the Lord Jesus (*Matthew 18*), I say they must sadly consider and know (lest their profession of the name of Jesus prove at last but an aggravation of condemnation) that Christ Jesus hath said they are but as heathens and publicans.[7]

By "the Beast" (*Revelation 13*) Williams understood Roman Catholic Christendom. Baillie quoted, almost verbatim, another significant sentence:

Woe be to me if I call that conversion unto God, which is indeed subversion of the souls of millions in Christendom, from one false worship to another. . . .[8]

Within the complicated web of thought that Williams spun out of the Bible around his missionary calling we may detect what usually lies at the centre—a fixed attention to what Williams believed about the words and person of Christ Himself. He did not tire of recollecting the closing words of Christ in Matthew's Gospel, with their close association of the nations, the Church, baptism, and the anticipated Last Day:

> Go therefore, and make disciples of all the nations, baptising them into the name of the Father and of the Son and of the Holy Spirit: teaching them to observe all things whatsoever I commanded you: and lo, I am with you always, even unto the end of the world (*Matthew 28.19–20*).

Williams correctly pointed out at the beginning of his small treatise that the words "heathen" and "nations" are the same, each a translation of a Greek original so that he could rebuke Europe with the implication:

> Some will say, "Have there not been great and mighty conversion of whole nations—England, Scotland, French, Dutch, etc., from popery to be good Protestants, &c?"
>
> I answer, "If the Holy Scripture, the first pattern, and doleful experience may be judge, as an eminent person lately spake (upon occasion of a debate touching the conversion of the Indians): 'We have Indians at home, Indians in Cornwall, Indians in Wales, Indians in Ireland', yea, as to the point of true conversion and regeneration by God's Spirit, who can deny that the body of this and of all other Protestant nations (as well as popish) are unconverted and, as formerly, ready to be converted and turned forward and backward, as the weathercock, according as the powerful wind of a prevailing sword and authority shall blow from the various parts and quarters of it?"[9]

He followed Christ in accordance with the repeated summons in the Letter to the Hebrews, as a member of a persecuted and suffering Church *in via*, a Church that waits for the revealing of a goal which it has not yet attained:

> Jesus . . . that he might sanctify the people through his own blood, suffered without the gate. Let us therefore go forth unto him outside the camp, bearing his reproach. For we have not here an abiding city, but we seek after that which is to come (*Hebrews 13.12–14*).

Christenings Make Not Christians pondered in a concise way what Williams had tested in practice. The fruit of his experience, published soon after his arrival in London on his first visit, was his *Key into the Language of America*. This practical word-book was "cast" out of "Materialls" drawn "in a rude lumpe at Sea, as a private helpe to my owne memory, that I might not by my present absence lightly lose what I had so dearly bought in some few yeares hardship, and charges among the Barbarians."[10]

While still at New Plymouth Williams had begun his fraternisation and concern. He used the good offices of the Plymouth men, who had dealt honourably with the Wampanoags, in order to come to know some of their leading sachems, or chiefs, and begin his acquisition of the basic language common to the Indians of New England, though he found there were various dialects.[11] The story of the trust they reposed in him, as in no other New Englander, has been told in Williams's many biographies. Their strange names appear in his letters. He came, at Providence and at his trading post, among the Narragansetts, a central and influential tribe; but he was known and respected by the successive chieftains of the Pequots of Connecticut, the Wampanoags in the Plymouth jurisdiction, and the Nyantics of Rhode Island and vicinity. He shared the dislike of all these groups for the fierce Mohawks, the cannibals of the northwest, and quickly seized the logic of "honour" and custom that lay behind the Indians' feuds, alliances, and relations with the English. Massasoit, the Wampanoag sachem who made league with the Pilgrims, was perhaps his first contact of note; but his more enduring understanding of Indian movements and aims was through the Narragansett sachem Canonicus and his nephew and successor Miantonoumi. In the year before he died he gave testimony to what these men had meant to him in his statement "relative to his first coming into the Narragansett country":

I desire posterity to see the gracious hand of the Most High, (in whose hands are all hearts) that when the hearts of my countrymen and friends and brethren failed me, his infinite wisdom and merits stirred up the barbarous heart of Canonicus to love me as his son to his last gasp, by which means I had not only Miantonomo and all the lowest Sachems

my friends, but Ousamaquin [a Wampanoag chief] also, who because
of my great friendship with him at Plymouth, and the authority of
Canonicus, consented freely, being also well gratified by me, to the
Governor Winthrop and my enjoyment of Prudence [the island acquired
by Williams,] yea of Providence itself, and all the other lands I procured
of Canonicus which were upon the point, and in effect whatsoever I
desired of him; and I never denied him or Miantonomo whatever they
desired of me as to goods or gifts or use of my boats or pinnace, and
the travels of my own person, day and night, which, though men know
not, nor care to know, yet the all-seeing Eye hath seen it, and his all-
powerful hand hath helped me.[12]

As the grateful "son" of Canonicus, who held Indian authority
and wisdom in respect, Roger Williams did not fail, when
he wrote to the towns of Providence and Warwick from Sir
Henry Vane's Lincolnshire house, in 1653, to add:

P.S. My love to all my Indian friends.[13]

The *Key* and Williams's letters reveal why the mutual trust
between the lonely Englishman and his Indian friends was
so strong. He lived with them and was open to what they
could teach him. His was a missionary presence among them,
though without any attempt to lose his own identity by assimila-
tion in reverse.

This presence among the Indians can be sensed in the thirty-
two chapters of the *Key*, which is more than a word book.
Entries under each main heading are seasoned with "observations" between word lists. Each chapter closes with a few
stanzas of sententious doggerel verse. Whatever virtues Williams
had, he was no poet. Nevertheless both the prose observations
and the didactic religious verse teach us a great deal about his
life among the Indians and his affection for them.

Like many phrase books, the *Key* gives forms of greeting
first. The salutation with which Rhode Island tradition credits
the Indians who greeted Williams when he landed near the
future Providence is given at once:

"What cheer, Nétop?" is the general salutation of all English toward
them. *Nétop* is friend.[14]

In the chapter on "Eating and Entertainment" one observation has a typical comparison that honestly set the experience of Williams in America alongside what he knew of Christendom:

It is a strange truth that a man shall generally find more free entertainment and refreshing amongst these barbarians, than amongst thousands that call themselves Christians.[15]

and with an obvious reference to the experience of the Prophet Elijah he concluded his verse on the subject with the lines:

In wilderness, in great distress,
These ravens have fed me.[16]

Some of the detailed description has the quality of scientific observation:

Their women constantly beat all their corn with hand: they plant it, dress it, gather it, burn it, beat it, and take as much pains as any people in the world—which labour is, questionless, one cause of their extraordinary ease of childbirth.[17]

A remark about the dreaded cannibal Mohawks suggests the same unshockable curiosity, this time with compassion:

The Mauguauogs [Mohawks], or men-eaters, that live two or three miles west from us, make a delicious monstrous dish of the head and brains of their enemies; which is yet no bar (when the time shall approach) against God's call, and their repentance, and (who knows but) a greater love to the Lord Jesus. Great sinners, forgiven, love much [cf. *Luke* 7.47].[18]

Brotherliness in the *Key*, as in the letters of Williams, is tempered with realism about human nature and its capacities and limitations. In a "generall Observation from the parts of the bodie," a context that acquits Roger Williams of racism or complacent paternalism, he said that

Nature knows no difference between Europe and Americans in blood, birth, bodies, &c., God having of one blood made all mankind (*Acts 17*), and all by nature being children of wrath, *Ephesians, 2.*[19]

Without hiding his preference for Europe's creature comforts and advanced technology, Williams had much that was good to say for Indian society and customs. He gives no advance indication of the later myth of the "noble savage," but where he found nobility he conceded the fact, as in his comparison of European prudery, and prurience, with the Indian attitude to near nudity:

> Custom hath used their minds and bodies to it, and in such a freedom from any wantonness that I have never seen that wantonness amongst them as, with grief, I have heard of in Europe.[20]

The description of the religion of the Indians is especially detailed and acute. Here Williams recorded conversations about God, the origin of custom in legend and belief, and the Indian's moral expectations of the Englishman on account of English possession of the Bible and a reputedly superior revelation; thus he could describe how the sachem Miantonoumi could say of himself, Williams:

> He hath books and writings, and one which God himself made, concerning men's souls, and therefore may well know more than we, that have none, but take all upon trust from our forefathers . . .[21]

but he had already noted of the Indians that

> they, apprehending a vast difference of knowledge between the English and themselves, are very observant of the English lives. I have heard them say to an Englishman who, being hindered, broke a promise to them: "You know God. Will you lie, Englishman?"[22]

In one of his observations, on trade, it is as though the dawn of a genuine Americanism comes through:

> Europe, be not proud, nor America discouraged. What treasures are hid in some parts of America? And in our New English parts, how have foul hands, in smoky houses, the first handling of those furs which are after worn upon the hands of queens and heads of princes?[23]

Throughout, the *Key* refrains from passing adverse judgments on the Indians except in conjunction with even more severe judgments on the colonists and their homelands. Since the benefits of the Christian message and of material civilisation had come to Europe, it seemed to Williams that European ingratitude was,

if anything, more culpable than Indian blindness.[24] His reluctance about founding Indian churches sprang from more
than theological questioning. He shrewdly sensed what many
Christian missionaries who came before and after him failed
to see—that the act of assent and the rite of baptism may involve
subtle manipulation of the missionary, or self-deception on the
part of the convert. When the catechumen says he is receiving
the faith, he has his greedy inner eye on material benefits and
perquisites that seem to drop from heaven like cargo on the
heads of lucky new Christians. In the address to his readers
Williams went straight to this touchy point:

> They have no clothes, books, nor letters, and conceive their fathers
> never had; and therefore they are easily persuaded that the God that
> made Englishmen is a greater God, because he hath so richly endowed
> the English above themselves. But when they hear that about sixteen
> hundred years ago England and the inhabitants thereof were like unto
> themselves, and since have received from God clothes, books, etc., they
> are greatly affected with a secret hope concerning themselves.[25]

John Eliot, in Massachusetts, has won fame above Williams
as a missionary to the Indians. He and Williams were friends
and kept in touch with each other at times about Indian
affairs.[26] Eliot's Indian Bible, annotated in Williams's shorthand, survives.[27] Eliot gathered churches of baptised converts,
though none of them has endured. The work of these two dedicated men stands as a monument to their different approaches.
Eliot has correctly been described as the apostle *to* the Indians
while Williams was rather the apostle *among* them. Eliot did
not hesitate to establish congregations that worshipped and
behaved as the New England churches already did. Williams
had special reasons for not doing so; he could not "bring
in the result of a satisfying discovery"[28] that this was the will
of God at that time. Preaching was another matter; he
preached to the Indians until near the close of his life;[29] yet
we should not think of him as a black-coated clergyman, Bible
in hand, haranguing a submissive audience. There are many

passages in his writings that suggest, rather, patient exposition of his message, followed by conversations far into the
night, in settlements of the Indians, "in their very wild houses,
and by their barbarous fires."[30] The task of the preacher lay
for him in the art of more than linguistics. He was aware
of the problem of true missionary communication, which went
beyond terms and categories to modes of apprehension, complete transposition of cultural values. Only in such communication could there be a full and honest presentation of the message,
Williams taught. He avoided short cuts and worked patiently;
how patiently is casually revealed in the early 1650's in the
Bloody Tenent Yet More Bloody, where Williams gave his own
conviction in an analysis that includes an explicit contrast
of his own method and that of his friend Eliot:

> Were the Church true, and the messenger or apostle rightly sent forth
> with prayer and fasting, according to *Acts 13*, yet I believe that none of
> the ministers of New England, nor any person in the whole country is
> able to open the mysteries of Christ Jesus in any propriety [i.e.,
> appropriateness] of their speech or language; without which propriety
> it cannot be imagined that Christ Jesus sent forth his first apostles or
> messengers, and without which no people in the world are long willing
> to hear of difficult and heavenly matters.
>
> That none is so fitted, first, the natives themselves affirm—as I could
> instance in many particulars; secondly, the experience of the discusser
> [Williams] and of many others testify how hard it is for any man to
> attain a propriety of their language in common things—so as to escape
> derision amongst them—in many years, without abundance of conversing
> with them, in eating, travelling, and lodging with them, etc., which
> none of their ministers [of the Bay colonies], other affairs not permitting,
> ever could do . . .
>
> I may truly add a third, an instance in the book of their conversion,
> written by Mr. Thomas Shephard. There Mr. Eliot, the ablest among
> them in the Indian speech, promising an old Indian a suit of clothes,
> the man (saith the relation), not well understanding Mr. Eliot's speech,
> asked another Indian what Mr. Eliot said. . . .
>
> The native, not understanding such a common and welcome promise
> of clothes upon gift, would far more hardly understand Mr. Eliot's

preaching of the garment of righteousness, Christ Jesus, unto which men mutually turn the deaf ear, &c.[31]

Williams referred to an account of Eliot's missionary work called *The Clear Sun-shine*, written for English consumption to enlist support. The part mentioned is notable for its paternalism, its suspicion that Eliot was not immune from the danger of making proselytes for the wrong reasons. From Thomas Shephard's account we learn that Eliot had told the man concerned

that because he brought his wife and all his children constantly to the lecture, that he would therefore bestow some clothes upon him, (it being now winter and the old man naked).[32]

The force of the "because" and the "therefore" is difficult to escape, with its suggestion that if the old man had not brought his family he might not have had the material aid.

A further point of difference between Roger Williams and the Massachusetts Puritan ministers was that he was no sabbatarian. After 1600, observance of a strict rest on Sunday became part of the Puritan way of life in England.[33] Williams prayed and preached with groups of Indians or Englishmen on the Lord's Day, but he saw no scriptural reason to refrain from work. The question may seem of small importance in relation to missionary activity; but it became significant in the controversy about method and content between people like Eliot and Shephard and himself. In the same book Shephard says Eliot asked one of the Narragansett sachems

why they did not learn of Mr. Williams who had lived among them divers years? and he soberly answered that they did not care to learn of him, because he is no good man but goes and works upon the Sabbath day.[34]

This was perfectly true. What Shephard did not say was that the keeping of a strict sabbath was itself an idea implanted among semi-Christianised Indians by the New England clergy, so that both they and the Indians could use that con-

sideration as a stick for beating Mr. Williams. Williams knew
they did it. In his long letter to his Massachusetts acquaintance
Major Mason, written in 1670, he reminded the sabbath-keep-
ing Bostonians:

> You know that famous Calvin and thousands more held it but
> ceremonial and figurative, from *Colossians 2*, &c., and vanished; and
> that the day of worship was alterable at the churches' pleasure.[35]

To Samuel Hubbard, a Baptist minister at Newport, Rhode
Island, Williams was even more firm on the point:

> After all that I have seen and read and compared about the seventh
> day—and I have earnestly and carefully read and weighed all I could
> come at in God's holy presence—I cannot be removed from Calvin's
> mind, and indeed, Paul's mind. . . .[36]

Williams was singularly free from the danger of turning
the Christian message into a new legal bondage. He found himself in competition as a missionary with clergy, who considered
working on the Lord's Day a sin. Liberty at such a point
must have been the most difficult of all Christian ideas to expound to Indians, who were themselves sticklers for their own
brand of legality.

For all that, the presence of their convenient exile among
the central group of New England tribes was of value to Massachusetts. There was no separation in Williams's mind between
his duty as a political mediator and his presence as a preacher
or apostle. He often exhorted the Massachusetts General Court
and his personal correspondents in that colony and Connecticut
(see pp. 21f. and 33), to act with justice and mercy among
the Indians, to respect their conventions and sense of honour,
and to treat their eventual conversion as the aim. He did his
best in the Pequot War of 1636 and the revolt of King Philip
in 1675–6 to bring all parties to agreement short of war, which
he hated. He tried not to be sentimental toward either the
English or Indian negotiating parties, but when negotiation
failed and war seemed inevitable for defensive or punitive
reasons, he did not contract out of it. He was painfully conscious

of the English incapacity to understand the way the Indians' minds worked, but he could not countenance laying waste the countryside. He considered the tribes as barbarians to the end. The word barbarians was not used pejoratively. To Williams the Indians were wild, unsophisticated in government, industry, trade, agriculture, education. He was content to be European in his "civilising mission," but he strove to keep the content of it separate from his witness to Jesus Christ. The Indian world was a poorer and wilder world than the English; therefore just defence of the New England colonists' society was inevitable; but the person of Jesus Christ was a standard of more than relative discrimination. Christ was, to Williams, the Judge and the merciful friend of both English and Indians, without respect of persons; so that the conversion of all of them became a matter of far greater concern and urgency than the subjugation of the one by the other. To redress the balance of his preference for English material civilisation and law, Williams many times throughout his residence among Indians questioned claims by the English that they were rightful masters of the lands and persons of those they dispossessed.

A summary of what Williams tried to do is contained in a letter apparently addressed to the Massachusetts authorities in May 1668:

> I abhor most of their customs; I know they are barbarous. I respect not one party more than the other, but I desire to witness truth; and as I desire to witness against oppression, so, also, against the slighting of civil, yea, of barbarous order and government, as respecting every shadow of God's gracious appointments.[37]

The last-expressed sentiment was in line with what he believed about all forms of civil order. They were appointed by God among the people, even the Indian people, to enable them to live together with a degree of reasonable humanity. His dislike of any English attempt to disregard the Indian institutions and customs lay close to his generally sensitive appreciation of the finer points of Indian culture. Much earlier,

a letter he wrote to the Massachusetts General Court had included several of his guiding principles governing war against
and between the Indians. The date was October 5, 1654, soon
after his return from his second English journey; he wrote as
president of the Providence colony:

> We have in these parts a sound of your meditations of war against
> these natives, amongst whom we dwell. I consider that war is one of
> those three great, sore plagues, with which it pleaseth God to affect
> the sons of men. I consider, also, that I refused, lately, many offers in
> my native country, out of a sincere desire to seek the good and peace
> of this.[38]

After recalling his services to Massachusetts in the Pequot
War, Williams described the apprehensiveness of the Narragansett chiefs lest they "be forced from their religion, and,
for not changing their religion, be invaded by war."[39] He told
how he had conversed with Oliver Cromwell about New
England and Indian affairs there. Then he outlined his own
position:

> I never was against the righteous use of the civil sword of men or
> nations, but yet since all men of conscience or prudence ply to wind-
> ward, to maintain their wars to be defensive, (as did both King and
> Scotch, and English and Irish too, in the late wars), I humbly pray your
> consideration, whether it be not only possible, but very easy, to live and
> die in peace with all the natives of this country.[40]

The next point was in the form of a pertinent question:

> Are not all the English of this land, generally, a persecuted people
> from their native soil? and hath not the God of peace and Father of
> mercies made these natives more friendly in this, than our native
> countrymen in our land to us? Have they not entered leagues of love,
> and to this day continued peaceable commerce with us? Are not our
> families grown up in peace amongst them?[41]

"Honoured Sirs," he continued,

> Whether I have been and am a friend to the natives' turning to
> civility and Christianity, and whether I have been instrumental, and

desire so to be, according to my light, I will not trouble you with; only I beseech you consider, how· the name of the most holy and jealous God may be preserved between the clashings of these two, viz.: the glorious conversion of the Indians in New England, and the unnecessary wars and cruel destructions of the Indians in New England.[42]

Four points followed, setting out the balance of power among the major tribes at that moment, and giving shrewd advice on English policy. Ascassassotic, the Long Island chief, and Ninigret the Narragansett were weighed up in five more points, (with a disenchanted preface—"The former is proud and foolish; the latter is proud and fierce"[43]). Then advice was given against treating the Indians as subject peoples, as had been done, to their cost in fire and pillage, by the Dutch on Long Island in the 1640's:

I know it is said the Long Islanders are subjects; but I have heard this greatly questioned, and, indeed, I question whether any Indians in this country, remaining barbarous and pagan, may with truth or honour be called the English subjects.[44]

The reason given for this was characteristically unidealistic. Williams did not plead an abstract right for the Indians; he said none of them should receive the status of an English subject until they had shown themselves civilised enough to merit it.[45]

Justice, always a matter of difficult ethical judgment, was Williams's goal before and during the course of Indian wars. When the wars were over, he sought reconciliation on a basis of mercy. After the Pequot War in 1637 his letters were full of information on the outcome—treatment of prisoners, Indian conventions governing selling into slavery, treatment of women and children. In the midst of other intelligence he sent to Winthrop, Senior, he seemed to ask for the privilege of bringing up a little Indian boy orphaned by the conflict:

Much Honoured Sir—It having again pleased the Most High to put into your hands another miserable drone of Adam's degenerate seed, and our brethren by nature, I am bold (if I may not offend in it) to request the keeping and bringing up of one of the children. I have fixed mine eye on this little one with the red about his neck, but I will not be peremptory in my choice, but will rest in your loving pleasure for him or any, &c.[46]

At the close of the same letter he "rejoiced" that leaders in the Connecticut colony, after the Pequot War and during "mopping up" operations, were "almost adverse from killing women and children," and he added:

Mercy outshines all the works and attributes of him who is the Father of Mercies. . . .[47]

These conciliatory attitudes and actions followed soon after his direct action to sever the Narragansetts from the menacing Pequots and his part in securing the English-Narragansett alliance that won the short Pequot War. We have Williams's own account of what it cost him, written retrospectively as late as 1670, but with details that make it all real:

Upon letters received from the Governor and Council at Boston, requesting me to use my utmost and speediest endeavours to break and hinder the league laboured for by the Pequots against the Mohegans, and Pequots against the English . . . the Lord helped me immediately to put my life into my hand, and, scarce acquainting my wife, to ship myself, all alone, in a poor canoe, and to cut through a stormy wind, with great seas, every minute in hazard of life, to the sachem's house.

Three days and nights my business forced me to lodge and mix with the bloody Pequot ambassadors, whose hands and arms, methought, reeked with the blood of my countrymen, murdered and massacred by them on Connecticut river, and from whom I could not but nightly look for their bloody knives at my own throat also.

When God wondrously preserved me, and helped me to break to pieces the Pequot's negotiation and design, and to make, and promote and finish, by many travels and charges, the English league with the Narragansetts and Mohegans against the Pequots, and that the English forces marched up to the Narragansett country against the Pequots, I gladly entertained, at my house in Providence, the General Stoughton and his officers and used my utmost care that all his officers and soldiers should be well accommodated with us. . . .[48]

Towards the end of his life the veteran among the Indians tried again to be a reconciler, when a consolidation of Indian

forces, under the desperate leadership of the young Plymouth
sachem called "Philip," made such havoc for themselves and the
colonists in King Philip's War. He strove by personal negotiation, up to the outbreak of fighting in the Narragansett country,
to detach the Narragansetts from Philip. His interest was that
"the English may more securely and effectually prosecute the
quenching of this Philippian fire in the beginning of it."[49] He
failed. "Sir," he wrote to Connecticut's John Winthrop, Junior,
on June 25, 1675:

> my old bones and eyes are weary with travel and writing to the
> Governors of Massachusetts and Rhode Island, and now to yourselves.[50]

He had seen the trouble coming for a long time. In 1665
he had told Sir Robert Carr, one of the royal commissioners for
the New England colonies:

> They are a melancholy people, and judge themselves . . . oppressed
> and wronged; you may knock out their brains, and yet not make them
> peaceably to surrender, even as some oxen will die before they will rise;
> yet with patience, and gentle means [they] will rise and draw, and do
> good service.[51]

Among the saddest testimonials to his eventual failure to
persuade the Narragansetts against cooperating with Philip
is a letter he wrote to Governor Leverett, at Boston. The correspondence surrounding this letter shows that Williams saw
the coming war would be inevitable unless some miracle occurred. He clearly appreciated what the modern anthropologist
has come to understand—the defiant panic produced in in-
digenous peoples when their folkways are destroyed by the
impact of the West. King Philip had become the leading focus
of the defiance; but Williams described to Leverett the influence Philip had on a young Narragansett sachem, Nana-
nawtunu, the son of Miantonoumi and a "very hopeful spark."[52]
The young Narragansett leader had been with Roger Williams
in a canoe, when Williams told him that in being drawn into
Philip's doomed revolt he was losing his own independent
judgment:

I told him and his men, being then in my canoe, with his men with him, that Philip was his *cawkakinnamuck*, this is looking glass. He [Philip] was deaf to all advice, and now was overset, *cooshkowwawy*, and catched at every part of the country to save himself, but he shall never get ashore, &c. He answered me in a consenting, considering kind of way, Philip *cooshkowwawy*.[53]

Close reading of this letter, and the next, written to Governor Winthrop of Connecticut, helps us to share in the sorrow that pervades them. Philip saw the "canoe" of his hopes about to be engulfed, while the old man, Roger Williams, powerlessly watched the suicide of a society he had come to respect and love.

Love is a word he used many times in describing his relationship with Indians. He chose it less frequently in what he said about the colonists and himself, where loyalty and honour were generally the qualities involved. He was clear from his first arrival in Narragansett territory that he was there by Indian "grace and favour." He said of the old chief Canonicus, who permitted him to settle within Narragansett bounds:

'Tis true he received presents and gratuities many of me; but it was not thousands nor ten thousands of money could have bought of him an English entrance into this bay; thousands could not have bought of him Providence, or Pawtuxet, or Aquidnick, or any other land I had of him.[54]

Confidence, mutual trust, love; these were the attributes that gained an entry for the pioneer of Rhode Island. "God was pleased to give me a painful, patient spirit to lodge with them in their filthy smoakie holes (even while I lived at Plymouth & Salem)," he said, "to gain their tongue";[55] and he spoke of his gradual conquest of the affection of Canonicus, to whom he was probably introduced by Ousomoquin of the Wampanoags while at Plymouth:

I spared no cost towards them, and in gifts to Ousamaquin—yea all his, to Canonicus; and [gave] open tokens and presents many years before I came in person to the Narragansett [people]. And therefore, when I came, I was welcome, to Ousamaquin and that old Prince Canonicus, who was most shy of all English to his last breath.[56]

The account agrees with what he had told John Winthrop, Senior, by way of explanation after he had acted as agent in the acquisition of the island of Prudence in the Narragansett Bay:

Sir, concerning the islands Prudence and (Patmos, if some had not hindered) Aquidnick, be pleased to understand your great mistake: neither of them were sold properly, for a thousand fathom would not have bought either, by strangers. The truth is, not a penny was demanded for either, and what was paid was only gratuity, though I choose, for better assurance and form, to call it sale.[57]

(It looks as though Williams had wanted to call Rhode Island Patmos after the Mediterranean Island where the Book of Revelation was written; the "thousand fathom" refers to lengths of wampum, the Indian currency made of threaded shells.) The basis of all land ownership on Rhode Island lay in this willingness of the Indians to cede it freely, or so Williams afterwards wrote. The point he made was fundamental in his understanding of his own dealings with the Indians and the subsequent objection he took to those who, like his enemy William Harris, considered their later and more hard-bitten deals had more legal validity than Williams's informal concessions.[58] Although he used the word "feoffee"[59] of Harris and other land-hungry men, it is not right to suggest that he acted like some mediaeval lord by doing so. He used the word to try to embody what he thought he had himself received from the Indians—an honourably ceded "living," at their gracious pleasure. He wanted to emphasise later that this was the true foundation of proprietary right for himself or those who came later. Legally he was unrealistic; but the quality of the original agreements, love, was precious to him, and he had tried to preserve it in the giving of land to new colonists:

I have acknowledged (and have and shall endeavour to maintain) the rights and property of every inhabitant of Rhode Island in peace; yet, since there is so much sound and noise of purchase and purchasers, I judge it not unseasonable to declare the rise and bottom of the planting of Rhode Island in the fountain of it: It was not price nor money that could have purchased Rhode Island. Rhode Island was purchased by love; by the love and favour which that honourable gentleman Sir Henry Vane and myself had with that great sachem, Miantonoumi, about the league which I procured between the Massachusetts English, &c., and the Narragansetts in the Pequot War.[60]

A similar principle ruled Williams's conduct of trade among the Indians. They wanted European clothes, alcoholic liquors, gunpowder, and muskets. There were many who provided them unscrupulously. Richard Smith, who bought Williams's trading post from him, was not averse to it;[61] "that bloody liquor trade"[62] Williams called it. In common with most of the Puritans he himself regarded beer, wine, and strong waters as divine benefits vouchsafed to Europe,[63] but he drew the line at promoting alcohol among the Indians for gain. "I have long had scruples," he informed the younger Winthrop in 1654, "of selling natives aught but what may bring or tend to civilizing; I therefore neither brought, nor shall sell them, loose coats nor breeches."[64] Obviously he did not think dressing finely, like a vain Englishman, civilised them. As for "liquor," he declared that

they are willing to be peaceable, were it not for that devil of liquor. I might have gained thousands [of fathoms of wampum or pounds?] (as much as any) by that trade, but God hath graciously given me rather to choose a dry morsel, &c.[65]

In 1655 he had warned the Massachusetts General Court:

The barbarians all the land over, are filled with artillery and ammunition from the Dutch, openly and horridly, and from all the English over the country (by stealth). . . . For myself (as through God's goodness) I have refused the gain of thousands by such a murderous trade, and think no law yet extant, among yourselves or us, secure enough against such villainy; so am I loth to see so many hundreds (if not some thousands) in this colony, destroyed like fools and beasts without resistance.[66]

For all his humanity, some have said humanitarianism, Williams was and remained a missionary.

Mr. Williams used to uphold a public worship, sometimes, though not weekly, as many now alive remember, and he used to go once a month, for many years, to Mr. Smith's in the Narragansett, for the same end,

wrote John Callender,[67] about 1739. Some of the finest passages in *Christenings Make Not Christians* are devoted to the theme of the conversion of the Indians. He was aware of the wholesale "christenings" of the successful Jesuit missionaries in Canada and the West Indies:[68]

If the reports, yea some of their own historians, be true, what monstrous and most inhumane conversion have they made; baptizing thousands, yea, ten thousands, of the poor natives; sometimes by wiles and subtle devices, sometimes by force compelling them to submit to that which they understood not, neither before nor after such their monstrous christening of them! . . .

For our New-England parts, I can speak uprightly and confidently, I know it to have been easy for myself, long ere this, to have brought many thousands of these natives, yea, the whole country, to a far greater anti-Christian conversion than ever was yet heard of in America.[69]

He drove home the argument eloquently in a long statement giving his reasons for refraining:

For all this, yet some may ask why hath there been such a price in my hand not improved? Why have I not brought them to such a conversion as I speak of? I answer, "Woe be to me if I call light darkness, or darkness light; sweet bitter, or bitter sweet. . . ." America, as Europe and all nations, lies dead in sin and trespasses. It is not a suit of crimson satin will make a dead man live; take off and change his crimson into white, he is dead still. Off with that, and shift him into cloth of gold, and from that to cloth of diamonds; he is a dead man still. For it is not a form, nor the change of one form into another, a finer and a finer and yet more fine, that makes a man a convert—I mean such a convert as is acceptable to God in Jesus Christ, according to the visible rule of His last will and Testament. I speak not of hypocrites, which may but glister and be no solid gold, as Simon Magus, Judas, &c., but of a true external conversion. I say then, woe be to me if, intending to catch men—as the Lord Jesus said to Peter—I should pretend conversion and the bringing of men, as mystical fish, into a church estate, that is a converted estate, and so build them up with ordinances as a converted Christian people, and yet, afterward, still pretend to catch them by an after-conversion. I question not but that it hath pleased God, in his infinite pity and patience, to suffer this among *us,* yea and to convert thousands, whom all men, yea, and the persons in their personal estates *converted,* have esteemed themselves good converts before.[70]

How close he sometimes came to gaining heartfelt allegiance to Christ among the Indians may be discovered in his *Key*[71] and particularly in the account he gave of the death of his trusted Pequot guide, Wequash:

I closed with him concerning his soul. He told me that some two or three years before he had lodged at my house, where I acquainted him with the condition of all mankind, and his own in particular: how God created man and all things; how man fell from God, and of his present enmity against God, and the wrath of God against him until repentance. Said he, "Your words were never out of my heart to this present," and, said he, "Me much pray to Jesus Christ." I told him so did many English, French, and Dutch, who had never turned to God, nor loved him. He replied in broken English: "Me so big naughty heart; me heart all one stone!"—savoury expressions, using to breathe from compunct and broken hearts, and a sense of inward hardness and unbrokenness. I had many discourses with him in his life, but this was the sum of our last parting until our general meeting.[72]

Roger Williams believed that the decision about the eternal destiny of any whose hearts he had touched by his message could be left until the Last Judgment.

The modern anthropologist may reflect that Williams in his *Key* showed "an ethnographic interest and insight not equalled until the nineteenth century."[73] The historian of Christian missions will see in him qualities that invite comparison with the most skilful interpreters of the Christian message and the Christian life. The outlook and methods of Roger Williams remind us of Bartholomew de Las Casas in the sixteenth century, Christian Friedrich Schwartz in the eighteenth, William Carey in the nineteenth, Charles de Foucauld in the twentieth.

Roger Williams

"Miantonoumi kept his barbarous court lately at my house,"[74] he wrote to the elder Winthrop in 1637. Toward the Indians his door was open. They came to him, and he went out to be with them. He thought this was his reasonable service among "the wild yet wise Americans"[75] because of what he believed about Christ.

Christ's Kingdom: Seekerism

IN OCTOBER 1646, Oliver Cromwell wrote to his daughter
Bridget, the wife of the parliamentary army officer, Ireton, about
the spiritual condition of her "Sister Claypole":

> she seeks after (as I hope also) that which will satisfy. And thus to be
> a seeker is to be of the best sect next to a finder; and such an one shall
> every faithful humble seeker be at the end. Happy seeker, happy finder![1]

Cromwell was clearly not describing an organised group with
ministers, forms of worship, and discipline of its own. He
pointed to a familiar state of mind and confessed he was no
stranger to it himself. The English religious literature of the
middle of the seventeenth century contains many accounts of
men and women subject to melancholy and unable to settle for
any one of the main religious parties of the land. Sometimes
their difficulties went beyond a quest for spiritual solace. They
wanted to discover what the Bible required of Christians in
ordaining ministers, celebrating baptism, evaluating spiritual
experiences, and discerning the auguries of the imminent thousand year reign of Christ with his saints. Some were concerned
about the fact that even after they seemed regenerate they

still went on sinning and fretting. They wished to be free of such hindrances and to be satisfied by more than occasional foretastes of what they sought. These were all seekers, who tended to alternate between depression and hints of bliss, like doves (as they expressed it), mourning and seeking their mates.[2] Some, like the wife of Sir Henry Vane the Younger, were socially eminent; others were anonymous inhabitants of Lancashire, Westmorland, and Cumberland villages. They were all seekers, unfolded sheep.

In the pamphlet warfare that raged between the Independent political party (and the Congregational clerical spokesmen) on one side, and the Presbyterians and their sympathisers on the other, the Seekers tended to acquire a capitalised initial by about the year of Cromwell's letter, 1646. Their attitude of mind had become so widespread that they were regarded as a party of their own. As their ranks were internally split by factions, including antitrinitarians and Arminian dealers in "free grace," classification and vilification of Seekers became one of the duties of orthodox Calvinists like the sharp-eyed Robert Baillie, the spokesman of the Scots Commissioners in the Westminster Assembly of Divines, then in session. His *Disswasive from the Errours of the Time*, published in 1646, related the "sects and schisms" then proliferating with the tacit consent of the Independents, to the almost universally suspect virus of "Anabaptistry." The sequel to this work, published in the following year, gave an observant account of the seeker phenomena and adherents under the title: *Anabaptism, the True Fountaine of Independency, Brownisme, Antinomy, Familisme, And the most of the other Errours, which for the time doe trouble the Church of England, Unsealed.*

Anabaptism was a horrific word used to insinuate that theological heresy and social revolt were abroad. Baillie was shrewd enough to know that many Puritan exiles in the Netherlands had been exposed to the influence of the continuing Dutch inheritors of the sixteenth century Anabaptist movement. He was aware that some had doubted the ordination of their own ministers, and others had rebaptised. His information came through correspondence with his equally orthodox Calvinist brother minister in the Netherlands, William Spang.[3] "Many of the Anabaptists are now turned Seekers," wrote Baillie, "denying all Churches, all Officers, all Ordinances."[4] He amplified the marginal heading with the words:

Very many of the Anabaptists are now turned Seekers, denying the truth of any Church upon earth for many ages past, denying that there are any pastors now on the earth, that there may be any preaching of the word, any joining in prayer, any celebration either of Baptism or of the Lord's supper, any church discipline at all, or any church Act, church state, or church ordinance whatsoever; while God from heaven send new apostles to work miracles and set up churches, which for the space of fourteen hundred years at least have totally failed in the whole world. Hitherto Mr. Williams, Mr. Clarkson, Mrs. Attaway, are come from their antipaedobaptism.

"Mr. Williams" was the busy Roger, who had met Baillie while lobbying in the English parliament and among members of the Westminster Assembly and, notwithstanding their differences, had gained his friendship.[5] Williams, he was willing to concede, "if I mistake not the humour of the man, is very unwilling to report a lie of his greatest enemy." Baillie's portmanteau delineation of what Williams and the other two people believed may not apply in close detail to Williams's own views, but it gives the general drift of developing convictions about the "apostasy" of the churches, the need for a newly authorised ministry, and the hope of an early millennial intervention to obtain this end. Baillie quoted from the then recently published *Christenings Make Not Christians*[6] to substantiate his point, but he had also gathered it from personal conversations noted in his *Letters and Journals*:

Sundry of the Independent party are stepped out of the Church, and follows my good acquaintance Mr. Roger Williams; who says, there is no church, no sacraments, no pastors, no church officers, or ordinance in the world, nor has been since a few years after the Apostles.[7]

More interesting, however, in the further account Baillie gave in his *Anabaptism*, was his recognition that some Seekers had not slidden off all the way into antitrinitarian errors, or the "perfectionist" antinomian "sinnes of the flesh" the Ranters were charged with taking over from Familists and "libertines."[8] He suggests between the lines that they were sound Calvinists at heart like himself. He certainly had Williams in mind as one such, because this marked their common ground. "We are not yet come towards any period of the journey of these wanderers, for the spirit that is in them is restless, and keeps them in a perpetual motion," Baillie said. He then continued with a recognition of the more moderate and sober type of Seekers, who were sound enough, even though they were looking for a new Elijah from on high:

These who are only Seekers notwithstanding of all their enmity against the setting up of churches or use of ordinances, till Elias and new apostles come to kill the Antichrist, and reform these anti-Christian abuses, that have destroyed for so long a time, the true being of all churches; yet are they content in a private and personal way to embrace the Scriptures, and the most substantial truths therein contained . . .[9]

Baillie's colleague Thomas Edwards was an indefatigable chronicler of the sectarians; in Baillie's works he is quoted with approval. His insulting book *Gangraena*, which appeared in a third edition in 1646, lists 176 errors, including some quoted from Roger Williams verbatim. The "Sect of Seekers," Edwards warned,

grows very much, and all sorts of sectaries turn Seekers; many leave the Congregations of Independents, Anabaptists, and fall to be Seekers, and not only people, but ministers also; and whosoever lives but few years (if the sects be suffered to go on) will see that all the other sects of Independents, Brownists, Antinomians, Anabaptists, will be swallowed up in the Seekers, alias Libertines. . . .[10]

Roger Williams seems to be meant in one of Edwards's more savage remarks:

How many cast out of New-England for their Antinomianism, Anabaptism &c. have come over, and here printed books for their errors, and preach up and down freely, so that poor England must lick up such persons, who like vomit have been cast out of the mouth of other Churches? . . .[11]

From both Presbyterians, Baillie and Edwards, it may be gathered that Roger Williams, on the occasion of his first return to London in 1643, was industriously writing, speaking, and simply talking. As he wrote *Christenings Make Not Christians* and *Queries of Highest Consideration*, as he published his *Bloudy Tenent* and discussed the implications of his *Key into the Language of America*, he moved among many of his old associates, Independents he had known at Cambridge, in East Anglia, and in the City of London. Their seeker state of mind was vague enough; he sought to give it theological definition and turn them into such Seekers as he had himself by then become. He did not wish them to abandon their Calvinist convictions, summed up in the five points of the Synod of Dort in 1619. All these points safeguarded Williams's view of "the true Lord Jesus" as he believed the Scriptures presented Christ's work of election and regeneration. At the same time he was eager that they should seek for a more satisfying understanding of the plight of the churches and their ultimate rescue from their wandering through the wilderness. His prefatory address to "the Impartiall Reader" in his *Mr. Cottons Letter . . . Examined and Answered*, in 1644, drove this home and must have had its effect in the lives of many of his former friends who well knew both Cotton and Williams:

I rejoice in the goodness and wisdom of Him who is the Father of lights, in ordering the season both of mine own present opportunity of answer as also, and especially, of such protestations and resolutions of so many fearing God, to seek what worship and worshippers are acceptable to him in Jesus Christ.

Mine own ears were glad and late witnesses of an heavenly speech of one of the most eminent of that high assembly of Parliament; viz., "Why should the labours of any be suppressed if sober, though never so different? We now profess to seek God, we desire to see light," &c.[12]

The speech in parliament had been delivered by Sir Harry Vane, a man known for his millennial and rather elevated type of thought. Vane was another who had come back to England after some difficult times with the magistrates and ministers of the New England Boston over the Anne Hutchinson affair. He and Williams were friends. Vane's wife was known for her circle of friends, people who sighed and longed for the further light they believed to be breaking in on England's soil.[13] Williams admitted to his reader that there were times when seeking God came too late, and there was no divine response, but he continued:

> Love bids me hope for better things. God's promise assures us that His people, returning from captivity, shall seek Him and pray and find Him, when they seek Him with their whole heart *(Jeremiah 27)*. And God's angel comforts those against all fears that seek Jesus that was crucified *(Mark 16).*[14]

The words are charged with high hope. Williams urged study of *Jeremiah 27*, which compares a false with a true priesthood and promises return for exiles in Babylon, with restoration of true forms of worship. The reference in Mark's Gospel is to the words of the women at the empty tomb on Easter morning. It gives us the clue to the occurrence of the same phrase in Williams at other times.[15] Exceptionally, he had used the noun "seeker" in the margin opposite the passage, writing that "whole-hearted seekers" were "the only seekers of Christ Jesus."[16] In what immediately follows there is even a touch of the longing for perfection that marked the spiritual ardours of the Lady Vane's group:

> Thy soul so prosper, whoever thou art, worthy reader, as with thy whole heart thou seekest that true Lord Jesus, who is holiness itself and requires a spiritual and holy Bride like to himself, the pure and spotless Lamb.[17]

But the tone changed to the voice of the Separatist who chose suffering and self-denial as Williams gave his invariable definition of the true Lord Jesus, the man who chose to stand with the hunted and hurt, "that Lord Jesus, who purposely chose to descend of meane and inferiour Parents, a Carpenter, &c."[18] This was the Christ who disdained not to enter this world in a stable, amongst beasts, as unworthy the society of men; who passed through this world with the esteem of a mad man, a deceiver, a conjurer, a traitor against Caesar and destitute of a house wherein to rest his head; who made choice of his first and greatest ambassadors out of fishermen, tentmakers, &c.; and at last chose to depart on the stage of a painful, shameful gibbet.

If Him thou seekest in these searching times, makest Him alone thy white [target, aim] and soul's beloved, willing to follow and be like Him in doing, in suffering, although thou findest Him not in the restoration of His ordinances according to His first pattern, yet shalt thou see Him, reign with Him, eternally admire Him and enjoy Him when He shortly comes in flaming fire to burn up millions of ignorant and disobedient.[19]

The conclusion is that Roger Williams, on his first visit home to London, was not willing to remain an isolated seeker. He, and probably others who shared his basic Calvinist doctrines, were not refraining from making their additional preoccupations known. Out of the scattered flock of undecided Seekers they were trying to gather a more closely knit fellowship for hearing preachers and praying expectantly together. They hoped the curtain was about to go up on the last act of the world's history, and that the Jesus they sought at the Cross would be the chief actor, in some way not yet clear.

In 1647 John Cook, a leading lay Independent who was to become Solicitor General under the Commonwealth and one of the regicides, wrote a small book called *What the Independents Would Have*. It was an attempt to still the noise caused in the world by Presbyterians like Baillie and Edwards and gave a picture of the typical Independent being full of goodwill and moderation, though critical of extremists. By the time Cook wrote, the cause of toleration for the sects was on the way to realisation, but what he said on the subject of the Seekers did not upbraid them for being against the Trinity or as libertines guilty of moral misdemeanour. He appears to have in mind good Independents who were being cast into a state of doubt about their own ministers and sacraments by a definable Independent-Seeker wing that was having some success in subverting them. Cook's good Independent hopes Seekers find the way to heaven, yet counts it sad that any should wait for new apostles—they may as well seek a new Gospel—and that those ordinances which Christ hath purchased with his precious blood should be counted shadows, much derogatory to his love and wisdom; yet he suspects his own heart, and thinks that possibly some men live at a very high rate in spiritual enjoyments, being wholly at rest in God, and have the less need of ordinances. . . .[20]

Cook sounded as though he could be rebuking Williams while applauding the friends of Lady Vane; and the impression was reinforced when he added that his typical worthy Independent

knows no hurt in a million of millenary-like errors; who would not be glad to see Jesus Christ?[21]

Speculation about the millennium, in other words, was permissible; but open suggestion that the Independent churches were not true visible churches of Jesus Christ was going too far.

Richard Baxter, who knew people, their writings and affiliations as well as most men of his time in England, recalled this period of Roger Williams's first return to London some twelve years afterwards, when showing how the Baptists had fathered all kinds of additional errors in the progress of their movement. He discussed ministers who had been induced to question their calling and abandon the celebration of the sacraments. Of Roger Williams he wrote:

How far Mr. Williams in New-England went by this way, that plantation can sadly witness; but England far more sadly, who giving him kindlier entertainment than they, have received far more hurt by him, when he became the Father of the Seekers in London.[22]

In old England this was explicit evidence of the type of activity Williams employed in making his particular witness to the task laid down for the groups he "fathered"; they were to cast a kind of holy doubt on existing churches and ministries and to seek new power from God and the rise of genuinely apostolic men to supplant the unsatisfactory Presbyterians and Independents.

The other Independents in New England, under their respected clerical leader, John Cotton, certainly could "sadly witness" how far Williams had gone already before he set sail in 1643. Cotton's sad witness by 1647 was precise:

> Time was, when of all Christian churches, the churches of New England were accounted and professed by him to be the most pure; and of all the churches in New England, Salem (where himself was Teacher) to be the most pure. But when the churches of New England took just offence at sundry of his proceedings, he first renounced communion with them all; and because the church of Salem refused to join with him in such a groundless censure he then renounced communion with Salem also, and then fell off from his ministry, and then from all church fellowship, and then from his Baptism (and was himself baptized again), and then from the Lord's Supper and from all ordinances of Christ dispensed in any church way, till God shall stir up himself, or some other new apostles, to recover and restore all the ordinances and churches of Christ out of the ruins of anti-Christian apostasy.[23]

As he proceeded, John Cotton outlined the consequences of Williams's "seeking" for the doctrine of the visible Church, church-state relationships, and the Last Things:

> Conceiving himself to have received a clearer illumination and apprehension of the estate of Christ's Kingdom and of the purity of holy communion than all Christendom (yea, even Christendom itself is an unsavoury word to him), he therefore taketh it to be his duty to give public advertisement and admonition to all men, whether of meaner note (such as myself), or of more public note and place, of the corruptions of religion which himself observeth in their judgment and practice. Neither would I deny but that (to use his own words) *God sometimes stirreth up one Elijah against eight hundred of Baal's priests, one Micaiah against four hundred of Ahab's prophets, one Athanasius against many hundreds of Arian bishops, one John Hus against the whole Council of Constance, Luther and the two witnesses against many thousands, &c.* And therefore I durst not neglect, much less despise, any advertisement from him alone against so many, provided that the word of the Lord be found in his mouth or pen.[24]

This was the distinguished champion of the Independent party speaking. In England and New England the Independents seemed to wait upon his word as he took up his pen against

the annoying attacks of Williams. Obviously Cotton did not
intend to be moved away from the position on church government he and the five Independent champions in the Westminster Assembly had set out so firmly. Even the formidable
John Owen had been won for the Congregational way by reading Cotton on the Church.[25] What Williams had said about
solitary witness in his examples from church history was acceptable to Cotton as far as it went; but the words "the two
witnesses" at the close of Williams's list of people touched a more
sensitive nerve. John Cotton, Thomas Goodwin, John Owen, and
many other outstanding leaders of the Independent cause in the
middle and late 1640's believed fervently that the new light
required to complete the Reformation in England would take
the form of a peaceful reign of Jesus Christ, acting in Church
and State through His taking up His personal prerogative of
kingship in the rule to be established by His saints[26]—meaning,
for the Independents, chosen and obedient men of their own
mind. When Roger Williams alluded to the "two witnesses" he
was aware of mentioning one of John Cotton's own favourite
texts from the Book of Revelation (*Revelation 11.2*). Cotton in
America and Thomas Goodwin in England were among the
immediate inspirers of the millenarian fever that gripped the
mind of Independency at the time of the calling of the Long
Parliament, as early as 1640.[27] In the years immediately following, and until the collapse of the Nominated Parliament of
the "saints" in 1653, hopes ran high among the Independents
that they were not simply heralds, but personal instruments of
the millennial dawn. They broke a tacit agreement with the
Scots and the English Presbyterians to refrain from speaking
and writing, largely on account of their excitement over the
prospect of being used by God to fulfil what seemed to them
the clear promises of the last book in the Bible.[28] The mysterious
"two witnesses" had called forth much ingenious comment on
the part of the Bible scholars, Thomas Brightman and Joseph
Mead. Richard Bernard, Roger Williams's presumptive father-
in-law, had been another eager student of these mysteries, though

in his *Key of Knowledge for the Opening of the Secret Mysteries of St. Johns Mysticall Revelation*, published in 1617, he had run true to type by rejecting the implication of the earlier Brightman that the Church of England was to be identified with the Church of Laodicea (neither hot nor cold and therefore spewed out of God's mouth; *Revelation 3.16*). Bernard combined his speculations on Revelation, and particularly its early Letters to the Seven Churches, with fanciful expositions of the Song of Solomon.

These were equally important books of the Bible for John Cotton. He twice expounded the Song of Solomon in curious sermons. On the first occasion, when he was still at St. Botolph's, he ran riot with allegorical detail about the approaching glory of the Church. The atmosphere of these sermons is often perilously poised between enthusiastic religious transport and veiled erotic interest. Both Cotton and Bernard were influenced by Brightman. Both had connections with circles of seeking and sighing enthusiasts which proliferated about the Lincolnshire family of the Wrays. The wife of Sir Harry Vane the Younger was a Wray.[29] The frame of mind represented by these people may be described as emotionally charged expectation of the millennium. The "two witnesses" were believed, by both Williams and Cotton, to stand just ahead of the "new light" they expected would shortly break in on the world.

Roger Williams had read[30] one of the other books of millennial sermons Cotton preached by the time the *Bloudy Tenent* was written in 1644. This was his *The Powring out of the Seven Vials*, which Cotton called "an exposition of the sixteenth chapter of the Revelation, with an application of it to our times" and had printed in 1642. The sermons must have been delivered shortly beforehand. They breathe Cotton's apocalyptic hope for New England's place in the prelude of the coming Kingdom of Christ. They speak often and confidently of "new light" and are comparable with his expositions of *Revelation 13* preached in 1639 and 1640 before the calling of the Long Parliament in England, where the same eagerness was manifested. At the close of that series of sermons he had called for a day of fasting prayer for

England and the Scots alliance, "that the Parliament may be
for the better, not for the worse, but purity of ordinances (if it
be the blessed will of God) may be established."[31] Earlier in the
series Cotton had tentatively predicted that the papacy would
fall in 1655;[32] events in London were thus an overture to the
unrolling of the prophecies of the Revelation.

In the closing sermons of his *Powring out of the Seven Vials*
we can tell the prospect of victory in England for an Independent
polity in the Church was brighter than in 1640. The new light
by now seemed to be visible without much help from Scotland;
men, according to Cotton, would

> raise such an earthquake first, in church and commonwealth, as you
> will at length wonder at; for though it begin in a corner of the world,
> it will not cease till it have shaken all Christendom, . . . when men
> once begin clearly to see which is the true Church of God, that it is
> no Cathedral, nor Provincial, nor Diocesan, but Congregational only,
> the officers whereof are godly Pastors and Teachers and ruling Elders
> and Deacons.[33]

With this in mind the preacher called his people again to prayer,

> both night and day, in season and out of season, for our brethren in
> our native country, for whom God hath wrought all these great things
> and for whom greater things yet remain to be done; for whom our
> work is to wrestle with God that they may not perish for lack of
> knowledge, nor mistake a false church for a true—and false it is if it
> be either Cathedral, Provincial, National, or Diocesan.[34]

Presbyterian pretended solutions as well as prelacy were within
Cotton's sights here. A struggle lay ahead and New England
must not be found wanting:

> And great pity were it that they should want any light which might
> possibly be afforded unto them, and marvellous useful will it be that we
> should not be wanting on our parts, to help with what light we have,
> that so there may be no more refuges of lies in that land.[35]

One further sermon of Cotton, also published in 1642, is
still more pointed in its topical applications—his *The Churches*

Resurrection, expounding *Revelation 20.5–6,* which promised a thousand year reign, with Christ, to those who were still alive. It was believed that they would be joined by the faithful dead, resurrected for the purpose. Cotton pointed out that the text foreshadowed this happy condition:

The saints have a comfortable time of it (over what they had) . . . they do rule, and sit upon thrones, and judgment is given them. . . .[36]

He anticipated that the Church of Rome would fall soon and thereafter the Independent clergy, or others brought to share their opinions, would

by the power of the keys . . . take hold on Satan, that is to say, convince him and his instruments of all popish and paganish religion, and bind him by the chain, that is to say the strong chain of God's ordinances, word, and sacraments and censures. . . .[37]

The delightful prospect of this approaching power led him on to even grander claims that

those that were branded before for Huguenots and Lollards and heretics, they shall be thought the only men to be fit to have crowns upon their heads and independent government committed to them, together with the angels, that is the Elders of the churches, for a thousand years together. . . .[38]

John Cotton's reputation as a serious thinker has undergone some justifiable rehabilitation in recent years, but he could evidently indulge in dreams of grandeur. However, it was not firm delusion, simply a wish:

Therefore let not New England be secure and bless ourselves in our Resurrection because we have part in this Reformation. I cannot say, "Here is a Resurrection of churches such as the text speaks of, boiled up to that consistence which the text speaks to," though I hope the Lord will bring us to it.[39]

Roger Williams found the whole thing offensive in two ways. He could not believe that these dreams of wearing crowns were compatible with the seeking of the true, crucified, Lord Jesus;

nor could he be so sure as Cotton about the meaning of the
Book of Revelation. Years afterwards, in his debate with the
Quakers in 1672, he would say

> I know the counsels of the Father of Lights are very deep, yea, the
> *Revelation* needs a revelation, the prophecies and *Canticles* and *Daniel*
> need heavenly messengers and the most holy Spirit or finger of God to
> untie such knots.[40]

His perplexity by then was nothing new. He had been seeking
the meaning for years. The passages Cotton opened up for
his rapt Bostonians meant much to Williams. But he could
not work out the time sequences for the two events he expected
as surely as Cotton—the further "slaughter" of true Christians,
and the conversion of the Jews.[41] Nor could he reconcile the
contradictions between hopes of earthly power for the saints
and their instructions to use only spiritual weapons. These
thoughts lay behind his queries to the English Independents,
Presbyterians, and Parliament men in 1644:

> Can you unlock those mystical numbers of John's forty-two months,
> 1260 days, the three days and a half *(Revelation 11.2)*, the time, times,
> and half a time *(Revelation 12)*, and the thousand years *(Revelation
> 20)*, with divers others? . . .[42]

and again:

> 'Tis true, John tells us of Christ's great battles against the kings of the
> earth, against the Beast and false prophet, against Gog and Magog, but
> where speaks he of other ammunition and artillery, used by the saints,
> but what we find in Paul's Christian magazine *(Ephesians 6)*?[43]

The part of the letter to the Ephesians Williams mentioned described the "whole armour of God" as spiritual.

Thus the differences between the two men became defined.
Abstract analysis of toleration was foreign to their controversy.
Cotton's conscience was bound fast to his doctrine of the Church
and his vision of the beginning of the End. Williams's conscience
could not be persuaded at either point. He desperately needed
a "liberty of seeking." He was sure others did. Cotton found

Williams's openness maddening; Williams found Cotton's certainties stifling. Cotton said of Williams:

> Surely, if it be a further light which is held forth by him, it is such a transcendent light as putteth out all other lights in the world besides, as (they say) *majus lumen extinguit minus.* The churches of Christ have been wont to be counted lights, the ministry lights, the sacraments and censures lights. But this new light held forth by Mr. Williams hath put out all these lights, yea, and all possibility of their shining forth again, till the restitution of new apostles.[44]

Williams had noted that Cotton expected further light to shine. Since Christ's presence and reign upon earth were made visible only in His being persecuted, Roger Williams foresaw, for Cotton, dire consequences of Cotton's dream of imminent glory and saintly ascendancy. Williams warned that the persecuting Boston preacher, under the circumstances must, "expecting more light, (according to his way of Persecution) persecute Christ Jesus, if he bring it."[45] At this, Cotton was irate:

> Doth Mr. Williams hold me so far forsaken of common sense as to frustrate and destroy mine own expectations? . . . But thus, when a man's head runneth round, he thinketh all the house runneth round about him.[46]

The rupture between the two had been, in fact, unintentionally pinpointed in Williams's *Bloudy Tenent.* In a plea for liberty to be given to those who seek in the unsatisfied and desolate spirit of "that mournfull Prophet," the author of the *Psalm 74* Williams said:

> I see not that man, that prophet, that can tell us how long. How many excellent penmen fight each against other with their pens (like swords) in the application of those prophecies of David, Isaiah, Jeremiah, Ezekiel, Daniel, Zachary, John—when and how those prophecies shall be fulfilled![47]

The controversy between the two excellent penmen proceeded during the years Roger Williams spent between his first and second English visits as a trader in the vicinity of modern

Wickford Point, and at Providence. In 1647 Cotton answered Williams's *Examination* of the private letter he had sent him after his banishment from Massachusetts and also published his tedious and dutiful book, *The Bloudy Tenent Washed and Made White in the Blood of the Lambe*. In his wilderness we may imagine Williams vigorously writing out his long counter-blow, *The Bloody Tenent Yet More Bloody*, a book that has the zest of battle in it, for all its length, and contains much material of historical and theological interest to compare with the best of the *Bloudy Tenent*. All these controversial items are in the best academic tradition of point-by-point disputation and tend to be repetitious and exhaustive to the point of distraction. Those among the radical Independents and sectaries who followed the controversy, however, knew that the books were thrust and counterthrust in a warfare for the right to be a Seeker, erring or otherwise. Williams became an absent "father" and champion for hundreds of distressed and thoughtful men and women whose position in English society during the Civil Wars was similar to those sixteenth century radicals who could not find assurance in the Lutheran, Calvinist, and Zwinglian or English reformation, which had been implemented by civil magistrates.

In all the years that followed his defection from the Baptists in 1639 Roger Williams refrained from setting up a new church organisation, from the celebration of the sacraments of Baptism and the Lord's Supper, and from recognition of any clergy as the "apostles" he hoped would come from God. In these respects he has been compared with Hans Denck, Sebastian Franck, and Caspar Schwenckfeld, lay "witnesses against Christendom" among the radicals of the century before his own. In some ways he was possibly more akin, however, to the stormy Anabaptist Melchior Hofmann,[48] whose eventual "quiet eschatology" looked for the millennium as did Williams. Hofmann's suspension of sacraments and antipathy to the official clergy came to transmit themselves, as time passed, to the lonely Dutchman, Obbe Philips,[49] and to the Collegiants or Rijnsburgers, who nevertheless finally constituted regular churches of their own. At the close of the sixteenth and opening of the seventeenth century in the Netherlands the thought of men like these seeped into the doctrines and practices of English Separatists in exile. Even earlier, the influential John Bale,[50] whose image of the Church in the wilderness became so important to John Foxe when he wrote the *Book of Martyrs*, had admitted the influence of Hofmann.

Roger Williams knew Dutch, but we cannot trace direct evidence of Dutch writers in his books. More probably he absorbed the Seeker doubts and doctrines through his exposure to the Barrowists. Henry Barrow was not immune from anxious questionings about the derivation of "apostolic" authority for the ministers of the small Separatist groups which survived the work of Robert Browne. He had asked, probably following controversy with Browne himself in about 1587, about the ministry of the Church of England, "where they find that our Lord Jesus ever sent out any without giving them power" and "what then is to be done in these confused tymes, save that they buye gold of him that walketh between the seven golden candell stickes."[51] Barrow alluded to the vision of the supernatural Christ standing among the churches in *Revelation 1*. He was raising the Seeker problem of the relationship between the coming of a genuinely "apostolic" ministry and the imminence of Christ's final advent. The Seeker accent in the writings of the Barrowist John Wilkinson, who was a Separatist prisoner at Colchester in Essex between 1613 and 1619, could hardly have been unknown to Williams. Continuing Separatist traditions were still active in that county when Williams was living at Otes, but he might have been familiar with Wilkinson's opinions and record of persecution before that time. Others certainly were. Christopher Lawne, who broke with the Johnson-Ainsworth Separatists of Amsterdam and returned to the Church of England, was a biased witness, but we have no reason to doubt what he said of Wilkinson in 1612: "John Wilkinson and his disciples will have Apostles."[52] In 1623 Edmond Jessop, in his *Discovery of the Errors of the English Anabaptists*, confirmed the picture of a pre-Seeker body of opinion among the Separatists, with specific mention again of Wilkinson:

> Wilt thou have apostles again, to lay a new foundation, and must they ordain new elders before there can be a true constituted Church with her "offices and ordinances" as thou termest them? Is this thy judgment? It may be. . . . It hath been the opinion of some of thy predecessors that held themselves as wise as thyself, whatsoever thou art; as, for instance, there were (among others) three brethren, ancient Separatists from the Church of England, living sometimes in the city of London; their names were Legate. These held it stiffly that there must be new apostles before there could be a true constituted Church. . . . These Legates had a conceit that their name did (as it were) foreshew and entitle them to be the new apostles that must do this work. . . . There was also one John Wilkinson, another ancient stout Separatist, who with divers that followed him held the same likewise. . . .[53]

Jessop mentioned that the Legate Brothers, of whom Bartholomew was the last Englishman to be burned at the stake for heresy, at Smithfield in 1612, were guilty of "the Heresie of Arius,"[54] which means they did not hold an orthodox Nicene doctrine of the Trinity. He did not suggest that Wilkinson held such ideas, which tends to confirm what we know of him through his extant writings,[55] that he was as Calvinist about Christ as Barrow was before him and Roger Williams after him. On the other hand, one of Jessop's later descriptions shows a state of affairs among the Separatist split-off defectors in 1623 that looks surprisingly like a miniature preview of similar confusion among their successors in the late 1640's and early 1650's:

> People, being in distraction, have run from one sect and error to another, from separation to separation, dividing themselves into many several sects; to Anabaptistry, wherein [they] are divided (again) into five or six sundry sects, each hatefully condemning other, holding also many dangerous errors; some to expect new apostles; some to the heresy of Arius; and some others, who, being as it were distracted with these things, have fallen to another—the most blasphemous and erroneous

sect this day in the world—commonly called by the name of the Family
of Love. . . .[56]

Those who "expected new Apostles" were not necessarily
charged with the other distinct errors, though they seem to
have been responsible for creating an unsettled state of mind in
which antitrinitarian and antinomian groups spawned freely.

Spawn they did in Rhode Island, as in England, in the late
1640's. Williams, who detested the licentious and antisacramental
tendency of the followers of Henry Niclaes, the Familists, accused that blurry and colourful early American thinker, Samuel
Gorton, who had settled at Warwick, Rhode Island, of "denying
all visible and external Ordinances in depth of Familism,"[57]
surely a suggestive lead for investigators of Gorton's thought.
The words attest that Williams did not deny the importance of
visible ministries and sacraments; he simply could not make out
what God wanted them to be like. His was a suspension of
ordinances, not a derogation of them.

Properly administered sacraments depended, Williams believed, on properly installed and authorised ministers. The
dispensation of baptism and the Lord's Supper was a "feeding"
ministry, practised by pastors, shepherds of assembled flocks.
But as he read the New Testament, he came to the conclusion
that there was a prior ministry of greater importance, a converting ministry, sent to the wider world rather than the en-
closed fold. This was the genuinely apostolic, or sent out, ministry, on which the derivative "feeding," or pastoral ministry,
depended for its validity. Such a visible apostolic, converting
ministry, Roger Williams could not find. His "search" was for
"apostles," and for the evidence of their effectiveness in the
bestowal of the power of communication in other tongues. He
believed the Church was asleep and that Jesus Christ must come
to wake it up and make it apostolic, missionary-minded once
more. The ministry preceded the Church by going out ahead of
it and bringing in the nations. All these thoughts are set out
cogently, against the background of hope for an entirely peaceful
coming of Christ, in Williams's writings published in 1644.[58]

By the time Roger Williams reached London on his second visit, in 1652, the same teachings had been set out in another short book of sixty-four pages by an anonymous author calling himself "a lover of Truth and Peace." This was John Jackson, who became the "principal spokesman" of the Calvinistic Seeker groups during the 1650's.[59] His ideas mirror those of Roger Williams, though they are set out with more system and care. The book was called *A Sober Word To A Serious People*, subtitled "A Moderate Discourse Respecting As Well The Seekers, (so called) As The Present Churches, Wherein the Difference between them touching Visible Administrations, is Discovered and Discussed. And may serve as A Plea for the Nations Ministery." The attribution of the book and of two others by the same author to John Jackson is a matter of internal evidence and contemporary report. Jackson would have preferred to remain anonymous, but he was well enough known in London at the time to be detected by Richard Baxter and others.

Jackson appears to have been a layman. According to a letter addressed in 1659 to Baxter he was "formerly Grand Treasurer of the Excise,"[60] a tax official of some importance during the Commonwealth and Protectorate. His *Sober Word*, printed in 1651, is virtually a reply to attacks made on the Seekers by such opponents as Thomas Edwards and Robert Baillie. Its preface says the aim is

> to give thee an account touching a sort of people which some are pleased to call SEEKERS; of whom, several men, in several books, have spoken several things, shewing the dangerousness of their opinion and the dreadfulness of its tendency. . . .[61]

Reluctance to accept the name "Seeker" was very likely prompted by the prevalence of antinomian and antitrinitarian teachings among those who had come to be called by the name. Roger Williams's abstention from using it of himself may well have been for the same reason. "In a good sense," Jackson wrote, "it is a good thing to be a Seeker: In a bad sense it's not to be applied to them, which seek the Lord in sincerity, for wisdom, how to walk before him. Of this sort of Persons, and this sort of Seeking," he added, "this present discourse only treats."[62]

Jackson thus attempted to dissociate himself from unwelcome allies. His precaution was hardly called for; it was plain to any godly orthodox Independent or Presbyterian reader that Jackson stood where Williams did, where indeed they stood themselves, at least when it came to moral behaviour and the doctrine of the person of Christ. Neither Williams nor Jackson can be described as a Familist, Ranter, Arian, or Arminian. There is a passage in his first reply to John Cotton in which Williams also fenced himself off from any such people.[63]

The style of the *Sober Word* is modest, and in places almost colloquial. There is evidence in it of acquaintance with the Greek Testament. Polemic has been kept in check; objections are answered clearly in turn, but there are imaginative passages showing how deeply the author could be moved. Jackson can be thought of as a sorrowful "Congregational high churchman," in the sense that to him, as to Williams, correct commissioning of a true apostolic ministry, true faith, right discipline, sacraments following divine requirement, are of the essence of the life of the Church, not matters indifferent. Like Williams, Jackson emerges in the character of a "deprived saint," who seeks all this sadly in a wilderness of apostasy. The tone of brotherly charity is in happy contrast with Edwards's horror and the biting restraint of Baillie. The *Sober Word*'s verbal parallels with Roger Williams, like its main conceptions, suggest either a single common influence, or dependence of Jackson and his friends on the writing and speeches of Williams himself.

Williams's fundamental distinction between a converting and a feeding ministry becomes, in Jackson's book, a discrimination between what he calls, more memorably, a "breeding" and a "feeding" ministry. The first of these consists of apostles, prophets and evangelists, the second of pastors and teachers.[64] Jackson argued, on the basis of the New Testament, that there could be a true breeding ministry without a feeding ministry, but never the reverse. On this ground he looked with regret upon "the present Churches, and the present Ministery," and concluded that Seekers did not see "sufficient ground for their Practice."[65] Absence of a true apostolic and visibly empowered ministry in any of the churches he knew led, Jackson said, to the consequence that "a powerless People give Call to a Giftless Ministery."[66] His criticism was specifically directed against the practice of forming local churches by taking a covenant, the favoured method of procedure in Massachusetts and among the Independents generally. Williams had already clarified his reasons for opposing the practice of voluntary covenanting. There was, he claimed in his *Bloudy Tenent*, "no president [precedent] of any people in the Gospell converting and gathering themselves without some Messenger sent from the Lord to effect those ends."[67] Jackson made the same point in describing such willing association without external warrant as "altogether without precedent from the Word of God" and consequently said the covenanting people were "not to be acknowledged for the true Visible constituted Churches of Christ according to the Primitive Pattern."[68]

Williams's suspension of the sacraments is also present in the thought of Jackson, though he explained that Seekers accepted certain "ordinances" like assembling together for worship, mutual edification and study of the Bible.[69] Both men use the fate of the people of Jerusalem in being deprived of temple worship when in exile in Babylon as a "type" of the state of the Christian churches of their own day.[70] Jackson, an educated man, had Roger Williams's Separatist antipathy to regarding the universities as fit seminaries for the ministry.[71] Attention is drawn to the beginning of the apostasy of the churches "before the Apostles left the earth."[72] Joseph Mead, the Cambridge millenarian, is cited as authority on this subject. So is the Separatist Henoch Clapham, who had been minister in the English congregation exiled in Amsterdam about 1600, but whose book called *A Briefe of the Bibles History* had been resurrected in 1639. Finally Williams's concern for true mission and the conversion of nominal Christians as well as non-Christian peoples appears, as in the question:

> How is the end for which Christ ascended, and for which he gave gifts to men, accomplished, if the work of the ministry be not again restored unto its pristine and primitive constitution; as well to respect the nations which are without, viz., the outcasts of Israel, together with the worshippers of the sun and moon, the Moors and Indians, and the people that know not God nor ever have heard the sound of Him, nor of the salvation which through Christ Jesus He holds forth to mankind; as well as that sort of ministry which it's supposed is found among good people who judge they are in church estate already? . . .[73]

As prototype Seekers in New Testament times, John Jackson invoked the case of the noble inquirers of the city of Berea,[74] mentioned in *Acts 17.10–12*, who searched the Bible to test the message brought by Paul and Silas. These particular examples were better known generally among religious people of the middle of the seventeenth century than they are today, and were quite often held up for emulation, but it is of interest that Roger Williams, too, appealed to the noble Bereans' "searching" to give a scriptural sanction for his own.[75] A number of Williams's references to these Bereans happens to occur in works published during his second English visit, when Jackson was also writing. It seems the Bereans were favourites for the "orthodox" Seekers.

Richard Baxter read the *Sober Word* and conceded it a grudging regard. What he said is a recognition of Jackson's ability and a regretful observation about his defection from the ranks of those who thought as Baxter did about the Church and sacraments. In an account of the moderate Seekers he called John Jackson "the most rational and modest that hath wrote for this way," which gave Roger Williams second or some lower place. Baxter continued:

> A likely thing indeed it is that so rational a man should heartily believe that Christ hath planted so excellent a ministry and church and ordinances as himself describeth, and to those standing necessary uses

which he mentioneth, even in stead of Christ, to take men into the holy covenant; and yet that all 'should be left but for an age or two and that, ever since, there is no such thing, or at least no certainty of it. The style shows that this author is no such dotard as to think as he speaks.[76]

Difficult though it may be to reconstruct the size, membership and meeting places of Seeker groups in London when Roger Williams returned to the city in 1652, we may infer that they existed. Their convictions were crystallised in the writings of Williams and of Jackson. They appealed to serious and thoughtful people whose reading of the Book of Revelation continued the Separatist interpretation of the millennial books contained in the works of Henry Barrow and John Wilkinson. We know that Roger Williams expressed sympathy for the millenarian speculations of writers like John Canne[77] and Henry Archer.[78] Canne in particular was linked with the Separatists who tenaciously clung to the witness of the returned Netherlands exiles of the earlier years of the seventeenth century as the successors of these men continued their corporate life in the various splits and developments arising from Henry Jacob's London Church and in the other older Separatist congregation that survived alongside it. Some former Separatists practised adult baptism, but not all; others were "mixed assemblies" of Baptists and non-Baptists. Those who could not be satisfied with the local covenanting of the Independents or persuaded as to the correct form of administering baptism were liable to become Seekers of one sort or another. Through family, business, and legal connections in other parts of the country, and especially East Anglia, their notions remained current among radical gentry and their families, some of them close to Cromwell and the new "establishment" that emerged in the Commonwealth after the execution of Charles I in 1649. The King was dead; they looked with anguish for the establishment of Christ's kingdom in His restored Church. Their state of mind can be glimpsed in an account of Seekers given in 1647, when the crisis was brewing, by John Saltmarsh, who was one of Cromwell's army chaplains given to visions and trances:[79]

They wait, in this time of the apostasy of the Christian churches, as the Jews did in the time of their apostasy, and as the apostles and disciples at Jerusalem, till they were endued with power from on high, finding no practice for worship, but according to the first pattern.

They wait only in prayer and conference, pretending to no certain determination of things, nor any infallible consequences or interpretations of Scriptures. They wait for a restoration of all things and a setting up [of] all gospel officers, churches, ordinances, according to the pattern in the New Testament.

They wait for an apostle or angel, that is some with a visible glory and power able, in the Spirit, to give visible demonstration of their sending, as to the world; and thus they interpret those places of the Revelation.[80]

Among those in higher places known to have been participants in this general state of longing were some of Roger Williams's friends. Sir Harry Vane and his "Vanists" certainly expected a millennium. During his second visit to London Roger Williams was Vane's house guest, both in London and at his Lincolnshire home. The wife of Vane, Lady Vane the younger, was addressed in a dedication of Williams's *Experiments of Spiritual Life and Health*. The Wray family had sympathised with clergy of millenarian and even Separatist tendency and earlier had been patrons of Richard Bernard in obtaining him a Cambridge education. Roger Williams's wife appears to have been Bernard's daughter. The milieu is thus on the fringes of "Seekerism."

Into the circles prepared by Seeker questions and attitudes came a new and dynamic missionary movement. In the early summer of 1654 the followers of George Fox, the Quakers, came as "new apostolic men" from their heartlands in the Lake District and Lancashire into the midlands and London.[81] Their invasion of the south startled Seekers and unchurched religious eccentrics of all kinds. They brought the mentality of certainty. The revelation they said they had received was declared infallible. They said that the "new light" others sought had come. It was, in fact, within them; and the light was Christ Himself. He had come into his Kingdom of saints. They were the saints, the "extraordinary men" (and women) who would be the persecuted "seed" of the woman, the true Church, in the Book of Revelation. The last days had dawned. There could be no mistake about it. All others, whether churches or simply Seekers in quest of a true Church, would be still captives in "mystical Babylon," allies of Antichrist, if they failed to acknowledge The Light. Opponents of the Quakers were branded, in the apocalyptic language of the time, as obdurate participants in "the great Mistery of the Great Whore," which became the title of George Fox's large book setting forth his quarrel with all his detractors. The descent of the clamorous and remarkable Quakers on the South of England and indeed, the world, was summarised in these terms in 1659 by Fox on the title page of *The Great Mistery* as

> An invasion upon the great city, Babylon, with the spoiling of her golden cup and delicate merchandise, whereby she hath deceived the world and nations; and herein is declared the spoiling of her prey, in this answer to the multitude of doctrines held forth by the many false sects, which have lost the key of knowledge and been on foot since the apostles' days—called Anabaptists, Independents, Presbyters, Ranters, and many others; who, out of their own mouths, have manifested themselves not to be of a true descent from the true Christian churches; but it's discovered that they have been all made drunk with the wine of fornication received from the whore which hath sitten upon the Beast, after whom the world hath wondered.

Above this, on the same page, is Fox's categorical announcement that "the despised people of the LORD called QUAKERS" are "of the Seed of that Woman, who hath been long fled into the WILDERNESS."

Roger Williams was still in London in 1654 when the Quaker missionaries arrived from the north.[82] He talked with some of their leaders. He formed and retained a low opinion of their bearing and doctrines; inevitably so, since they clashed with his own carefully thought out theological conclusions in more than one way. His teaching about Christ derived from his belief about the meaning of the life of Jesus of Nazareth—that it was a "once for all," objective, scripturally attested Incarnation. The Quakers regarded all that as secondary. To them the subjective birth in them of Christ, as present Light and Spirit, was the Message to be shared. Williams believed that ministerial order was important. The Quakers believed they were all saints and apostolic people and that anything beyond that was for the "priests." Objective baptism and the Lord's Supper were vital to Williams, though he had lost them. The Quakers regarded them as at best secondary ways of mediating Christ; why bother with them when Christ was present in you immediately? Williams looked for external events for signs of the end of history and the reordering of churches and nations under Christ, the coming world ruler and judge. The Quakers spiritualised and internalised all that; for them the thousand year reign of peace had been inaugurated and would spread further in their own reception and diffusion of internally realized Truth.

Worse still, however, for "orthodox" Seekers like Jackson and Williams, was the attempt of these comparatively unlettered self-styled apostles to make proselytes among "orthodox" Seekers, their own friends and fellow "searchers." We may reasonably speculate that Williams's own meeting with leading Quakers in London arose out of attempted Quaker infiltration. From John Jackson's hand we have another curious publication, issued in 1655, called *Strength in Weakness, or The Burning Bush not Consumed*. This consists of a series of letters written by the leading Quaker James Nayler to Mrs. Mary Noell, wife of James Noell, which is bound together with her replies. Jackson became the editor of this collection, together with a further tract from Nayler's pen called *The Secret Shooting of the wicked, reproved*, and a final reply of his own; these "documents in the case," had Jackson's discreet initials, "J.J.," on the title page. George Fox, Richard Baxter, and Roger Williams had no hesitation subsequently in referring to the author as John Jackson.

Mary Noell had been "got at" by Nayler, who tried to turn her from orthodox Seeker to Quaker. Jackson, as her spiritual adviser, helped her to frame her replies and issued his own commentary on the attempted subversion. In answer to this commentary Nayler wrote *The Secret Shooting of the wicked, reproved,* the "wicked" being Jackson and the secrecy of the shooting being his modest preference for remaining anonymous. In the end Mrs. Noell, with the aid of her attendant theologian, held out for her former position. Both Quaker and Seeker apologists ran true to form. There was plenty of apocalyptic language on both sides, though it was used in different senses for the ends in view. We learn that Nayler, in the course of the exchange, called on Jackson for some "unexpected" face-to-face discussion,[83] which leads to the question whether this interesting (and rather sadly misled) early Quaker, who later entered Bristol in Messianic garb,[84] was among those Roger Williams also "talked with."

The whole affair is described in a preface addressed to the reader of Jackson's compilation, which gives a good idea of the impact of the Quaker missionaries on the "moderate" London Seekers and may act as a partial clue to Roger Williams's frontal tactics when he had the chance of personal debate with Quaker representatives:

> This daughter of Abraham (who is the subject), having been visited by many of the persons distinguished and commonly known by the name of the Northern People at sundry times and in sundry manner of ways, which occasioned (as in her self) much inquiry, accompanied with many prayers and soul-searchings, not without great and sore temptations from that terrible Adversary, who was not wanting to help on the affliction to the utmost; which conflict was repeated and renewed (as oft as opportunity was given by her new visitors) and hath produced, in many persons whose eyes were fixed upon her, much thinking and some speakings . . .[85]

Publication of the records of the encounter is justified as evidence of a Seeker victory,[86] and it is clear from other places in the text that the publisher hoped it would serve to confirm that the Quakers were not the expected heralds of the Last Days. One of Mary Noell's letters to Nayler said so firmly:

I have received of my spiritual sonship in Christ Jesus, and by this holy union with Christ Jesus my head have been by him taught, many years past, to try the public teachers of this nation, with those private also, who have held forth themselves to be sent messengers from Christ Jesus, and by his Holy Spirit, to which I am united [I] am taught to turn from them, and from thee also, who hast run, before thou wast sent, with this false message, to me. . . .[87]

Who was Mary Noell, the wife of James Noell? The answer to that question leads us a step nearer to the discovery of the personnel of the orthodox Seeker groups. James Noell was the publisher of John Jackson's *Sober Word*[88] in 1651. He may therefore have been a responsible and financially well-provided man with an interest in making Jackson's writing known. The printer of the *Sober Word* was James Cottrel, who also printed *The Examiner Defended* in 1652. This tract, as Perry Miller remarked, although anonymous, is unmistakably by Roger Williams;[89] the internal evidence is overwhelmingly strong. Jackson and Williams thus used the same printer at about the same time. Did the two ever meet? It has been thought that they could not have been personally acquainted on account of the fact that later on, in 1672, Roger Williams, in his Rhode Island debate with the Quakers, referred to the author of a book called *Hosannah to the Son of David*, published in 1657 anonymously, as "the unknown heavenly author."[90] This book was really by John Jackson. It is another, lengthier anti-Quaker tract by the "Lover of Truth and Peace" who produced the *Sober Word*. Elsewhere in his own record of the debate he staged with the Quakers in America Roger Williams followed George Fox in calling John Jackson by name[91] as the author of *Strength in Weakness*, in spite of the fact that its title page, at least in surviving copies, bears only the initials, "J.J." In the case of *Strength in Weakness* the secret was obviously out and there was no point in trying to hide the author's identity. But in *Hosannah* Jackson had given explicit reasons for wishing to be anonymous:

If any person enquire touching the author, and take offence because he is not named, let such know that, for that very reason, viz., to avoid offence, is the name withheld, considering how common an error it is for persons to judge of books by the author, rather than of the author by the book . . . and partly to give content to my own genius, who am a lover of retirement and privacy.[92]

There are, on the evidence, conflicting possible reasons for Williams's not revealing a definite relationship with John Jackson. He may genuinely not have known or met him. Or he may have known him very well and chosen to obscure the connection, both because he did not want to give the impression that the "Seekers" were yet another delimited sect and because he knew and respected Jackson's reason for being anonymous. We can tell that Jackson was no man to boost his case by virtue of official prestige. He had Williams's distaste for social climbing and wrote:

I have reason to believe that there are many persons dear and precious to the Lord whose spirits are fallen asleep on the Delilah's lap of this world's enticing pleasures and preferments. . . .[93]

Until the end of his life Roger Williams adhered to his "Seeker" variation on the theme of Christ's sole kingship. The "crown rights of the redeemer" were as dear to him as to any of the notable Independents; the irony for him lay in what he believed to be the usurpation of Christ's power in the Church by officers whose function and business should have been purely political. When the parliament assumed direction of the future of the Church in England under Cromwell he lamented "the setting of the Spiritual Crown of Christ Jesus upon Henry VIII, his head, and so ever since."[94] His "search" was for a Church that would be universal in its mission, apostolic in the original sense of the word; but he looked also for the disentangling of the jurisdictions of Church and State so that the kingly reign of Christ could be seen in the Church, where it belonged, and no longer remain obscured by continuing synthesis of imperial and ministerial power. He fought to gain a new freedom for the Church:

What king and governors of Israel are now to be found in the Gospel but Christ Jesus and his servants, deputed in his absence, which are all of a spiritual consideration? What is this to the nations, kings, and governors of the world, where few kings, few nobles, few wise are called to profess Christ? Is not Christ Jesus the only King of Israel, and are not all his holy ones made kings and priests unto God? And unto his saints and his spiritual officers' administration in the midst of them is his Kingdom's power committed in his absence. This spiritual power, however, the pope and prelates, kings and princes, parliaments and general courts, and their respective officers of justice (to be honoured and obeyed in civil things) . . . have challenged, and assumed this kingly power of the Son of God. Yet the King of kings, Christ Jesus, hath begun to discover, and will never leave until he hath made it clear as the sunbeams, that he is robbed of his crown and will shake and break all the nations and powers of the world until his heavenly crown be again restored.[95]

8
Caesar's Dunghill: Politics

A YARMOUTH SHIP'S CAPTAIN, Joseph Ames, brought a present of a young deer in 1655 from New England to Oliver Cromwell, the Lord Protector.[1] It was a gift from Roger Williams, then president of Providence Plantation, and a token of the gratitude Williams felt toward the "eminent" man who had been pleased, during Williams's second English visit, "to send for me," Williams wrote, "and to entertain many discourses with me at several times; which, as it magnifies his Christian nobleness and courtesy, so much doth it magnify *His* infinite mercy and goodness, and wisdom, who hath helped me, poor worm, to sow that seed in doing and suffering. . . . I hope for God. . . ."[2]

The recipient of this information concerning the interviews between colonist and regicide, was Mrs. Anne Sadleir, royalist daughter of Sir Edward Coke, who was not favourably impressed. But what Roger Williams said showed the mixture of political shrewdness and piety that runs through most of his career. The politician quotes the Bible; the biblicist quotes canny saws about political tactics. "As your honourable father was wont to say," he ran on at once to Mrs. Sadleir, "he that shall harrow what I have sown, must rise early."[3]

We are apt to think a religious man who enjoys the compromises and subtle chess of politics must be something of a hypocrite; or alternatively that politicians who talk religion must have something to hide. In the case of Williams, the politician and theologian are distinct but integrally united. The political doctrine and practice derive from a particular view of law and government; the religious motivation is invariably bound up with Williams's view of the person of Christ and Christ's power. Politics and religion in his thought are both subject to his belief that the Bible is the guide; but the Bible, on his reading of it, demands and portrays "a civil, a humane and political medicine, which," Williams told his old friend Major Mason in Connecticut, "if the God of Heaven please to bless, you will find it effectual to all the ends I have proposed. Only," he added sagaciously, "I must crave your pardon, both parties of you, if I judge it not fit to discover it at present."[4]

In the letter in question he had been urging constitutional and legal points on both Mason and Governor Thomas Prince of Connecticut. In 1670, after the restoration of Charles II to the English throne, he was still having trouble in getting the other New England colonies to agree to a sound compromise with Rhode Island about proper relationships. As though to concede that whatever was decided would be subject to the overruling providence of God, Williams put in the words "if the God of heaven please to bless." Yet he spoke as though the realm of political negotiation had its own divinely permitted provisional autonomy, for so he believed. By comparison with the glimpse of eternal glory he found in "the true Lord Jesus," Williams looked upon "these children's toys of land, meadows, cattle, government, &c.,"[5] as "leaves and flowers, and smoke and shadows, and dreams of earthly nothings."[6] The "dunghill"[7] of this present world had such trivia as its gods and goddesses; for that very reason it was unthinkable that it could be ruled by Christ, since his authority was obviously not acknowledged in the greater part of it. On the contrary, it was ruled, under God's permission and providence, by Caesars, with their own criteria of power, to which limits could be set through good laws and the expression of the will of the governed.

The distinction between the Kingdom of Christ and the kingdoms of this world is fundamental in the political thought of Roger Williams. Both are subject to the total sovereignty of the "Father of Lights," whose name is skirted in many places in this way because of the awe in which God was held. The Kingdom of Christ became visible in the true Church, which bore the stigmata of the "true Lord Jesus" as its authentic signs. About the Church, Williams was not merely idealist, as many of the Puritans were; he was, as many have pointed out, a perfectionist in a minority of one. When he came to politics everything worked quite differently. He took such a low view of human possibilities that he expected the worst and became highly skilful in the arts of adjustment and compromise. This was Williams's type of "humane and political medicine." There was little trace of utopia or even moral idealism in it; much less the illusion that he was constructing a Christian society. Politics for Williams was the cunning involved in keeping a sick patient, society, as comfortable as possible, pending the fatal inroads of death and the devil. These were the reasons Williams had at the back of his mind for telling Major Mason:

> If you please to ask me what my prescription is, I will not put you off to Christian moderation or Christian humility, or Christian prudence, or Christian love, or Christian self-denial, or Christian contention or patience. . . .[8]

At the top of his long letter to Mason he had written his own address and the date, "Providence, June 22, 1670, (*ut vulgo*)."[9] The English translation he sometimes supplied in other letters for this qualification of the date was "so called." Williams did not regard 1670 or any other year as the "year of our Lord." Christ did not reign visibly over the wilderness or dungheap of time and its kingdoms; to pretend that He did was to confound the human power of the sword with the divine power of the Word; the crown of gold with the only possible crown of Christ while time endured—the crown of thorns.

A total "segregation" of the two spheres, of Grace and Nature, is not involved in this significant aspect of Williams's thought,[10] as though Nature could safely be left to lawyers and politicians, Grace to theologians and clergy. The mediaeval separation of the spheres, described in such a way, is not found in his writings, or even to be suspected in his political method. He does not seem to use the word "grace" of the Church as compared with the State. Probably that was because he found the traditional language of "Christendome" rather "unsavoury,"[11] particularly after he wrote the *Bloudy Tenent* and thought the issues out in his own terms. He was, however, willing to agree with John Cotton and all his godly former friends about the legitimate division of the Ten Commandments, the basis of the code of Moses. These ten divinely revealed injunctions were divided into two "tables"; the first, of four commandments, was concerned with God and the worship of God, and was called "ceremonial"; the second was to govern human relations and was called "moral." Cotton and the New England clergy tended to argue that Moses continued to be a valid lawgiver, and that the functions of judges and kings in the Old Testament state of Israel continued to hold good for all time. Both the ceremonial provisions of the first table and the moral provisions of the second continued in force; their enforcement was the task of the magistrates and ministers acting together. Williams argued that the Ten Commandments remained valid, not as coming from Moses, but coming from God. Moses, he said, recalling the argument of the Letter to the Hebrews, had been a servant in the divine household. Now that the Son, the true Lord Jesus, had come, the old worship had been abrogated and a new put in its place. The new worship was spiritual. It was not celebrated in temples made with hands, but by buildings made figuratively of "saints," people in whom Christ ruled. In laying out his new laws of worship Jesus had supplanted the old office-bearers, judges, kings, and magistrates. In their place he had appointed his own officers to oversee the ceremonial provisions of the first table. These matters belonged purely and simply to his Church and Kingdom. Since his coming the magistrate was to have nothing to do with them. Williams described the change by saying in many places that the old state of Israel was unique and that its function was merely to provide a "type," or preliminary outline sketch, of the general shape of the Christian Church as it ought to be. This ancient Israel, said Williams,

> I have proved to be a none-such, and not to be paralleled, but in the antitype, the particular church of Christ, where Christ Jesus alone sits King in his own most holy government.[12]

The distinction thus made was not a private fad of Williams. He had many parts of the New Testament and plenty of evidence from the early history of the Christian Church on his side, so that John Cotton squirmed in the tight grasp of the argument as he tried to counter the *Bloudy Tenent* in his *Bloudy Tenent, Washed.* By the time Williams sat down to write *The Bloody Tenent Yet More Bloody* in 1651, the drift of English politics and the force of his biblical evidence in the *Bloudy Tenent* made him sense victory. The ironic remarks, alluding to politics, give Williams's second and longer book a flavour of its own. Building on his biblical differentiation between the power of the Church in the first table, and the power of the State in the second, he remarked rather insolently of Cotton's opposite position:

> After a new refined fashion and dress, he projects how to turn this whole dunghill of the corrupt and rotten world into a most sweet and fragrant garden of the Church, or Dove, of Christ.[13]

For all his derogatory adjectives about the world, the humane and political world, Roger Williams enjoyed playing by the rules that governed behaviour on the dunghill. He thought those rules belonged broadly to the second table of the Ten Commandments and were laid down in civil and common law, to be administered with more or less common justice and equity by the recognised civil officers of the "heathen." The provision made for government, administration of justice, taxation, and service of the "commonwealth" in all countries, whatever their religion, was part of the providential divine ordering of the world. There,

where men had not heard of Christ or had taken no notice of
Him or of his message, things were not utterly desperate. Most
men, according to Williams, were never likely to take Christ
seriously, let alone be numbered with the remnant of the elect;
so as to protect them from Caesars, tyrants, "bloody emperors"
of all kinds, God had located the sovereign, original, and foundation of all civil power in the people. The famous passage in
which Williams asserts that this is the case has so often been
quoted out of context to support the contention that he was a
forerunner of the doctrine of natural human right as self-evident
truth that it is necessary to detach his affirmation from that
framework of ideas. Williams would not only have been scan-
dalised by the removal of the idea of right, or justice, from the
idea of God; he would not have been content to think of it as a
secondary quality implanted in the nature of things by an all-
wise Creator who took no personal account of what happened
thereafter. When Williams spoke of God he meant the Calvinist
God, a living being with a perpetually "all seeing eye,"[14] who
ordained and supervised, moment by moment, the minutest
developments of the universe and human history. His God, in
other words, was the God of the Hebrews, not Pascal's rejected
"god of philosophers and learned men." What came immediately
before the celebrated passage in the *Bloudy Tenent* has to be
read, with the whole statement, in this light:

I acknowledge the proposition to be most true, both in itself, and
also considered with the end of it, that a civil government is an
ordinance of God, to conserve the civil peace of people so far as
concerns their bodies and goods, as formerly hath been said; but from
this grant I infer, as before hath been touched, that the sovereign,
original, and foundation of civil power lies in the people, whom they
[the Massachusetts authors of the law code called *A Model of Church
and Civil Power*] must needs mean by the civil power distinct from the
government set up; and if so, that a people may erect and establish
what form of government seems to them most meet for their civil
condition. It is evident that such governments as are by them erected
and established have no more power, nor for no longer time, than the

civil power or people consenting and agreeing shall betrust them with. This is clear, not only in reason, but in the experience of all common-weals, where the people are not deprived of their natural freedom by the power of tyrants.[15]

There is no intended platform here for manhood suffrage or secular libertarianism. All Williams said was that sensible thought and experience of the actual processes of government everywhere led to the conclusion that God watched over politics to the extent that he gave people enough wit to frame decent laws and set limits to the excesses of autocracy. He personally was a great defender of the rights of property in the elective process and the conceding of honour, rank and obedience to office-bearers. In recognising the authority of magistrates he was acknowledging the ordering and restraining power of God at work in them; not the power of Jesus Christ, (for the only Kingdom of Christ was the true Church), but the real power of the all-wise Father, God, who ruled the "lights" above and the earth below. This God, he believed, had set limits to chaos by establishing government, and had set limits to the power of the governors by locating His restraining and legislating power in the people. For this reason he wrote later in the *Bloudy Tenent*, using the heading "Magistracy in general from God, the particular formes from the people":

> The gentile princes, rulers and magistrates—whether monarchical, aristocratical, or democratical . . . , though government in general be from God, yet receive their callings, power, and authority, both kings and parliaments, mediately from the people.[16]

The word magistrate, as used by Williams, had the primary connotation of duly empowered master, or ruler. This meaning was more than etymological. It derived in the thinking of the Puritans from their careful study of *Romans 13.1–7*. They all took this to be a charter for civil government since the coming of Christ and a Christian interpretation by Paul of the duties of magistrates in administering the "second table" of the Mosaic Law. Williams was no exception. His affirmations about secular power

and government should be read with the understanding that
he thought *Romans 13* was part of the "last will and testament"
of the Lord Jesus Himself, or, as he curiously put it in his debate
with the Quakers, "the love letters of Christ Jesus to His
Church."[17] He had to come to terms with the plain literal sense
of "there is no power but of God," with "the powers that be are
ordained of God," with "he [the ruler] is a minister of God to
thee for good." His life as a citizen was bound by the injunctions
to pay civil taxes, render deference, awe, and honour to the
masters of the civil order for the time being. Everything therefore
followed; he read it in *Romans 13* and behaved accordingly. In a
certain sense too, he was willing to concede to Cotton that the
right ordering of the civil state was an "appointment" of Christ
and in keeping with Christ's explicit will.[18] What he refused to
allow was that *Christ* ruled *in* civil rulers and that they were
therefore *Christ's* ministers, or servants, not merely servants of
God the Father. Williams agreed that Christ's rule would
eventually be manifested in relation to all the rulers of the
world, but the time for that was not yet. Had not Christ himself
"refused to manage" both swords, the sword of the Word and
the sword of steel?

> Yea, he was the true heir to the crown of Israel, being the Son of
> David; yet being sought for by the people to be made a king *(John 5)*
> he refused, and would not give a precedent to any king, prince, or
> ruler to manage both swords and to assume the charge of both tables.[19]

There is a distinction to be made, therefore, between an
ordinance and an appointment of Christ. Civil government was
not ordained by Christ to be an instrument of his visible Kingdom
in the world, but it was one of his appointments. That is to say
he indicated, in his sayings about the respective functions of God
and Caesar, *how* things were to be ordered, but without taking a
direct and personal hand in the ordering himself. The saying of
Jesus, "render to Caesar the things that are Caesar's and to God
the things that are God's" *(Matthew 22.21)*, was taken[20] with a
seriousness equal to *Romans 13*. "God will not have Caesar

wronged," Williams said, as he attacked Massachusetts for depriving merchants (himself naturally included) of civil privileges on account of religious deviation:

Christ Jesus was of another opinion (who distinguisheth between God's due and Caesar's due: and therefore (with respect to God, his cause and religion) it is not lawful to deprive Caesar the civil magistrate, nor any that belong to him of their civil and earthly rights. I say in this respect, although that a man is not godly, a Christian, sincere, a church member, yet to deprive him of any civil right or privilege, due to him as a man, a subject, a citizen, is to take from Caesar that which is Caesar's, which God endures not though it be given to himself.[21]

In this fashion the Old Testament distinction between the types of duty, ceremonial and moral, to be rendered under the two tables of the Law of Moses, was refined and consolidated by Williams's use of the classical New Testament citations from *Romans 13* and *Matthew 22*. But the question remained; what is God's due distinct from Caesar's? At this point Williams was forced to define what he meant by conscience. Standing as we now do at a later stage in the development of the Western political tradition, we are inclined to attribute to him more than he said. To us conscience suggests an honestly held belief on almost any subject short of deliberately provoking violence and turmoil. To him conscience, or "soul liberty," had reference only to the first table of the Ten Commandments; it was an affair of the God or gods a person worshipped. Williams maintained that everybody worshipped something in practice. He liked to recall the dramatic scene described in *Acts 19* when the people of the great city of Ephesus staged a riot against Paul because he threatened their goddess Diana[22] (and their greed, profit, and pleasure) by introducing Christ. The worship of Diana, like that of all men (the attitude or "spirit" that drove them on toward their chosen goals), belonged to the realm of worship and conscience; not merely to the outward forms, but to the inner motives. The definition of conscience that Roger Williams gave to Governor Endecott after Massachusetts had whipped its Baptist visitors from Rhode Island in 1651, points especially to the stubborn consciences of Englishmen; Williams was a faithful reader of the patriotic English martyrologist John Foxe. The application may be provincial; but the definition is general, loud and clear:

> That thing which we call conscience is of such a nature, (especially in Englishmen, as once a pope of Rome, at the suffering of an Englishman in Rome, himself observed) that although it be groundless, false and deluded, yet it is not by any arguments or torments easily removed. I speak not of the stream of the multitude of all nations, which have their ebbings and flowings in religion, as the longest sword and strongest arm of flesh carries it; but I speak of conscience, a persuasion fixed in the mind and heart of a man, which enforceth him to judge—as Paul said of himself, a persecutor—and to do so and so, with respect to God, his worship, &c. This conscience is found in all mankind, more or less: in Jews, Turks, papists, Protestants, pagans, &c.[23]

Williams's definition is consistently upheld. He asked, rhetorically, but inwardly sure of his scriptural evidence,

> whether Caesar's sword was not God's sword? *(Romans 13)* And whether, by giving unto Caesar his submission, honour, tribute, &c., was not a giving unto God *His* due, in a true sense, *by* giving this his due to Caesar? And whether there can be any other characteristical difference imagined, but only that of matter of conscience—spiritual and religious—"which Caesar himself," as the old martyrs, witnesses of Jesus, were wont to say, "had no power over"?[24]

The same unity of the two kingdoms in God, and their distinction from each other among men, is found in the long and boring debate[25] between Williams and Cotton over the parable of the wheat and the tares *(Matthew 13.3–43)*. Briefly, Cotton said magistrates could help Jesus Christ by pulling offending weeds out of the field of the world. Williams said that was none of their business, except in matters of the second table of the Ten Commandments, which concerned misdemeanours affecting men's bodies and goods. In matters of the first table, dealing with God and His worship, Jesus had given instructions for the wheat and the weeds to grow together until the harvest in the world outside the Church, which was, in any case, a wilderness by nature. Christ's Church, His garden, was different. There He had given orders to His ministers (whoever they might turn out to be) to do the weeding thoroughly and keep it pure. Let Caesar's ministers do Caesar's work and let God's do God's.

Williams's doctrine of "the two realms" is strikingly like the teaching of Luther. His affinity with Luther can be shown in several ways. Indirect indebtedness is more clearly established through the Baptist author of the *Humble Supplication*,[26] which he quoted as he introduced his plea for liberty of conscience in the *Bloudy Tenent*. The "close prisoner to Newgate,"[27] who wrote the *Humble Supplication*, quoted several of Luther's books, including the decisive early treatise *On Secular Government*. One of Luther's sentences in particular became a recurrent motif in Williams's own argument:

> The laws of the civil magistrate's government extend no further than over the body or goods, and to that extent which is external; for over the soul God will not suffer any man to rule; only he himself will rule there. Wherefore, whoever doth undertake to give laws unto the souls and consciences of men, he usurpeth that government himself which appertaineth unto God . . .[28]

Calvinist or no Calvinist, Roger Williams could not bring himself to go all the way with John Calvin and Theodore Beza in their attempt to build and discipline a godly commonwealth in Geneva. True, he could hardly have approved either, of the relationship between prince, lawyers, and clergy in the Lutheran territories. He knew that Geneva, Wittenberg, and London all gave the civil government power over the Church; in all these places the custodians of the second table of the Law had invaded the prerogatives of Christ over the first. Caesar had used his temporal power to force nations to come to Church. This was state-compelled "hypocrisy, which if suffered, will leaven the whole lump and render the garden and spouse of Christ a filthy dunghill and whore-house of rotten and stinking whores and hypocrites."[29]

Earthy talk, also worthy of Luther! But when he dealt with the Geneva experiment he was gentler—possibly because he owed so much in other ways to Calvin—but none the less definite:

That Christ's ordinances and administrations of worship are appointed and given by Christ to any civil state, town or city, as is implied by the instance of Geneva, that I confidently deny. The ordinances and discipline of Christ Jesus, though wrongfully and profanely applied to natural and unregenerate men, may cast a blush of civility and morality upon them, as in Geneva and other places—for the shining brightness of the very shadow of Christ's ordinances casts a shame upon barbarism and incivility. Yet withal I affirm that the misapplication of ordinances to unregenerate and unrepentant persons hardens up their souls in a dreadful sleep and dream of their own blessed estate and sends millions of souls to hell in a secure expectation of a false salvation.[30]

There was still a further classical text from the Old Testament to challenge Williams's ingenuity. The New England clergy were fond of it; they regarded it as addressed to their latter-day Canaan; *Isaiah 49.23*: "kings shall be thy nursing fathers, and their queens thy nursing mothers." The challenge was picked up without hesitation. Here again Williams disappoints those who think they see in him a precursor of the doctrine that no government must help and favour the Christian Church. He maintained that it was good for the magistrate to "cherish the saints." Williams was not asking for special privileges, but he was not averse to accepting kindness and protection from the civil arm when this was spontaneously offered.[31] The logic of his position was that similar kindnesses and support could be extended toward other "consciences" if that seemed right and desirable to the civil authorities:

I know each sect is apt to plead, "Mine interest, being Christ's, the purse and sword of the state is not only mine, but 'tis Christ's due," but I also maintain that 'tis not true civility, not true Christianity, that draws the sword for one or other. Christ's interest in this commonweal, or any, is the freedom of the souls of the people. I confess that all nations, all peoples, kings, princes, judges, &c., ought to kiss the Son, to be nursing fathers and mothers to Christ Jesus and his followers; but what a dreadful mistake is this, that no people must live but Christians?[32]

Further on, in his *Examiner Defended*, Williams dealt more trenchantly with the original meaning of the phrase "nursing fathers" in its Old Testament context and modern application. He set out his case under nine headings and summarised the duties of magistrates in maintenance of the autonomy of religious institutions. He suggested that rulers who tried to exercise spiritual functions "have ever forced down poison instead of food . . . from Constantine to the last Presbyterian Magistrate."[33] The year being 1652, Williams reflected that "the doctrine of Kings & Queens being nursing fathers" was "the axe that cut off the last King's head." Charles, he said,

> being flattered and bewitched into this dream of a nursing father and a judge of wholesome food and poison for his people, he forced poison for food upon the Scotch nation and, upon that occasion, was persuaded to maintain his stewards and cooks the bishops by commencing and prosecuting those fatal wars which, by a naked hand from heaven, justly plucked up root and branch—both ceremonies, bishops, and King—together.[34]

A new twist was given to the whole idea of magistrates as nursing fathers by Williams when he pointed out that in the Bible some of the most friendly and effective guarantors of religious liberty had been "idolaters."

> Thus Cyrus proclaims liberty to all the people of God in his dominions, freely to go up and build the temple of God at Jerusalem, and Artaxerxes after him confirmed it,[35]

he wrote in the *Bloudy Tenent*, while in the *Bloody Tenent Yet More Bloody* he went further:

> I remember that some of eminent note for knowledge and godliness have not stuck to affirm that the gentile prince, Cyrus, as he was called God's servant, "anointed," (or Christ), *(Isaiah 44* [45.1]); I say that he, in a respect, as a restorer of God's people, was a figure of Christ Jesus.[36]

Appreciation of the qualities of Cyrus and others like him was characteristic of Williams, who had a breadth of view on the world beyond most English Puritans. His openness had geographical dimensions, because the diversity of mankind and of human forms of government appealed to him. He opposed his own perception of the virtues of other people's laws to John Cotton's rather pompous certainty that the conscience of New England was rightly informed, but all others wrongly. "One thing," Williams observed, "is shrewdly to be suspected in this matter,

and that is a most unchristian partiality in directing the sword of the magistrate to fall heaviest on such seducers only as trouble *his* conscience, his doctrine, worship, and government. Suppose in some of the cities of Holland, Poland, or Turkey (where some freedom is) that Jews, pagans, anti-Christians, and Christians (that is Christians of Master Cotton's conscience), together with Turks, were commingled in civil cohabitation and commerce together. Why now shall that Turk that hath seduced one of Master Cotton's conscience to Mahometanism be more punished for that crime than for turning a Jew, pagan, or papist to his belief and worship?[37]

It was a good question, foreshadowing the plural society and aimed with deadly irony at a man who could be provincial and oracular.

Within the universal society where he felt himself to be a member Williams had also acquired the capacity to shed the taint of clerical condescension toward the non-Christian. "Alas," he admitted,

too frequent experience tells us in all parts of the world, that many thousands are far more peaceable subjects, more loving and helpful neighbours and more true and fair dealers in civil conversation, than many who account themselves to be the only religious people in the world.[38]

As a Christian Williams looked out on the world of men and affairs and understood well that non-Christians could be well-governed and happy. At the "humane and political" level, once he had taken the plunge and decided to become involved in playing the power game, this Puritan enjoyed himself immensely. The pleasure was not the same thing as the life he found in the Kingdom of Christ, through the Bible, and through his faith that the Hand that formed the universe had been laid upon him for good; but it was absorbing and rewarding, for all its evanescent quality of "a shadow vanished, a bubble broke, a dream finished."[39] Williams saw this in practice:

> Yea, and there is a moral virtue, a moral fidelity, ability and honesty, which other men, beside church members, are, by good nature and education, by good laws and good examples, nourished and trained up in, [so] that civil places of trust and credit need not to be monopolized into the hands of church members, who sometimes are not fitted for them, and all others deprived and despoiled of their natural and civil rights and liberties.[40]

As usual the practical good sense was supplemented with an appropriate justification from the Bible, in this case the words addressed by Jesus to his followers (*John 16.20*): "You shall weep and lament, but the world shall rejoice: you shall be sorrowful, but your sorrow shall be turned into joy." Williams noted the saying in his *Bloudy Tenent*:

> So many stately kingdoms and governments in the world have long and long enjoyed civil peace and quiet, notwithstanding their religion is so corrupt, as that there is not the very name of Jesus Christ among them; and this every historian, merchant, traveller, in Europe, Asia, Africa, America, can testify; for so spake the Lord Jesus himself; *(John 16): The world shall sing and rejoice.*[41]

Lawyers and politicians, soldiers, and public administrators were better friends to Roger Williams than the clergy. Among Presbyterian, Independent, and Baptist ministers he felt ill-at-ease. They were all attempting to design a form of theocratic civil government, or at least refusing to break with existing forms of government that had underlying theocratic assumptions. For a short time in the middle 1640's the Presbyterian system was the established religion of England.[42] When the Presbyterian power gave place to the rising Independents they vacillated, but did not abolish the livings and tithes of the Church of England.[43] Many inherited these perquisites and did not wish to forego the wealth and status they obtained. When the Baptists became powerful in the army and in Cromwell's Council of State from

1653 onward, they in turn found their motives mixed and were embarrassed by their former zeal against state power in the Church.[44] Aside from the temptations of power, however, which Roger Williams well understood, and for himself conscientiously and conveniently foreswore, his friends in both Independent and Baptist parties held a kind of last minute trump card. The Independents until about 1655, and the Baptists until after the death of Oliver Cromwell, remained theocratic in their hopes. They longed for the personal reign of Christ through His saints, meaning they hoped, themselves. Williams was realist enough to know that if an assembly like the Nominated Parliament of 1653 were to turn out to be the godly remnant who would judge the nations, with Christ in the midst, the "sword of steel" would need to be used by them to cope with dissenting elements—possibly for internal and external war. He himself looked for the reign of Christ; but it would be a spiritual reign, through the Word, not through the magistrates' sword. Those who embraced the full implications of the hope reposed in the Nominated Parliament of one hundred and forty "saints," were full of impatience and balked when it voluntarily dissolved itself. Many became Fifth-Monarchy Men, thoroughgoing theocrats who were prepared to use the army to open a path for the entry of Christ into the troubled world of the later Protectorate. Many were Baptists.

Williams rejected both routes toward theocracy—the moderate "Genevan" discipline, with its use of the government to compel people to Church; and the radical millenarian, with its belief that Christ would do what men could not—use the State's means to make men worship rightly. His distaste for these two alternatives helps to explain his alienation from most of the clergy he knew well. Some, like John Cotton and Hugh Peter, combined both types of theocratic theory. Cotton's book, *Moses His Judicialls* set forth a plan for the government of Massachusetts which applied the Mosaic ordinances to the requirements of what was regarded as a Christian Commonwealth. In the event his recipe was not accepted in detail; Massachusetts tempered his biblicism with English-Common Law in the document called *A Model of Church and Civil Power*, which Williams discussed in detail in the second half of *The Bloudy Tenent*. Cotton must have been disappointed. He envisaged his outline legislation as possibly a ground plan for the millennial society. Baptists in Rhode Island were equally taken with Old Testament patterns of civil government when William Coddington[45] and John Clarke first settled together at Pocasset in 1638. Coddington was called a Judge; his assistants in government were elders. Later on in his career John Clarke showed he was an ardent millenarian in the closing part of his *Ill Newes from New England*. Very probably the title "Judge," in the original and short-lived Pocasset experiment, had reference not only to the period of occupancy of the promised land by ancient Israel, when "the judges ruled," but to St. Paul's flattering question:" Do you not know that the saints shall judge the world? and if the world is judged by you, are you unworthy to judge the smallest matters?" (*I Corinthians 6.2*).

All such clerical dreams about wearing diadems on the "dunghill" were avoided by Roger Williams. To him the prophecies about Christ's return were "dark." When He came, and however He came, it would not be with the deterring and avenging weapons of man's government. In the meantime the laity who also believed in God, but were more modest in their hopes for this world, became Williams's co-workers in the pursuit of his aims for the assorted farmers, traders, hunters, and religious cranks who made up the refugee communities of Rhode Island and the Narragansetts country. The medicine he tried to devise was a mixture different from John Cotton's or William Coddington's. He had seen it mixed many years before by the political intimates of Sir Edward Coke.

The great body of judgment built on adjustment of claims, established precedents and practical wisdom, called the Common Law, was the great passion of Coke's life. He and a multitude of local justices in the England of his day had come, not *a priori*, but through living in a particular legal tradition, to believe in the majesty and autonomy of law so conceived. God was supreme over all. However, under God the law ruled. The established wisdom of law defined the power of the throne as well as the people. The King, the lawmakers, the courts of justice, the Church, had their own autonomy and prerogatives. The power of each was spelled out by law. No one was to invade the prerogatives of another. All should know their places in the temporal order, without aspiring to dominate and invade others' spheres.[46] The men who believed in this needed a person of Coke's stature and ability to articulate it for them. They rather felt and lived it than formulated it. The common lawyers who made the English revolution against the Stuart conception of royal power into a permanent mark of English life were not, however, anticlerical on principle. They became somewhat anticlerical in practice because they could not consider the theocratic and millennial aims they heard laid down from pulpits to be within reasonable grasp. Law was made for forgiven sinners, not potential saints. (This conception of law also prevailed in Puritan Massachusetts.) Coke's *Commentary on Littleton* had rather more to say to England (or Virginia, or Massachusetts) than "Moses, his Judicialls."

The unquestionable leader of the lawyers was Coke, "probably the man most feared by James and Charles. A person of great acumen, he has rightly been called the intellectual leader of the opposition to the crown."[47] Roger Williams sat at Coke's elbow when the conflict was brewing. He saw the law in action in the person of its most impressive exponent. Williams was not a lawyer, but saw so much of the law and of its political surroundings that he developed legal skills, insights, and habits of mind. He became a drafter and negotiator who won the respect of the Winthrops, of a succession of Massachusetts governors, and of some of England's most influential parliament men and courtiers between 1630 and the late 1670's. He was an unusual man—a godly minister who was living in the lawyers' world. Most Puritan godly ministers tried to get the lawyers to live in theirs, unsuccessfully.

When he came down from Cambridge and went to live in Essex, Williams was strategically placed to become acquainted with some of the future leaders of the Commonwealth.[48] The house of Sir William Masham at Otes was one of the meeting places of those who combined in parliament around Coke. Barrington Hall was not far away. Lady Joan Barrington, who had turned away Roger Williams's request for the hand of her niece, was an aunt of Oliver Cromwell. Jug Altham, her other niece, the stepdaughter of Sir William Masham, became the first wife of Oliver St. John, the brilliant Puritan lawyer who later became Lord Chief Justice under Cromwell. Barringtons, Mashams, and Hampdens were involved together in resisting the forced loans of Charles I. Their marriages and financial schemes led to comings and goings between their houses and those of the Earls of Warwick and Lincoln. These lords had their lawyer-retainers, relatives and advisers, the Riches and the Wrays. In Suffolk, not far away, an able Puritan lawyer, the elder John Winthrop, had renounced state office for his convictions in the year 1629, when Williams was at Otes. He and the younger Harry Vane, of Lincolnshire, were known to Williams. Within the "clan" of families connected with the Barringtons, there were fifteen relatives of Oliver Cromwell. The future Protector himself entered the wider environment of Roger Williams during those years. The contact established would be strengthened later; mutual regard and similarity of religious experience were there already.

During the sessions of the dramatic parliament of 1629, when the speaker was held in the chair and Sir Thomas Barrington's group of members were among the main actors behind the scenes, Roger Williams had been in London and brought back reports to Otes and to Barrington Hall. Among parliamentary leaders after the withdrawal of Sir Edward Coke was John Pym, who came to coordinate and lead the "middle group" that held the balance of power in the early days of the Long Parliament between 1640 and 1642. Pym's relationship with the Mashams and the Barringtons was close. We learn that only the plague prevented his spending the summer of 1630, six months before Williams went to America, at Barrington Hall.[49] Pym has been represented as a consummate political manager; so he was; from the methods which he and his colleagues used, Roger Williams absorbed detailed lessons about the responsible use of power such as he could not have gathered direct from Coke. But Pym was more than a "politique."[50] This lawyer statesman was involved in the ensuing ten years in brooding over more than parliamentary techniques. He and all the others with him, set their kind of religion against Archbishop Laud, the Prayer Book, and the Articles. They had remonstrated in the Commons against Arminianism in 1629. They ridiculed the attempt of King and bishops to hold them loyal to the hierarchical structure of the Church by the use of the Etcaetera Oath.[51] The Bible and their faith had shaped the minds of Pym and his friends. Their legal and political method derived from what they thought about God, the King, and the law. When Roger Williams returned to England in 1643 Pym was still alive. He died on December 8 of the same year. Roger Williams had known the men who played their parts in the work of this master politician; he was to work with them for many years more. One of them, who occupied an important place on the English political scene until his death in 1656, was Sir William Masham, his patron at Otes.

When the policy of the King and the bishops drove him from England in 1630, Williams had a taste of politically enforced religious compulsion. On arrival in New England he discovered that his Separatist position was no more acceptable to the government there than his Puritanism had been in Essex. As he meditated on the meaning of his rejection on both sides of the Atlantic he began to formulate his case for the distinction between the powers of Church and State, with its consequences; the command of Christ was that church officers stick to administration of the first table of the Ten Commandments, civil officers to the second. Church officers are not to meddle in state business except as private citizens. State officers are not to meddle in church matters except as office-bearers elected from among church members. His doctrines proved unacceptable at Boston, at Plymouth, and eventually at Salem.

In the latter town Williams repeated what he had conveyed in writing to the governor at New Plymouth—that the grant of the King of England did not confer right to hold title to the lands of the Indians. The assertion was linked with a rebuke to King James[52] for having thanked God that he was the first Christian prince to discover that part of the world. The expression of thanks was conveyed in the Patent of the Bay Colony. It has generally been thought that Williams was objecting on behalf of the Indians and in the name of civil rights. On Winthrop's account of what he said and on the evidence of his own later description of a letter he wrote at the time to King Charles, his objection was on another ground. He remonstrated against the naming of God in a civil document and the claiming of Christian power over other men's land by virtue of being in some way Christ's representative. Recalling the trouble in 1651 he wrote of

the sin of the patents, wherein Christian kings—so called—are invested with right by virtue of their Christianity, to take and give away the lands and countries of other men . . . also . . . the un-Christian oaths swallowed down, at their coming forth from old England, especially in superstitious Laud's time and domineering . . . I know these thoughts so deeply afflicted the soul and conscience of the discusser [Williams] in the time of his walking in the way of New England's worship, that at last he came to a persuasion that such sins could not be expiated without returning again into England, or a public acknowledgment and confession of the evil of so . . . departing. To this purpose, before his troubles and banishment, he drew up a letter, not without the approbation of some of the chief of New England then tender also upon this point before God, directed unto the King himself, humbly acknowledging the evil of that part of the Patent which respects the donation of land, &c.[53]

Similar misgivings lay behind his successful plea to remove the cross of St. George from the colonial ensign, the King's colours. Cotton Mather's *Magnalia* says the action was taken by "one in some authority, under the heat of some impressions from the ministry of Mr. Williams,"[54] but Mather reserves several diverting pages for all the subsidiary issues that were raised in the colony for fifty years. Our knowledge of the general cast of Williams's political thought leads to the conclusion that the presence of the cross in the flag outraged him because it suggested that His Majesty was a sacred person whose badge bore the authority of Christ.

The last source of friction at Salem arose from the denial by Williams that the government had the right to impose an oath, invoking God.[55] Religious oaths belonged to the first table of the Ten Commandments. They were therefore not to be administered by magistrates, who were to be custodians only of the second table. Oaths seemed to him to be an invasion of Christ's temple by Caesar, or alternatively an attempt by Caesar to drag Christ into his bloodstained guardroom. He would admit neither. All the charges preferred against him had a strong religious colouring; but they amounted to sedition in a society that accepted the assumptions of the *corpus christianum,* that church ministers and magistrates were part of Christendom, christened, anointed, literally messianised by the consequences of Christ's incarnation. Williams's "turbulent and singular" advocacy of his opinions did not help, but he was not banished merely because of his temperament. He was sentenced at a time when the beacon had been placed on Beacon Hill, Boston, to warn of any invasion from England;[56] when the founders of the colony had differences enough already with the personal government of Charles I, without adding to the offence by permitting a challenge to his right to be called a Christian king in Christendom. Williams later reported:

After my public trial and answers at the General Court, one of the most eminent magistrates, whose name and speech may by others be remembered, stood up and spake: "Mr. Williams," said he, "holds forth these four particulars: first, that we have not our land by Patent from the King, but that the natives are the true owners of it, and that we ought to repent of such a receiving it by patent; secondly, that it is not lawful to call a wicked person to swear, to pray, as being actions of God's worship; thirdly, that it is not lawful to hear any of the ministers of the parish assemblies in England; fourthly, that the civil magistrate's power extends only to the bodies and goods and outward state of men, &c." I acknowledge the particulars were rightly summed up. . . .[57]

Cotton used the word "seditious" to describe these offences. "The truth is," he wrote,

> his banishment proceeded not against him, or his, for his own refusal of any worship, but for seditious opposition against the Patent and against the oath of fidelity offered to the people.[58]

Williams, in his maddening way, was willing to accept the description under the circumstances. In doing so he claimed he was in the best possible company:

> Christ Jesus deceived the people, was a conjurer, and a traitor against Caesar in being King of the Jews—indeed he *was* so, spiritually, over the true Jew, the Christian. Therefore he was numbered with notorious evil-doers and nailed to the gallows between two malefactors. Hence Paul and all true messengers of Jesus Christ are esteemed seducing and seditious teachers and turners of the world upside down.[59]

Roger Williams named his new town Providence. The name indicates that God provides a refuge for hunted and afflicted consciences. When he and his first handful of companions were joined by more refugees and adventurers he had to proceed to make a compact for the temporary and provisional governing of relations between them. Having done this he sent it off to Winthrop in Boston for his private advice about the legal form of the document, which was later subscribed with only minor changes by the newcomers.[60] The form is not an oath, but a promise; the one mention of the name of God refers to general dispensations of providence available to all mankind, with no word of Christ or of the Trinity. The draft proves Williams's ability as amateur lawyer and is of peculiar importance as his first original contribution to the realisation of the secular state, in touch with Western Christendom, yet already beyond it. In language and outlook it is in the spirit of the Common Law. The whole letter attests Williams's capacity to think ahead, improvise, and work by simple precedent rather than grandiose general principles.

His political talents in the same direction were seldom displayed better than on the occasion of his first return to England in 1643. He started at a disadvantage. Passage through the port of Boston was out of the question. The agents of Massachusetts were already representing in London the claims of the Bay to jurisdiction over the territory around Providence and Rhode Island.[61] Thomas Weld and Hugh Peter, who had been charged with Massachusetts business, were prestigious men within the circles that had now come to power in England; they would be hard to forestall. On November 2, 1643 a commission was formed by Parliament to determine future colonial affairs. The president was the Earl of Warwick. Fortunately for Williams, Hugh Peter was absent in the Netherlands when he and Weld were putting their respective cases before the members of the commission. Weld had to work alone. He found himself outwitted by the active Williams, who during the winter ingratiated himself with Parliament by acting as an agent to find alternative fuel supplies for the poor in London following the stopping of coal supplies from Newcastle through the war in the north. In this work he probably reestablished bonds of confidence with members from Essex, and the East Anglian shires, who would know of sources of good faggots in their heavily forested constituencies. As London would be the recipient, the task also gave him valuable personal access to members and aldermen in the city. In other ways he rode the rising wave of radical power, while Weld seemed caught in the backwash of the preceding alliance between the more moderate Presbyterians and the Scots. His publication of the *Key Into the Language of America*, the *Answer* to John Cotton's letter about his banishment, his *Queries of Highest Consideration* and *Christenings Make Not Christians* were like so many smaller items around the larger book, his central piece, *The Bloudy Tenent*, which appeared in 1643, with a second printing in 1644. The last three of these were written "in change of roomes and corners, yea sometimes (upon occasion of travel in the country, concerning that business of fuell) in variety of strange houses, sometimes in the fields, in the midst of travel; where he hath been forced to gather and scatter his loose thoughts and papers."[62] The authorship of the *Bloudy Tenent* was an open secret, but the worst the

Presbyterian majority could do was burn it. The author was *persona grata* with new men now moving into power, the "war party," and the more radical Independents.

Williams received his charter on March 14, 1644. On December 10, 1643, the Warwick Commission had made an impotent gesture of goodwill toward Weld by handing him a patent signed by nine members of the Commission, excluding Warwick, when ten were required.[63] Williams had gained his effective support from behind the scenes, with the aid, no doubt, of his powerful friend, Sir Henry Vane. Both men knew that politics and law consist in more than formal diplomacy and appearance in court or committee; Williams was expert in the processes of personal consultation and interpretation that lead to favourable decisions. The signatures he obtained for a letter of commendation[64] to the Massachusetts authorities, when he took ship to the Port of Boston without fear of molestation, tell the story. Significantly the name of Sir Harry Vane is absent from the list. His opinion of the Massachusetts General Court and ministers was too well known after the unhappy Anne Hutchinson crisis to endear him any longer to the Bay colonists.

The cleverly phrased letter had the desired effect in Massachusetts, as John Winthrop's journal entry for September 17, 1644, shows: "Here arrived . . . Mr. Roger Williams of Providence . . . He brought with him a letter from divers lords and others of the parliament, the copy whereof ensueth."[65] Who drafted the letter? Was it one of the signatories? Or Williams himself; or Williams in collaboration with Vane? We do not know, but the choice of signatories is indicative of the ability to form a balanced group in order to effect a specified end. Winthrop noted the "lords" especially; their impressive names were on top. Algernon Percy, the tenth Earl of Northumberland, and Philip, fourth Baron Wharton, headed the list.

Northumberland[66] was contemporary with Williams, being born in 1602. He was a Cambridge man and, like Vane, had suffered a Puritan revulsion against the policies of Charles I and Laud; but he was, and remained under the parliament, Lord High Admiral. His opinions ran close to Pym's; he was therefore judged a safe man, favouring peace; but when more radical Independents came to power he cooperated with them in organising the new model army. When the king came to trial he refused to go further in that direction and withdrew from public office. Wharton, a more colourful figure, "was in his younger days one of the handsomest men and the greatest beau of his times; he had particularly fine legs and took great delight to show them in dancing."[67] This elegant Puritan peer followed the trend toward radical policies in the Long Parliament further than Northumberland. Despite differences on policy, he and Cromwell remained friends until the Protector's death. His sympathy toward dissenting consciences remained unaffected by his support for the Restoration. This great landowner, with "a taste for architecture and gardening" and "a very fine collection of the paintings of Van Dyck and Lely" was also a disseminator of Bibles and catechisms; the kind of man to receive all due deference from the many members of John Cotton's congregation who had something in common with the socially aspiring Malvolio in Shakespeare's *Twelfth Night*.

All the other names were chosen with the same insight into their bargaining value. Sir Robert Harley[68] of Brampton Bryan Castle in Herefordshire, was Master of the Mint, an active participant in the work of the Westminster Assembly and one of the champions of parliament against the King's forces in the West. In July of 1643 his castle withstood, under the personal leadership of his third wife, Brilliana, a siege of six weeks. Sir William Masham of Essex signed, proving his constant trust in Williams. John Gurdon,[69] of Gray's Inn, a radical and regicide, represented Ipswich in Suffolk, a part of the world where Williams had many friends in common with the men of Massachusetts. Cornelius Holland,[70] probably born at Colchester in Essex, was educated in London and became a servant of the younger Vane at court and under the Commonwealth; an indisputably religious "man on the make" who successfully weathered all the crises of civil war and interregnum to die in apparently comfortable exile in Lausanne. John Blakiston,[71] member for Newcastle, became a radical and regicide. He was a rich mercer and appears to have coordinated the interests of Sir Arthur Haselrig, one of the most powerful beneficiaries of the spoils of the revolution. Sir Thomas Barrington's name was there, with all it meant for grateful Puritan churchmen, loan-resisters and colonists. Redoubtable Oliver St. John,[72] who had become the leader of the "war party" by 1643 and was personally known to Williams as the sombre man who had married Joan "Jug" Altham, his own wife's former mistress and companion, had been a hard-driving leader among Puritans since the days of Sir Edward Coke's last parliaments. St. John became the greatest lawyer of the Commonwealth period. Isaac Pennington[73] repre-sented the City radical cause; he had been High Sheriff and had, by the date of signing, become Lord Mayor of London. He had estates in Norfolk and Suffolk and was "a sturdy and austere Puritan." Sir Gilbert Pickering,[74] who married into the influential Eastern family of the Montagues, ran the gamut in time from Presbyterian, to Independent, to Separatist, to Baptist; he appears to have had sincerely held views on toleration and was later to prove a valuable man to Rhode Island as one of Cromwell's Baptist Lords, "finical, spruce, and like an old courtier." Miles Corbet,[75] of Lincoln's Inn and Yarmouth, was another radical member who combined interests in London and the Eastern Counties. Like Harley, he married into the Barrett family of Avely in Essex. The whole group was composed of what the savage Presbyterian chronicler of Independency, Clement Walker, thought of by the 1650's as "a Combination or Faction of Pseudo-Polititians, and Pseudo-Theologitians, Hereticks, and Schis-maticks both in Divinity and Polity,"[76] except perhaps for the two "lords," who certainly struck a chord in Winthrop. Harley, Masham, and Barrington also added solidity; but all the others were valuable for Williams, as things then stood in England and New England.

On the Rhode Island political scene Roger Williams was less at home. He was not himself a party to the first Providence Compact, believing that as the founder and first landowner it was his prerogative to cede privileges to new arrivals. There is an aristocratic remoteness about this. Williams never was a "frontier democrat." He was prepared to be summoned to office as a magistrate, but he could be, and often chose to be, a voice against the people. He disliked all self-made men, including the Baptists and Quakers, who often turned out to be as much interested in their acres and profits as in their religion. Cotton Mather remembered that Williams "was by the people sometimes chosen governour: but for the most part he led a more private life."[77] His heart was in England. He passed on to the younger Winthrop in Connecticut the detailed intelligence he received about the progress of politics there. Most of it is surprisingly fresh from the source; his own evaluations of what he had heard still strike us as discerning and prescient. In the tedium of his trading life in the remote forest fringe of the Narragansetts Bay he had time to think. There were few with whom he could share his deepest pondering. When he corresponded with the university men and lawyers of Connecticut and the Bay, he could unburden himself to people who understood his remembered Latin tags and allusions.[78] In so far as early Rhode Island was a busy society of unlettered opportunists it foreshadowed the independence and terseness of an America not yet fully born. At that point Williams was thoroughly un-American. The "calm midnight thoughts" he gave to the uncontemplative getting and spending of his cruder neighbours led him to look stonily on their "depraved appetite after the great vanities, dreams, and shadows of this vanishing life," their

great portions of land, land in this wilderness, as if men were in as great necessity and danger for want of great portions of land, as poor, hungry, thirsty seaman have, after a sick and stormy, a long and starving passage. This is one of the gods of New England, which the living and most high Eternal will destroy and famish.[79]

When King Charles I[80] died on the scaffold in 1649, the reaction of Williams was far from praise for regicides and republicans. The first reaction we have from him seems sober enough, and ominous. When the *Eikon Basilike,* the royalist "King's Book" on which the portrait of Charles as martyr is founded, came to his hands in 1650, Williams's mind was working on the question of the king's death and looking upon it as a kind of judgment implicit in the nature of royal folly. "Doubtless," he told John Winthrop, Junior, "*viis* and *modis* [in his ways and means] he was guilty of much blood." But he went on to say: "All that seems weighty in my eye are the popular tumults alleged as the artifice of the Parliament."[81] He then used several scriptural incidents to show that the people had been used before as instruments for ending the careers of unjust men; but his conscience was not quiet on the matter. By 1651 he was writing to Governor Endecott about Cromwell in terms that suggest he saw the Lord General in much the same way as Luther saw any government, however unsatisfactory and provisional, as a containment of worse chaos. He pointed out to Endecott, whom he was attacking for approving the persecution of John Clarke and his companions, that persecution would be generally let loose,

had it not pleased the God of Heaven who bounds the insolent rage of the furious ocean, to raise up a second Cromwell (like a mighty and merciful wall or bulwark) to stay the fury of the oppressor, whether English, Scottish, popish, Presbyterian, Independent, &c.[82]

The parallel with Thomas Cromwell's work under Henry VIII suggests that Williams had been looking about for justifiable precedents for this commoner's intrusion into supreme power. For all his regard for Cromwell and the opportunity of access to him during his second English journey, we can read into many of his statements Williams's sense of impending return to monarchy, together with his ill-smothered aversion to the court sycophants that he had to cultivate in Cromwell's circle. After his return to Providence in 1654 he wrote frankly to Connecticut's Winthrop, who was a son-in-law of Hugh Peter, Cromwell's chaplain, then living in the Whitehall lodgings of the late Archbishop of Canterbury. Williams brought news of him, then added a long excursus on English affairs, which began with quiet irony and foreknowledge of the end by saying that Peter

and all the people of God in England, formerly called *Puritanus, Anglicanus,* or late *Roundheads,* now the *Sectarians,* (as more or less cut off from the parishes) are now in the saddle and at the helm, so high that *non datur descensus nisi cadendo* [there is no way down except by falling].[83]

Williams was talking to a man trained in English law, who had absorbed the teaching of Coke, that King, law, and parliament formed a balanced harmony of powers, all in their own spheres and subject to a God of order. Winthrop would be willing to accept the forewarning on the fate of his father-in-law.

By comparison with the high politics of England, most of what went on in Rhode Island failed to draw Williams out of his "beloved privacy"[84] at any time. Two great issues could do so—the unity and "common liberties" of the colonies, and the promotion of peace with the Indians. The first of these was the occasion for his second visit to England, when he sold his assets to go. Williams followed hard after William Coddington, who departed in 1651, with a view to having himself made chief magistrate in the Rhode Island settlements under a new charter. After the king's death some new form of recognition had become inevitable. As he had forestalled Weld and Peter in 1643, so Williams set out this time to put a better case than Coddington or the representatives of Plymouth and of Connecticut. He was accompanied by John Clarke whom he regarded highly as a friend and a relatively disinterested pursuer of the public good of the colonies. It was politic to have a Baptist; in England the Baptists were already strong. In the Nominated Parliament of 1653 they dominated. When effectual government was vested in the Council of State about the Protector they became more powerful than any other religious group. Sir Harry Vane fell from favour. Sir William Masham and Cornelius Holland were no longer members of Cromwell's Council after May 1653. In April the changes had not occurred. Vane was still in power; Williams wrote to the town of Providence[85] to report that their existing charter had been confirmed as valid for the time being. By remaining friends with Vane, Cromwell and the President of the Council of State, Sir Henry Lawrence, who was a Baptist, he managed to hold all available doors open for the granting of a future charter along the lines that the four towns of the Rhode Island colony desired. But his sense of strategy did not fail; he left the long-range diplomacy to Clarke, who negotiated further for nearly eleven years and came back in triumph, as Williams had done in 1644, bearing the charter.

All the adverse shifts in power during 1653 tended to nullify the advantages Williams gained as negotiator by his five publications of 1652. The plea he made in *The Fourth Paper Presented by Major Butler*, "to the Honourable Committee of Parliament, for Propagating the Gospel of Christ Jesus" had its effect in the preparation of far greater religious toleration. His *Hireling Ministry None of Christs* was less influential; its exposition of the principle of purely voluntary support of the Christian ministry was more difficult to relate directly to the economic realities of the Church and country. *The Examiner Defended* tried to hold the line, in the name of a soundly reasoned theology, the mounting criticism that the sects were breaking all bounds of reason and sobriety. Then in 1654 the Quakers arrived in London. The emotional tone of Roger Williams's denunciations of George Fox and his movement can be partly explained by the fact that their coming was associated with the queering of his political pitch and with his decision to depart for home with his mission incomplete.

There was something abortive, too, about the appearance of the largest publication of the five, *The Bloody Tenent Yet More Bloody*, his reply to John Cotton's painstaking and pathetic *Bloudy Tenent Washed*, which had been printed in 1647. Cotton died in 1652 and probably never saw the huge counter-blow he had provoked. The battle for toleration had, by then, been won in principle. When Cotton was buried at the foot of Beacon Hill his friends and family must have known the peculiar sadness that comes from expenditure of mature talents in a lost cause; the bitterness comes through in subsequent correspondence Williams had with Cotton's son.[86] By 1653, the most valuable tactical item in *The Bloody Tenent Yet More Bloody* turned out to be the publication of the memorable letter Williams had sent to Governor Endecott[87] on the occasion of the persecution of John Clarke and his friends in Massachusetts in 1651. This, with

Clarke's own *Ill Newes from New England,* ensured that the predominantly Baptist Council of State would provide legal safeguards for Rhode Island against Massachusetts. Williams returned through Boston, armed with a letter from the Council of State requesting free passage for him through the Massachusetts ports. He insisted, on his return, that the letter be inscribed in the official transactions of the colony.[88]

John Cotton's death gives a sour taste to some of the witticisms Roger Williams directed at him while he was writing his long sequel to the *Bloudy Tenent,* but they illustrate his vein of "worldliness," his ability to set an opponent by the ears. "Some say Mr. Cotton is wise," he observed,

and knows in what door the wind blows of late; he is not ignorant what sad complaints in letters, printings, conferences, so many of God's people (and of his own conscience and judgement of Independency) have poured forth against New England's persecuting, &c.[89]

When he came to criticise Cotton's mingling of the administration of the two tables of the Law in one, Williams indulged in a classical quip; "he speakes too like the doubtful oracles of Apollo, which will be true however the event fall out."[90] The hint that Cotton was a kind of Delphic prophet for the city of Boston is irresistible. Sometimes the crowing verges on bad taste; Cotton is sarcastically referred to as "this holy man."[91] Elsewhere outrage and eloquence are fused with shattering effect in passages that reveal Williams's passionate hatred of religious persecution:

If Mr. Cotton, or any of his bloody judgment, wore the imperial crown of the world's majesty, what slaughters shall we imagine the world should hear and feel? Whither would such fiery zeal transport men? Yea, what an earthly dunghill religion and worship should the most high God be served with, fit only for the dunghill gods and goddesses, "whom all Asia, (as the town clerk speaks) [*Acts 19.27*; wrongly attributed to the town clerk] and the world, worshippeth."[92]

Cotton, according to Williams, made the magistrate "the Cleargies Cane[93]"; he wanted to force the magistrate "to see and read with the Cleargies Spectacles."[94] John Cotton had already rebuked him for having fun in the *Bloudy Tenent*, when the issues between them were a serious business. Williams justified himself. He felt his pressing home of his advantage in a situation with political aspects could be justified out of the Word. He said he did not dare

willingly to profane the holy name of the Most High with lightness, no not with those fine turnings of wit which the Word forbids . . . and yet there *is* an holy wit and pleasantness in Samson's riddle, in Jotham's and Jesus's parables, yea, and in Elijah's sharp and cutting language. . . .[95]

On the occasion of his second English visit Williams thus continued to consort with the great and measure his political skills against the best others could do. At the same time he resisted most of the temptations of power successfully and returned to find petty bickering worse than ever among the hard-handed sectarians around the Narragansetts Bay.

How could a political thinker and administrator of his capacity choose to play his role occasionally, with little applause, on such an unrewarding stage? His praise for the cobbler-preacher Samuel How of London, written in 1652,[96] gives the answer. Williams was more at home among the powerful and wise Englishmen of his time; but he chose to consort equally with the unlearned and obscure. The Separatists' insistence that the true Church and the true Christian would be found among these "low mechanicks" affected him permanently. What he said may be stripped of its scriptural background and roughly translated in the proposition that spiritual power is found in the renunciation of material power and in service of the weak; but Williams would never have thought of it in those terms. He found it in Christ's pattern of action, which he wished to follow. A bold phrase in *The Examiner Defended* summed it up. Williams would no doubt have been ready, in his own free way, to address the thought to Oliver Cromwell himself, and may have done so:

The great Lord General, Christ Jesus, carried his cross and gallows; and professeth it impossible for any to follow him, without a denying of himself, and taking up his cross, or gallows, also.[97]

In old age Williams, as politician, reaffirmed what he had learned from Coke—that justice is based on equitable adjustment of competing claims and rests on respect for the crown and the law. After the arrival of the Quakers and the heated extremism of the Fifth-Monarchy Men, the country justices and city lawyers made common cause with clergy like John Owen in a cooling-off process that prepared for the Restoration of the monarchy within the limits imposed by the followers of Coke's doctrine.[98] When something of the kind emerged on paper, Roger Williams welcomed the effects in Rhode Island. The new charter Clarke brought back was quite exceptional; it embodied provisions for religious liberty undreamed of in England under the returning cavaliers; but Clarke brought word that the easy-going King was satisfied to indulge his subjects across the Atlantic in a way that reflected his promises about toleration in the message he had sent from Breda before his return to the throne. All this must be remembered in accounting for the many loyal and grateful words about Charles II that are scattered through Williams's later letters and his book against George Fox.

Old Roger Williams, in "the long winter of this retirement,"[99] when he was not often called as president or mediator to the duties of making just compromises among his neighbours, probably seemed to many to be wasting those late years among the "muskeetoes and wolves";[100] but his "beloved privacy" gave him time to remember what had determined his politics and his religion:

I affirm that state policy and state necessity, which, for the peace of the state and preventing of rivers of civil blood, permits the con-sciences of men, will be found to agree most punctually with the rules of the best politician that ever the world saw, the King of kings and Lord of lords, in comparison of whom Solomon himself had but a drop of wisdom, compared to Christ's ocean, and was but a farthing candle compared with the all and ever glorious Son of righteousness.[101]

9

Quaker Upstarts: Theology

THE QUAKER MOVEMENT came to Rhode Island in the summer
of 1657, three years after Roger Williams came back from
England.[1] Newport and Providence soon had Quaker groups
at work. The soil was fertile for the new seed. William Coddington and his sympathisers had been originally adherents
of Mrs. Anne Hutchinson's faction; they were emotional enthusiasts and longed for "perfection"; the Quakers responded to
their needs. In language that announced the millennium had
arrived they promised the realization of sainthood—influx
of the full light of Christ, ecstasy without necessary use of the
older visible means of hard Bible study and the two sacraments.
In contrast with the small body of the Elect, which was the best
the Calvinists could offer as a Church, they were an ever-expand-
ing missionary brotherhood; the Spirit was being poured out on
all flesh. The small candle of grace was alight in every man
and needed only to respond to the message of the Quakers to
flame with the complete illumination of the indwelling Christ.

With such exciting prospects and face-to-face with Quaker
missionaries who did not fear suffering, former Antinomians,
Baptists, millenarians, and unattached neurasthenics became

recruits in Rhode Island for the new "apostles." Much to the
irritation of Massachusetts, all four towns of their neighbour
colony around the Narragansett Bay produced emissaries who
felt constrained to preach weal and woe to Boston and other
towns nearby. Plymouth and Connecticut were also visited.
The stricter Puritan régimes remonstrated with Rhode Island;
it was, from their point of view, one thing to have a cess-pit
on the outskirts of your property, something more grave to
have it seep back into your own soil. They wanted the Quakers
controlled and supressed. Rhode Island declined, naturally,
since permission of all consciences was fundamental to the
terms of their original charter. Even though more sober magistrates in Rhode Island, particularly the better educated Baptists,
may have disliked the teachings and immoderate enthusiasm
of the Quakers, they had no intention of proceeding against
them unless they defied decency or public order. Roger Williams
was necessarily of the same mind; little could be done, short
of public debate; for many years he refrained from doing battle
on that front, probably because he was deeply involved already
with prominent Quaker converts on other fronts. They included
William Harris, who seemed to Williams to be an unscrupulous
land-grabber; William Coddington, who was a bold and slippery
politician; and William Dyer, whose unhappy wife had given
birth to a misshapen child at Boston while under the spiritual
direction of Mrs. Anne Hutchinson.[2] In attacking their religion
Williams would be accused of adding a final insult to his
standing warfare with them. These could have been the reasons
for his silence. He needed a clear-cut situation, free from
side issues, or at least as free as possible.

To make things worse, Massachusetts was provoked into severe
persecution of the Quakers, who came into their towns like
moths to an open flame. The case of Mary Dyer,[3] who returned,
fatally, after the magistrates had tried to get rid of her, was
the worst. The poor woman's state of mind, a sort of peace
that succeeds years of distraught terror, is hard to praise, blame,
or comprehend. She left the hard letter of the law little alterna-

tive and was hanged on Boston Common on June 1, 1660. The severity of their treatment led other women among the Quakers to hysterical gestures; Deborah Wilson walked naked in Salem in 1662, Lydia Wardwell in Newbury, Connecticut, in 1663.[4] To the Quakers it was testimony to the naked truth and all one with the symbolic acts of the Old Testament prophets who cried woe on "the bloody city." Sober Puritans believed this behaviour was a step toward the promiscuity of the Ranters, who said they could do anything, because Christ was in them and Christ was perfect. Williams fully shared the theological horror of the men of Massachusetts; he may not have approved of the severe sentences passed on the Quaker missionaries, but his own teaching countenanced measures against public nakedness. The extreme behaviour of the women had been a breach of civil order and was, by his standards, punishable as going beyond the limits of soul liberty. It had been a violation of the public peace. This explains why he denounced it so fiercely[5] and does not seem to have attacked the Massachusetts court for what had been done. By the time all the harsh counter-measures against the Quakers were being taken Williams had this reason for drawing closer to the leaders of the neighbour colonies. His anger in 1654, when he had witnessed the Quakers at work among the London Seekers, had been reinforced and became canalised into serious thought and study about their movement. He could hardly expect his Connecticut and Massachusetts "friends of old" to share his Seeker resentment; but he approved of their cold appraisal of the swarming Quakers in so far as he and his friends were firm Calvinists. After 1660 the millennial temperature of nearly all the old guard leaders in New England had dropped suddenly. They became much less sure than they had been about their high destiny as the saints of the Last Time. They were aghast when the Quaker legion of mean and ill-educated people came pouring on to their stage, making the claims they had themselves once made, but in a louder voice and with more assurance.

With the collapse of the Protectorate and the restoration of

the monarchy in England came a reinforcement of two connected kinds of conservatism among the Independents. The
laity rallied to the reaffirmation of the rule of law; the clergy
recalled what had united them in the "good old cause" before
1640—the intellectually impressive systems of Calvin and the
Calvinists. Roger Williams, living in isolation from the community he had founded, shared in both kinds of newly prized
conservatism. The crusty and impulsive old man had fight
left in him. His mind was keen and still devoted to its old
loves. What could be better than an enlistment of the allies
of 1629 against the religious puerilities (as he saw them) of
this "new upstart party or Faction"?[6] He waited for his moment, which came when George Fox in person visited the
Quakers in Rhode Island and was challenged to a serious
academic disputation on fourteen theses put forward by Williams.[7] Fox, for reasons not his own, never came to debate. Three
of his followers did, and felt they had won the day in the midst
of audiences packed with Quakers who disliked Williams. But
the elderly theologian held his backlash in reserve—a book.
When it appeared many Puritans who chuckled over it rec-
ognized that it was a massive Calvinist demolition of the major
Quaker positions as they had then been stated in the mouths
of early Friends. This book was his own accurate and earthy
summary of the debates, spanning five hundred pages in the
modern reprint, by turns acute, jeering, and sore. *George Fox
digg'd out of His Burrowes* is as occasional as the rest of
Williams's output. Its seemingly scrambled appearance and
personal rancour should not put us off; in the context of that
uncouth colonial society it was a revelation of the old gentleman's mind, a recapitulation of his theological position, and
a document of unusual savour.

Some have thought it inconsistent of Williams to plead for
toleration and then so intolerantly to attack the Quakers; but
there is no real inconsistency. "It is not lawful for Israel, that
is, the Church of God, to tolerate,"[8] he had written in 1652.
His purist doctrine of the Church had led him to tolerate

practically nobody but himself in spiritual matters. Intolerance
of error became a duty to him, but his intolerance was restricted
to the questions specifically at issue—matters of faith, worship,
and morality. The instruments of his intolerance were in line
with his idea. No words were barred in the attempt to rebut
and subdue other religious opinions. Sticks and stones, swords
and staves, racks, thumbscrews, and similar "weapons" were
barred. Williams was thus not in favour of restricting allegedly
"offensive" clashes between Church and sect. He thought blunt
controversy was a Christian duty. "It is no civil injury," he wrote,

for any man to disturb or oppose a doctrine, worship, or government
spiritual. Christ Jesus and his messengers and servants did, and do,
profess a spiritual war against the doctrine, worship, and government
of the Jewish, the Turkish, and other pagan and anti-Christian religions
of all sorts and sects, churches, and societies. These all, again, oppose
and fight against His doctrine, worship, government. And yet this war
may be so managed, were men but humane, civil, and peaceable, that
no civil injury may be committed on either side.[9]

In preparation for the day when he could meet the Quakers
in this "spiritual war" Roger Williams equipped himself by
reading as many Quaker books as he could.[10] His real guide,
however, was George Fox's "book in folio,"[11] written with
Edward Burrough, *The Great Mistery of the Great Whore*.
He said he had acquired it "some years since."[12] Its wildly
apocalyptic preface must have set him by the ears and led
him to study carefully the many tracts by opponents of the
Quakers which it purports to answer. The preface, or address
to the reader, concludes with a bit of doggerel verse and has the
signature of Burrough and the date 1658. Many have lamented
the tone of *George Fox digg'd out of His Burrowes* and of Fox's
reply, *A New-England Fire-Brand Quenched*, but usually without reading (or trying to read) the *Great Mistery*. This tirade
set the style of the whole encounter. It is difficult to tell how
much of it is from Fox and how much was ghost-written by
Burrough and given the *imprimatur* of his leader. Regardless of
this, it must be said that the *Great Mistery* is chaotic, illogical,
and crude. After the first eruption from Burrough, a proces-

sion of anti-Quaker authors is exposed in its pages to indecorous scolding. In this latter and longer part of the book the reader is treated to some embarrassingly assertive and ungrammatical dialogue with John Bunyan, the author of *Pilgrim's Progress*, with the Fifth-Monarchist Christoper Feake, Richard Baxter, the Baptist Jeremiah Ives, the Presbyterian Giles Firmin, the London Seeker John Jackson, the leading Independent John Owen, and many others. The "great whore" of the title is the strumpet who has in fact claimed the love of such "Protestant priests" as these, whose sin, in the thought of the compilers, is continuous with that of the Church of Rome and the Church of England. To these besmirched whoremasters Williams, in a fit of eagerness to close the ranks of the intellectually presentable, addressed one of the prefaces to his own outraged rejoinder. He made special mention of two of the more eminent, Baxter and Owen, and called the whole group "those many Learned and Pious Men, whom G. Fox hath so sillily and scornfully answered in his Book in Folio."[13]

As the *Great Mistery* is generally passed over with small notice, it is necessary to resurrect some of it for the sake of balance. The tone of infallible certainty was what offended Williams and many others. "The Lord God everlasting, who is true, and faithful, hath fulfilled his promise in us, and unto us,"[14] readers were told. Williams, who had been a Seeker for so long predictably trembled to read:

And after our long seeking, the Lord appeared to us, and revealed His glory in us, and gave us of His Spirit from heaven, and poured it upon us, and gave us of His wisdom to guide us, whereby we saw all the world, and the true state of all things, and the true condition of the Church in her present estate. First, the Lord brought us . . . to know and understand, and see perfectly that God had given to us, every one of us in particular, a Light from himself shining in our hearts and consciences, which Light, Christ his Son, the Saviour of the world, had lighted every man, and all mankind withal.[15]

He could hardly have become calmer at the words "and also by the Light in us, we perfectly came to know the way of restoration, and the means to be restored,"[16] or by the flat statement that the Quakers were the seed, or saving remnant, born to the pregnant Church of the wilderness[17] (*Revelation 12*). "We are of the royal seed elect," Burrough claimed again, "chosen and faithful, and we war in truth."[18] The Quakers' arrival in London was recalled in language far from complimentary to the Independent and Baptist clergy and politicians:

Then, in the year 1654, as moved of the Lord, we spread ourselves southward and entered into these south parts, and came the first of us into this city of London, in the first month that year [March 1] . . . and we were set at nought and rejected by the fat beasts of the south.[19]

Within the snatches of verse at the end of the preface is the unvarnished representation of the Quakers as the fulfilment of the predictions of the Revelation about the true and final Church on earth:

And the woman that long hath fled, into that place of mourning,
And rested in the wilderness, she is again returning,
And her seed is again springing, and shall replenish nations,
And the man-child must come to rule, forever through gen'rations.[20]

There is much question-begging and jumbled nonsense in the replies to the Puritans that follow. Often the case of the antagonist is summarised—or said to be summarised—in a "principle," which is then answered. As a specimen of irrelevant dialogue out of its depth we may take a reply to a book of Jeremiah Ives:

Pr. He saith, "It is a rare thing to see any of the seed of the Devil grown up to that degree of impudence to charge a man, that he hath done that which he never did do, &c.
Ans. The seed of the Devil always said that which was not true, so not a rare thing to find them; for the Devil and his seed is out of the truth, and when he speaks a lie he speaks of himself, and so speaks a thing that is not, and there thou art.[21]

Giles Firmin's defence of sound learning is countered simply, but with the grammatical crudeness Williams later noted, in the following antithesis:

Pr. He saith *take away learning and England becomes a dunghill.*
Ans. Peter, and John was unlearned men, yet was no dunghill.[22]

The conclusion of the Quakers' "discussion" with Firmin is worse yet:

thou must eat thy own dung; and drink thy own piss that comes from thee, for all that in thy book is but dung . . . ,[23]

a sentiment that evidently predates the "gentle Quaker" tradition. Some other parts of the *Great Mistery* have flashes of more serious and courteous intentions, as in the replies to John Jackson, but on the whole, it must be judged as low-grade and railing controversy.

In the course of the address to the reader, the authors of the *Great Mistery* had declared themselves "willing to engage with these Priests, and all, or any one of these Sects, in a lawful tryal, in disputes, or writings, for the tryal and searching out of the truth, and the true Religion."[24] Roger Williams was to note the challenge. His two large books on persecution had been cast in this ancient form, the academic disputation. The repetitious and punctilious parts of them were, indeed, merely strict adherence to the rules of the game. They were no more tedious than their drawn-out predecessors of the sixteenth century in Germany. When Fox came to Newport Williams saw his chance. He formulated fourteen theses[25] and sent them in proper form to be conveyed to Fox for debate. Williams knew quite well that he was standing on the right foot at that moment. Fox had his own genius, but no training in dialectic. Then no reply came. Fox left without any word. Roger Williams assumed the worst; that Fox had seen his propositions and declined to appear.[26] The subsequent denials that this was the case exonerate Fox, but do not speak well for the Newport Quakers, who had received copies of the theses from Williams and appear to have taken fright.[27] An attempt to reconstruct what really happened in that late summer of 1672 points to a manoeuvre whereby the local Quakers, who disliked Williams and wanted to keep him in his retired corner, withheld the sealed message from Fox and let him depart without knowing what was in the wind. Williams had let his civility steal a march on his tactical sense and lost the pleasure of direct debate with his adversary. But there are not sufficient grounds for Williams's accusation that "this old Fox thought it best to run for it, and leave the work to his Journey-men and Chaplains to perform in his absence for him."[28] The judicious management was rather due to some of Williams's Quaker neighbours, one of whom upbraided him roundly in letters, another calling him a "blind sot" in the street.[29]

After the departure of Fox, the Newport Quakers passed the theses on to three Quaker missionaries who remained. They, with four others, then waited on Williams at Providence to accept his challenge. It was agreed that the first seven propositions should be debated at Newport on August 9 and the last seven at Providence thereafter. Williams made the journey down the sound by boat on August 8 and did not arrive until midnight. At his age he must have been accompanied, and it is unlikely that the boat had no sail over such a distance, but probably August calms prevailed or he took a hand in pulling an oar under lea shores, because he said "God graciously assisted me in rowing all day with my old bones so that I got to Newport toward the Midnight before the morning appointed."[30] There is a melancholy dignity about this old man clambering ashore, bearing his copy of Fox's "grand Alcoran"[31] in folio and the notes he had prepared; a Pembroke College man come to do battle as he had been taught, on this remote shore among people who owed him so much, yet credited him with so little.

The three opponents who faced him the following morning were at an advantage. "When I came into the place. . .," wrote Williams,

I found three able and noted preachers amongst them, viz., John Stubbs, John Burnet [Burnyeat], William Edmundson, sitting together on an high bench with some of the magistrates of their judgment with them. I had heard that John Stubbs was learned in the Hebrew and the Greek, and I found him so. As for John Burnet, I found him to be of a moderate spirit and a very able speaker. The third, W. Edmundson, was newly come, as was said, from Virginia, and he proved the chief speaker; a man not so able nor so moderate as the other two. For the

two first would speak argument, and discuss and produce Scripture or
any other learning; he had been a soldier in the late wars, a stout portly
man of a great voice, and fit to make a bragadocia, as he did, and a
constant exercise merely of my patience . . .[32]

The audience assembled in view of the three Quaker disputants
was largely composed of eager Quakers, flushed with the memory
of Fox's recent visit. In order to be generous toward them (he
said he "knew and did love and honour"[33] many of them)
Williams decided to debate without a moderator, which led
to his being frequently interrupted,[34] especially by people in
the crowd and by Edmundson. "Though J. Stubs and J. Burnet
were more civil and ingenious," he remarked, "yet W. Edmondson
was nothing but a bundle of ignorance and boisterousness."[35]
Williams's position in the assembly suggested a suppliant rather
than an equal.[36] Whereas he was old ("I desired to be sensible
of my many decays of my house of clay")[37] the three Quakers
were in their prime and "placed on high in their desk."[38] On
the first day at Newport Williams spoke so long and had to strain
so hard to make himself heard that he became hoarse. His
conception of the disputation, as set out in his invitation, had
been that speakers should have as much time as they liked to
develop their cases under each heading. Although this formula
had been accepted, Roger Williams's length and excessive detail
became burdensome to most of his hearers. After a queer coin-
cidence, a solar eclipse, on the first day, the night proved rainy.
On the second morning Williams was hoarse and had a head-
ache. Gossip said he was drunk, but he afterwards firmly rejected the slander.[39] The second day was a Saturday. The debates
were adjourned on Sunday and resumed on Monday morning,[40]
with revised rules calling for a maximum of fifteen minutes in
speaking to the remaining propositions on the list for Newport.
Williams stayed with his daughter, the widow of Thomas Hart
of Newport; he was supported in his case for a fair hearing by
a letter from his brother, Robert Williams, a Newport Baptist
and schoolmaster, and by Elizabeth, Robert's wife. Robert
Williams evidently was the first to try to declare publicly what

the record of the debates reveals—that the old man was sub-
jected to taunting and disrespect; the letter was handed sealed
to Roger Williams with the request that its reading be permitted
at the opening of the third day's discussions, but the Quakers
protested this as irregular and Roger Williams left the letter
unopened. However, he published it in *George Fox digg'd out of
His Burrowes*. Elizabeth Williams, for her part, gave a touching
"Unexpected yet Seasonable and true Testimony"[41] as her
brother-in-law left for home. As Roger Williams stepped down
into the boat that sailed him home to Providence, against the
background of Quaker cries that he had "proved nothing,"
she "said aloud: The man hath discharged his Conscience: He
hath fully proved what he undertook to prove against you, and
the words that he hath spoken shall Judge you at the last day."[42]

Word of how things had gone at Newport must have come
back to Providence by the time the second part of the disputation
began there on August 17. Providence Baptists and John Green
from Warwick, a magistrate, called for the reading of Roger
Williams's letter and for fair play in debate respectively. After
Quaker objection, the letter was again voluntarily set aside by
Williams. Green wanted to know "whether Mr. Williams be
here as a Delinquent Charged to Answer at the Barr, or as a
Disputant upon equal Terms."[43] Another Warwick man, Mr.
Caverly, moved for the appointment of a chairman, but the
Quakers insisted on the letter of Williams's document nominating
"every mans Conscience and Judgement"[44] as the sole moderator
of the disputes. Williams again did not insist. None of the
details of this and other procedural reports in *George Fox digg'd
out of His Burrowes* was denied by Burnyeat when he and Fox
replied to it.

At Providence, on the last day, there was more support in
the crowd for Williams. Burnyeat was not there, and the fifteen
minute rule prevailed. Samuel Gorton was present and intervened[45] at one point to support Williams on a matter involving
simple logic; the Providence audience included people who had
been trained to think; even Gorton, whose doctrines were

different from those of Williams, had the Puritan respect for sound learning. Another incident was stage-managed by Edmundson, with the assistance of Williams's old enemy, William Harris. Edmundson denounced Williams for having supported the execution of Charles I, "the King's father" as he put it, thus implicitly drawing attention to the well-known courting of Charles II by both the Quakers and the Rhode Island Baptists. Harris handed him one of Williams's books to prove his point. This was most probably *The Bloody Tenent Yet More Bloody*, with its highly complimentary prefatory address to the High Court of Parliament. After some altercation, the document was ruled to be inadmissible evidence in the case; but Harris's collusion with the rambunctious Edmundson was not forgotten and became the pretext for a fierce excursus in Williams's book about the debates.[46]

We do not know whether Williams had a shorthand writer apart from himself. At home, after the debates, he set everything down fully and quickly. *George Fox digg'd out of His Burrowes* is a large book. Its biblical allusions, lashing invective, and theological niceties are daunting to the student. However, when its structure is understood and the personalities are illumined a little, it becomes a colourful source for understanding Williams's character and theology. It consists of a formal offer of a disputation, followed by a narrative account of the two conferences, at Newport and Providence. The whole book was addressed to "The Kings Majesty, Charles the IId: &c., Whom the King of Heaven long and eternally Preserve." The ornate address to the King is followed by a letter to the People Called Quakers and another to Baxter, Owen, and the others whose works had been treated by Fox in his *Great Mistery*. The narrative begins with an account of what led to the debates, including an acrimonious set of letters[47] exchanged between Williams and his old Providence neighbour John Throckmorton[48] (J. T. in the correspondence) who had become a Quaker. Williams called this "the Skirmishings of my Forlorn-Hope" and proceeded to "the relation of the main Battle."[49] After the detailed report of the two contests, he added the "Appendix," in the form of about two hundred pages of examples, drawn from the pages of the *Great Mistery*. This material was (mercifully) withheld in public debate when the time limit was applied. In it Williams, without too much trouble, demonstrates from this specimen text "That the Quakers Writings are Poor, Lame and Naked (not able to defend themselves, nor comfort the Souls of others with any solidity)."[50]

The address to Charles II had several purposes. Williams was genuinely grateful for the royal charter John Clarke had brought back with him from England. His picture of Charles II was idealised in terms of this bountiful preservation of Rhode Island's "liberties." It was also necessary for Williams to demonstrate that he remained royalist at heart, even though he had been a friend of Cromwell and of the regicides, or some of them. His attitude to the Restoration is much what we might expect of one who had been close to Edward Coke. He had cloaked his misgivings under Cromwell, but his relief in 1660 was genuine. He knew, too, that the Quakers were bidding for royal support and protection; he did not hesitate to attack and outbid them. The florid compliments flow fast, with an eye on the King's knowledge of French. "The crown of all, the Sanctifier of all must be *L'esprit de Djeu*, or else all that is under the Sun *in fumum abeunt*,"[51] wrote old Williams. He spattered various other courtier-like Latin remarks through the text and said:

> I humbly importune your Majesty's continued grace and patience to this poor New England, which, though a miserable, cold, howling wilderness, yet *l'Eternel* hath made it his glory, your Majesty's glory, and a glory to the English and Protestant name.[52]

These sentiments were also suitable for Massachusetts and Connecticut, whose support he solicited in his battle of words against the Quakers.

The fourteen propositions Williams put forward as a structure for the arguments between the parties look categorical and angry on paper; but they are worked out fully in the conven-

tional style of Calvinist scriptural exegesis within the body
of the text. Williams began with analysis of the nickname
"Quaker" and his own account of the origins of the movement.
In his second thesis he defended the orthodox doctrine of the
Incarnation of Christ. The third point he made was that the
Quakers' "Spirit" was not the Holy Spirit of Christian orthodoxy.
Fourthly, he tried to show that the Friends put their own
revelations above Scripture. In his fifth thesis he tried to show
contradictions and hypocrisies in Quaker teaching; in his sixth
he deplored their betrayal of Reformation worship and the
Reformation's teaching on justification and repentance; in his
seventh he alleged their religion was a pastiche of various
heresies. At Providence, in his eighth thesis he attacked the subjective habit of mind of the Quakers in locating God, Christ,
and the Kingdom of God in man; his ninth charged them with
having a superficial religion of cheap grace, easily come by;
the tenth made his central charge against them, that they
were guilty of spiritual pride, "although many truly humble
Soules may be captivated amongst them, as may be in other
religions." The eleventh proposition suggested that the enthusiastic simplicity of the Quakers' conversion obstructed real
repentance and contrition and stood in the way of true faith.
Quaker sufferings, Williams argued in the twelfth place, are
no guarantee of the truth of Quaker doctrine. The thirteenth
proposition began Williams's contemptuous exposure of the
piecemeal illogicality of George Fox's writing, an exercise he
continued in his *Appendix*. And finally he tried to detect among
the Quakers tendencies to incivility, arbitrariness, abrupt dis-
missal of opponents, and a disposition to persecute if they
gained power.

Obviously the angry old warrior was unfair to the early
Quakers at their best; but Barclay's able *Apology*,[53] also presented to Charles II in 1676, had not yet appeared. Williams
worked with what he had seen in England and Rhode Island
and with the major document the earlier Quaker missionaries
used to justify themselves—*The Great Mistery of the Great*

Whore. Certain of his charges contain more than a grain of truth and may help toward demythologising early Quakerism.[54] What were these charges?

In the first place Roger Williams's derivation of the Quakers from the influence in England of the Familists and similar antinomian sects is of interest, if only because it was more usual until recently to derive Quakerism from the more amorphous phenomena of the Northern "seeker" groups. What Williams said suggested that the special revelations, incipient pantheism, and claims to sinlessness of the followers of Henry Niclaes had seeped by untraced routes into the popular enthusiastic religion of the seeking common people in the North of England. The milieu of James Nayler, who was of equal importance with Fox in the first days of the Quaker movement, has recently been described as Familist.[55] Roger Williams drew attention early in his big book to these affinities of many of the writers whose works he examined; he was probably not simply denigrating the Friends, but trying to give a rational explanation of the presence among them of ideas found elsewhere from the Middle Ages onward:

'Tis probable they are the offspring of the Grindletonians in . . . Lancashire . . . who held those two grand points, though many wicked paths of doctrine and practice were amongst them, viz., 1. That God doth all; 2. They could not sin, taking it according to the letter. These Grindletonians were the offspring of the late Nicolaitans, as all of them are in truth justly so called [*Revelation 2.6*] from Henry Nichols [Niclaes, the Familist], who put forth his books of the same poison in King James's time, which long since I read, and were confuted by many, and by Mr. Ainsworth and Mr. Robinson, precious and powerful witnesses of Christ Jesus. H. Nichols and his Nicholaitans were the litter of those Spirituals and Libertines which spread in Germany and France in Calvin's days; against whom that heavenly soul gave his powerful and heavenly witness in his book against the Libertines. These Libertines Satan raised up about the Protestant Reformation from the ruins and rubbish of the old Manicheans and Gnostics, and other blind guides who swarmed in the first, third, and fourth centuries, until the pope swallowed up all the lesser serpents and so became a Dragon with seven heads and ten horns. . . .[56]

When Williams traced this supposed ancestry at the outset he hung out several signals of his major quarrels with the Quakers. He regarded their doctrine of Spirit as bordering on pantheism; he intended to press them on the exposed nerve where they pretended they were infallibile and could not sin; and he would associate what he considered to be their errors with similar teachings of the Pope and the Jesuits. The crux of the matter lay in Roger Williams's defence of the Calvinist teachings on the "rottenness" of human nature, the objective work of God in retrieving the true Elect by the incarnation and death of Christ, and the need for receiving all this by repentance and faith. He objected to the Quakers' seeing of the Light in every man, because he said such natural light was deceptive darkness; he detected a dissolution of the doctrine that what counted was Christ's flesh and blood, with a preference for the idea that the birth of Christ in every man as the Light was the essential; he saw few signs of repeated admission of error and evil on the part of the enlightened Quakers, with the result that he doubted whether their faith could be what the Bible meant by faith at all. Most persistently of all, he drew attention to the way many Quakers set their Light and insight over the Bible, instead of listening to the meaning of the literal words and doing the hard work needed to discern their original sense, as distinct from the preferred current meanings the Quakers tended to attach to them. He genuinely believed himself to be fighting Calvin's fight against the Spirituals and Libertines of the sixteenth century, only now in a different stadium. The language he used to come to grips with his opponents had the insulting vigour of Calvin, without Calvin's eloquence, but with a touch of frontier humour that makes it less poker-faced, more forgivable.

With Calvin and Augustine, Roger Williams saw the root of evil in human nature as pride, inability to say repeatedly "I am sorry; I am wrong." He thought the Quakers, when they said they had received the Light or that Christ was in them, were concluding that they were then "saints" in the sense that they could not sin, because the Light was pure and

Christ was perfect. When he saw these assumptions hand-in-hand with surly self-assurance and lack of humility in many members of the early Quaker society (which was a tight "in-group") he was led to write:

This is the main ground of my controversy with the proud Quakers; they stir up . . . their illuminations in themselves, and condemnations against others, but they magnify (with the papists and Arminians) cursed, rotten nature; their converts and proselytes have but a painted, formal repentance, faith, &c. Only if they can come to their church, &c., and "thou" and "thee" and disrespect all superiors, then are they high saints, cannot sin, &c.[57]

In the course of the Rhode Island debates Williams noticed that his opponents "could not endure to be Informed, Admonished, Counselled, least of all Reproved by any,"[58] and toward the end of his book he commented particularly on this reluctance of the early Quakers ever to admit they were fallible or evil, which for him was a sure sign of the subtle working of the sin of pride. He asked,

why then doth the Lord Jesus command us to pray daily against temptations, yea, and to pray daily for the pardon of sin, if his followers be forever escaped out of the reach of sinful thoughts, words and actions and many thousand sinful omissions?[59]

Soon after this he particularly upbraided George Fox himself for going out of his way to deny that any true messengers of Christ can come short of their duty. "I reply," Williams commented caustically

this deluded soul (as it is written) must grow worse and worse, except the Lord wonderfully awaken him, to all eternity. Instead of seeing any failing against God and Christ, the Spirit, and servants of God, &c., he claps his wings upon his dunghill, and vapours that, in all these transactions, he hath not failed, no not in a sinful word or thought.[60]

Thomas Weld and others had made the same general criticism in their anti-Quaker book called *The Perfect Pharisee* and a sympathetic modern scholar has said of early Quakers: "Practically never in my researches have I come across a Friend who acknowledges a mistake."[61] This arose from the fact that "in Quaker preaching the doctrine of perfection and infallibility, taught uncritically, was at first well nigh universal."[62]

Infallibility was one of the ideas Williams used to plead parallels between the Quakers and the papacy. At first the comparison seems extravagant and far-fetched. It looked as though the critics were stretching evidence in order to brand the Friends with the favourite taunt of "Jesuit." Richard Baxter had used the same accusation.[63] Of course the charge that Jesuits somehow "fathered" the Quakers was wide of the mark, but the grounds for the suspicion in the minds of conservative "reformed" theologians lay in the common assumptions of "natural theology" underlying Quaker teaching and the definitions of the Council of Trent. Williams scornfully declared in *George Fox digg'd out of His Burrowes* that the supposed Holy Spirit had been smuggled into the Council at Trent in a "cloak bag"[64] in order to fabricate infallible definitions in the "chemical laboratories"[65] operated by the Council fathers. He objected to the thought that the pope and the Church were master interpreters of the Scripture; like all Calvinists he taught that they must simply submit to the Scripture and be ruled by it; that they had no final light for determining its meaning, but were to be judged and reformed under its total influence. The claim to infallibility, he said, rested on the exaltation of purely human natural light as though it were the light of final revelation. Church traditions were pushed into the center of authority where only the Bible should be arbiter. In place of the Reformation's teaching of justification by grace through faith, both "papists" and Quakers had devised the idea that God, by cooperating with man's natural goodness, simply aided him to become holy. Williams, as a Calvinist who believed in the mysterious *fiat* of predestination and free unmerited grace, came to think of Quakerism as a sort of poor man's back door into the "hellish" error of the Counter-Reformation, human effort disguised as God's gift.[66]

Williams was greatly irritated by the way Quakerism's early apologists used precise terms interchangeably, as though they all really meant the same thing. He attacked their habit of using the word Light and equating it with Christ and the Spirit. They liked to refer to their experience as the coming of the Light to the Seed, so that Christ dwelt in them. Williams's theological training made him rebel violently against the submergence of the carefully drawn distinctions between the persons of the Trinity in this "Babilonian Jugling, & Egyptian canting." Williams had been taught to clarify by distinguishing terms and demonstrating their common and peculiar properties. One of his most devastating *jeux d'esprit* emerges from his examination of a passage in which George Fox has used a number of theological terms as equivalents for what he means by The Christ Within, culminating in the statement, *None sees Iustification and Redemption, but with the Light within which comes from Christ who hath enlightened him.* Williams warmed up for his counter-blow by the observation that "he usually, and here (as before I have opened) confounds Justification and Light, and Christ, and Faith, and obedience, (after his Babylonish wont) all in a Juglers box within together: So that the English of Faith is Christ, Obedience is Christ, Justification is Christ, Light is Christ, &c."[67] Shortly afterwards Williams arrives at the consequence: "that Fox his words may be in plain English thus rendred, *None sees Christ and Christ but with the Christ within, which comes from Christ who hath Christed him.*"[68] And the voice of sober Puritan logic draws the inference:

it is a mystery of iniquity to darken any, much more heavenly matters with confounding, and not distinguishing aright, when matters are in examination.[69]

A related impatience is felt in Williams's attempt to pin his opponents down on the question of the primacy of the "once for all" appearing of Christ in the flesh over his indwelling of man through the experience of the Spirit. He was at pains to prove that the sequence of events in the New Testament— Christ's birth, life, death, resurrection, outpouring of the Spirit

on the Day of Pentecost (*Acts* 2)—mattered supremely. He said
no Spirit could be the authentic Holy Spirit unless bearing
witness to the past and accomplished acts of this "literal and
historical Declaration."[70] The internalising of history, the assertion that what really matters is "what happens to us now"
was certainly characteristic of the Quaker arguments. Both the
historic events of Christ's earthly life and the anticipation of
a future culmination of history tended to be subordinated to
the collective rapture of present experience. The historical sequences set out in the old Christian creeds and the idea of
an Incarnation defended by the formulation of the doctrine of
the Trinity were prized by older Puritans, but not so highly by
the Quakers. Fox and his followers were so radical in internalising the meaning of both the Incarnation and the future
Kingdom that they drove Williams back to defend "old authors,"[71] the church fathers and the reformers. "I affirmed,"
said he, in his defence of his "true Christ Jesus" against their
accustomed emphasis,

> their Christ was but half a Christ, a Light, an image, or picture or
> fancy of a Christ, made up of the godhead and their flesh. I said they
> had set up a Christ within them which was but an imagination, an
> image, a Christ in the mystical notion, but in reality nothing.[72]

In the margin next to these words he charged "the Quakers'
Christ" with "destroying the history." They denied the charge,
but he had threatened them at a point where they were vulnerable.

It seemed to Roger Williams that many other false notions of
the Quakers could be traced to their arbitrary wresting of the
plain sense of the Bible[73] to support them in their own type of
private assurances. He was an uncompromising biblicist. The
literal words in the original languages were, to him, love-letters
addressed by the Lord Jesus to his spouse, the Church; they
were Christ's last will and testament, left as an infallible objective guide to his intention after his death; they were the document that contained the good news of the reprieve of a condemned man, under the "broad seal"[74] of the King who sent

them. He frequently reminded the Quakers of Christ's words "it is written" and deprecated their tendency to dispense with the external paper and ink once they felt sure they had the Word in their hearts.[75] He took care to chide Quaker authors for relying on English translations in stating their case. He took this to be as bad as Roman Catholic reliance on the Latin. When John Stubbs used his Greek and Hebrew Bibles in the course of the disputation Williams was glad of it and duly impressed. He said,

> it may be he understood the Hebrew and the Greek and other languages as well as myself, and better, too. I was about to say that they were wonderfully altered and changed from their former principles and practices; for heretofore they have professed to me that they had no need of books, no not of the Scripture itself, for they had the Teacher within them that gave forth Scripture, &c. If now they were persuaded to study the Holy Scripture and the translation of it, and to examine the translations and the copies of them, then they did err and sin before—which they say the saints cannot, in so wonderfully neglecting and slighting them as useless and needless things.[76]

Williams, like John Owen, drew attention to one of the more serious Quaker *gaffes* caused by reliance on wrong translations. This concerned their announcement that Christ the Light shone in every man who came into the world. A text they used to support their teaching was the mistranslation[77] of *John 1.9:* "That was the true Light, which lighteth every man that cometh into the world." Williams used the Greek to point out the real meaning in context,[78] that the true light, as *it* came into the world, shone objectively on every man, but that some received it and others refused. For all his sympathetic former attitudes toward such "mechanick preachers" as Samuel How, the Baptist, Williams rallied to the Reformation's call to close study of the Bible in the original texts. "The scriptures put both papists & Quakers to flight," he wrote:

> It is no wonder this spirit of lying cries out so fiercely against the schools of learning in Old and New England. It knows that the right

and regular propagation of natural, of civil, and especially of divine knowledge, scatters the thick fogs of the Quakers' affected hellish ignorance.[79]

Probably "affected" meant "emotional," suggesting that the anti-intellectual "enthusiasm" of the Quakers was the source of their unclear conceptions. When he wrote thus he seemed to be feeling passionate enough himself—and reminiscent of his own days as a Pembroke man, because he went on to recall how the martyr-bishop Ridley "had got most of the holy Epistles in Greek by heart, even before he left Pembrook Hall in Cambridge."

In view of the later, more pacific, developments of Quakerism, we are startled to find Roger Williams accusing the Friends he knew of entertaining dreams of earthly power and being possible persecutors of the future. Here it must be remembered that he was dealing with two specific environments—London in early 1654 and Rhode Island during the influx of the early "messengers of truth." Fifth-Monarchy Men, who were by no means all bent on using the existing army units in England to bring in the Kingdom, joined the Quakers in good numbers. They brought their dreams of a Last Great Battle with them and were not at first counselled by George Fox to put up their swords.[80] Edmundson's voice and presence, by 1672, obviously carried over parade ground atmosphere into the debating room. In England by 1659 the Quakers were involved in politics. Their aim was to spread their movement all over the world, and they became the inheritors of the frustrated dreams of the preceding twenty years when the Protectorate collapsed, and they absorbed the split-off remnants of many disillusioned millennial and enthusiast sects. Their behaviour, as their literature and contemporary observers attest, was more pentecostal than mystical.[81] They were not called Quakers for nothing; like some of John Wesley's early converts after 1738, they quite often shook physically, tumbled on the floor in strange ecstasies, spoke in incomprehensible tongues and generally alarmed respectable people.[82] As in all grand revivals, they attracted their quota of the mentally unbalanced. The reality of their persecutions was accompanied by the usual compensating mirage of grandeur. Even the classic background of economic depression is present; many of these rapidly emigrating "high saints" had suffered for years in their home counties of Lancashire and the Lake District under the straitened conditions of a decline in the wool industry.[83]

Some of these phenomena were unkindly described by Williams, from personal experience or the reliable reports of others. He was severe on the extreme "prophetic" witness of running naked in the streets,[84] but he reserved his most stinging language for their conviction that they were already in a state of glory and triumph, judging the nations and all things because they had the Light and the Spirit. The claim to be already entered into the Kingdom and to be members of the promised Church of the millennium was the antithesis of his own continuance in bereft isolation, knowing only the wilderness and the command of the Cross, but waiting for a glory to be revealed. He could not bear the thought that his far-from-humble Quaker neighbours should say they were the saints in light. He told his friend, the Quaker convert John Throckmorton:

> now all on a sudden . . . you are got up into the lofty chair of judging, and ready to say, "God, I thank thee I am not as this Publican." I beseech the Lord to make you savingly to remember that Word, "God resisteth, that is 'sets himself in hostility against' the proud, but he giveth grace unto the lowly."[85]

Speaking of the Quakers generally as rejecting any thought of an objective future "personal coming of the Lord Jesus," he took the same occasion to reprove the internalised millennial conceptions of the Quakers on the ground that they led to pride:

> these deluded and deluding souls, in their dark prisons of willing blindness and the hellish chains of the pride and hardness and security of their hearts, they dream they sit in robes of glory themselves and now keep open the high court of eternal judgment and pass sentence upon this Christ without as a poor outside Christ—and all that worship him.[86]

It does not seem to have occurred to him that in speaking like this he was himself judging high and hard, but we can be consoled by the quality of theatre about the whole scene. "These

high Saints who now keep Judgment Day,"[87] he called the
Quakers in that rather scruffy Newport audience. He ironically
contemplated their effort "to mount up into their saddles and
thrones of the eternal power and Godhead, that so the earth may
be theirs by authority."[88] He called it "a dangerous counterfeit
court," and compared it (in a voice like Sir Edward Coke) with
"a company of drunken sots that kept a court in Hartford-Shire,
and feigned themselves judges, and justices, and officers, & had
almost brought themselves all to the gallows, &c. by hanging up
one man until he began to look black, and some of them began
to fear their own necks, and to repent of their rash madness."[89]

All this does not fit the usual picture of the Quakers as a peaceful people who abjured the sword; but George Fox was not immune from visions of power. He wrote in his *Journal*, "And ye
Nations will I Rock being on them atopp."[90] On another occasion, in 1657, he advised English soldiers:

to them that do well the sword is a praise . . . and, if ever you
soldiers and true officers come again into the power of God which hath
been lost, never set up your standard until you come to Rome, and
[when] it be atop of Rome, then there let your standard stand.[91]

A section of Williams's book against the Quakers is devoted to
his conservative objections to their use of "women apostles." In
this he again reveals himself as biblicist. When he had been an
officer of the Church at Salem he had contended against Puritan
custom by drawing attention to the fact that women are supposed to have their heads covered during worship. The Massachusetts Puritans were disposed to keep peace with their wives
by turning a blind eye to the injunctions of St. Paul on this
matter (*I Corinthians 11*). Williams had kept this passage under
scrutiny, together with Paul's reminder that he did not give
women leave to raise their voices in the assemblies of the Church
(*I Corinthians 14.34–35*). The Quakers gave offence to him by
tolerating "nakedness of women" to make a prophetic point,
which was far worse than merely worshipping without a veil; and
they designated women as "apostles," a title that connoted for
Williams the highest order of the Christian ministry, reserved by

New Testament practice, so he believed, for men. He gave the customary Puritan "solid" reasons against women preachers by expounding the relevant Bible passages.[92]

On the subject of oaths Williams wrote an interesting analysis of George Fox's position (enlivened by offensive asides), followed by the most complete and lucid account of his own stand that we have from him at any time. He rejected Fox's refusal of all oaths and made out a New Testament case for swearing oaths on religious occasions with proper solemnity. He then applauded another Quaker author for describing a formula that could invoke the name of God as witness to a solemn affirmation in civil matters, without the overtly religious formality of the traditional oath.[93] Williams's proposal here demonstrates his willingness to stand alongside sober and thoughtful Quakers where he can make common cause with them. The number of times he indicates such readiness is unfortunately obscured by the surrounding flood of "sharp scripture language" in *George Fox digg'd out of His Burrowes*, but the present instance is a good one. Williams constructively said,

> I believe this highly concerns the high assembly of Parliament and all law makers, to search well and to appoint a committee of searchers to examine if the laws, upon new appearances from heaven, have not need of rectifying, and some of cancelling. . . .[94]

Social conservatism and aristocratic preferences appeared in Williams's comments on "Quaker ways," which he called invented traditions and regarded as a bumptious disdain of ordinary civilities. "The Quakers (if they had their scope)," he wrote,

> scorn to come behind the Jews or papists for ceremonies and traditions, which it was necessary for them both to add, as apples and nuts, &c., to still poor children from crying after God's worship.[95]

He listed "dumb worship," "brutish salutations," and particularly handshaking,

> their new way of feeling and grabbing the hand in an uncouth, strange, and immodest way, and this instead of kissing, called the holy kiss amongst Christians, and a token of love and reverence to men also in sober and civilised nations.

Other complaints concerned their "brutish irreverence to all their superiors, either in age, or in any other way of preeminence," their "crying down of musicians and music—so excellent a gift of God—as a foolish and devilish practice," their own "fantastical singing," "their condemning of the commendable and ingenious arts of carving, embroidering, and painting, so approved of and commended by God himself in Scripture" and

their crying out against ornaments, of garments and otherwise, against that order God hath set in his works and that variety of his gifts for necessity, for conveniency, for delight, even to astonishment and admiration in all his glorious works.[96]

John Milton, Williams's friend, might have heard this with pride.

Williams took special exception to their familiar forms of address. Though he reports it, and afterwards George Fox did the same thing to him in print, he does not seem to have complained that they repeatedly addressed him as "Roger," but he objected to their return to the "thou" they employed in speaking to all ranks. "They can now 'Thou' the King himself,"[97] he said, in the course of a long passage of amusing comment on the comparative ease with which they seemed to become "ravished" and transported by what he sadly called "one of the easiest religions in the world."

Equally amusing are the grammar lessons he administered to Fox over what he variously castigated as "this boys' English," "un-English nonsense," "the talk of aged doting women" and "bastard and false English."[98] Williams felt there were more ineptitudes here than he could "impute to his northern dialect (having been so long in the South, and London, and read and answered, as he dreams, so many English books): nor to the printer (the faults of that kind being so numerous)."[99]

Throughout his book Williams went out of his way to underline his agreements with the Calvinist centre group of the English Puritans. When he came to points that might have involved him in expounding his Seeker beliefs he did not expand as fully as usual. His address to Baxter, Owen, and Fox's other critics observed:

As to matters in difference between yourselves and me, I willingly omitted them, as knowing that many able and honest seamen in their observations of this Sun (one picture of Jesus Christ) differ sometimes in their reckonings, though uprightly aiming at, and bound for, one port and harbour.[100]

Williams went out of his way to praise the work of the Synod of Dort for trouncing the Arminians;[101] he had just previously thanked God for Calvin; William Perkins,[102] the Cambridge scholar who had been a leader in the Calvinist scholastic development of the early seventeenth century was acknowledged for his aid. When the Quaker spokesmen contended that the reality of the Church was spiritual and invisible because it dwelt within, Roger Williams took his stand for the outward visibility of churches, offices, and sacraments,[103] as all good followers of Calvin did. They taxed him with inconsistency because he attended no visible congregation himself and did not acknowledge the sacraments. Williams replied

that it was one thing to be in arms against the King of kings and his visible Kingdom and administration of it, and to turn off all to notions and fancies of an invisible kingdom, and invisible officers and worships, as the Quakers did; another thing, among so many pretenders to be the true Christian army and officers of Christ Jesus, to be in doubt unto which to associate and to list ourselves.[104]

And finally, in true Genevan style, *George Fox digg'd out of His Burrowes* repeatedly downgraded unregenerate human nature as corrupt. On the last page of the book he went through his own penitential duty to stress his case:

We shall then for all our pretences cry out with Peter, "Depart from me for I am a sinful man, O Lord," and with Job, "Once have I spoken, yea, twice, &c., but no more, &c., I abhor myself as a loathsome, rotten, stinking carrion in dust and ashes." But alas, I fear G. Fox is so taken up with his sitting with Christ in heavenly places, with immediate dictates of his supposed holy spirit, that God's speaking thus to his poor worms after the way of men and by these outward means, stinks in his nostrils.[105]

Most probably, when the Quaker missionaries left after these contests, they thought they had given Williams satisfaction and seen the last of him. To him, the encounters had been a first round only; he wrote everything out with surprising accuracy and sent the manuscript to Governor John Leverett in Boston with a request for publication. "I humbly hope the Lord hath showed me to write a large narrative of all those four days' agitation between the Quakers and myself," he wrote, apparently soon after the debates, to Samuel Hubbard. He continued: "If it please God I cannot get it printed in New England, I have great thoughts and purposes for Old."[106] Leverett later admitted he had raised the money and contributed himself. George Fox, who was furious about the transaction, quoted a letter from Leverett to William Coddington, in which the admission had been made, "I am not asham'd to own my taking care for, and being at the charge of the coming forth of Roger Williams's Book, entitled, *George Fox digg'd out of His Borrows . . .*"[107] The book was published in Boston in 1676. No doubt it was carefully disseminated in England so that Williams could put subtle three-way pressure on the Quakers in retaliation for the grilling they had given him, particularly at Newport; they were attacked now from Providence, from Boston, and from London. Williams obviously derived sinful enjoyment from the transaction; he took great pleasure in the pun on the names of Fox and Burrough in his title, which he said he had not intended until it was suggested to him by his opponents in the debates having pointed it out to him.[108]

Burnyeat spent three weeks at the country house of William Penn, in Sussex, in the summer of 1677,[109] assisting Fox to write the long reply, in two parts, which was published in 1678. *A New-England Fire-Brand Quenched* proves that Williams had achieved his aim of annoying his Rhode Island Quaker neighbours. It contains two irate but interesting letters[110] from William Coddington and Richard Scot, who wrote to Fox to remonstrate against Williams and give a certain amount of rather biased biographical background about him. Coddington described what Williams had done in publishing his book against Fox in picturesque but revealing terms:

He was for the priests, and took up their principles to fight against the truth, and to gratify them and bad magistrates, that licked up his vomit, and wrote the said scurrilous book; and so hath transgressed for a piece of bread. And so are all joined with the Red Dragon to pour out their flood against the Man-Child.[111]

This was loyal support from a reader of the *Great Mistery of the Great Whore*; more soberly, Coddington added he had been "credibly informed" Governor Leverett had said "he would give twenty pound, rather than this mocking, persecuting book should not be printed—and the governor of the New Plymouth jurisdiction other five pound." Thus the picture of financing and publication seems to be confirmed.

In content, *A New-England Fire-Brand Quenched* is much like the *Great Mistery* for both matter and manner. Fox was very angry that Williams presumed to present his book to the King "for Truth concerning G. F."[112] He pictured Williams as the Newport Quakers did: "I think he is an old doting man, and few mind him."[113] The refutations are not logical; the taunts are embarrassing to read, unlike Williams's barbs, which were also uncharitable, but at least not pointless. Frequently Fox asked, "Nay Roger . . . Is this good sense, Roger?"[114] Sometimes he sounded like the man who abused Williams in the street at Newport: "Where hast thou been? Hast thou lost thy Bible as well as thy religion in the woods?"[115] In reply to Williams's special section devoted to his own bad English and triviality, Fox inserted a postscript to Part II of his book in the form of a twenty-four page *ad hominem* "catalogue of R.W.'s envious, malicious, scornful, railing stuff," followed by another five pages of incriminating extracts from the *Bloudy Tenent* and *Hireling Ministry*, intended to try to set Williams at odds again with Massachusetts and the English government. Fox's book was reissued in 1679.[116]

A last relic in writing of the debates of 1672 is a rare item from the pen of George Fox called *Something in Answer to a Letter*, published in 1677. It is a reply to a letter written by Governor Leverett to William Coddington, "wherein he mentions my name, and also wherein John Leverett justifies Roger Williams's book of lies."[117] Evidently Williams's book was by then in print, or possibly circulating in proof. In this pathetic little tract by Fox there are some poignant protests against the whipping of Quaker women at Boston. He cried out against such injustice— "to whip men and women till you cleaved the teats of their breasts (as you did to Anne Coleman) . . ."[118] He warned Leverett: "Herod and Pilate were made friends when they turned against Christ; and it's like you and Roger Williams are made friends in your turning against God's people and his truth now."[119] In spite of the *non sequitur,* that because Williams chose to refute vehemently in speech and writing he was therefore in favour of physical persecution for religion, the small book shows Fox's love of the cause he embodied and his care for all its despised and hurt witnesses.

As for Williams, his case against the Quakers had seemed to him to be a defence of the Incarnation and a reunion with one of his first loves, theology.

10

Christ and Christendom

Hᴏᴡ ɪꜱ Rᴏɢᴇʀ Wɪʟʟɪᴀᴍꜱ to be assessed?

He thought of his own life as a vocation. He had been called by God to be a witness, and the form of obedience he followed must bring him close to the Cross. His model was Christ; therefore the coherent pattern of his career is best unravelled by reference to his understanding of the presentation of Christ's life and demands in the New Testament. Having chosen this standard, Williams declared he had found joyfulness and assurance.

The price he paid for his stand was a certain isolation. He chose to break with the state-church system of old Europe and to attack the doctrine that Church and State are two aspects of a single, divinely ordered *corpus christianum*. Mediaeval Christendom stood for divinely sanctioned monarchy. Around the monarch, invested by God with sacral power, lords sacred and secular were disposed in their functions. Through the anointed royal person the civilising and hallowing reign of Christ was diffused into the natural order. From the time when the Roman *imperium* adopted Christianity as its official religion it was assumed that the spread of this central conviction would lead to the Christianising of the world. The imperial myth in this form had the Church's blessing. In the sixteenth century the same blessing passed to the nation-states of Portugal and Spain. Later, the Netherlands and British empires embodied the secular-sacred imperial dream. Roger Williams, by thinking theologically, became a clear-sighted critic of this European myth. He criticised Christendom in the name of Christ.

Williams taught that Christ's rule can never be furthered by an established Church, because the idea of an establishment, or compulsory religious uniformity, is incompatible with the "powerless authority" revealed in the Incarnation and on the Cross. The assumptions of a crowned monarch are necessarily arrogant, in the sense that the crowned person arrogates to himself the necessary civil power he delegates to his office bearers, who maintain human order by the "sword." The civil ruler has a right to uphold good laws by physical force and make disobedience physically painful. Christ's actions in founding the true Church, however, were a renunciation of this kind of kingship. Christ refused to use the sword. The power He arrogated to Himself lay along the path of suffering, service, and rejection—a way of personal authority without the use of physical force. This personal power of Christ, according to Williams, was delegated subsequently to the true ministers of his Church, but not to secular governors and magistrates. The new law of Christ concerning His "worship" (a word that means "service" in the original New Testament language) must be interpreted and enforced by the Church's ministers only; nor should officers of the civil government ever have any part in supervising it.

These conceptions are not original to Williams. The radical reformers of the sixteenth century had held the same opinions. In England, Baptist pioneers of the early seventeenth century influenced Williams and others by their lives and writings; they too denied the "crown rights" of the royal house in the true Church of Christ. Williams's originality lay in his explicit use of the word "Christendom" and the idea of "christening" as targets for attack, as he argued a case for the practical separation of the jurisdictions of Church and State; and in his sponsoring the first community to make the separation. So Williams, the herald of "secularity," happened to be both a strict biblicist who held Christ's Kingdom was not of this world, and an astute politician who insisted that this world's rulers keep their fingers off the keys of the Kingdom.

In making his witness Williams removed himself beyond the normal boundaries of the Christendom of his day. He believed that what happened to him was correctly interpreted as banishment and persecution. He took steps to prepare for what happened to him and tried to give his stand more integrity by foregoing the prerogatives and perquisites of clergy. Out of the harsh fringe of New England, "a miserable, cold, howling wilderness,"[1] he aimed his arrows back across the frontiers at the clerics and magistrates of the more conventional Puritan brotherhood. His life spoke louder than his books. Place-seeking ceased to be one of his sins. He became unaligned with any major church or sect. His spiritual isolation may be compared with that of Sören Kierkegaard in nineteenth century Denmark. Kierkegaard also used the word Christendom to stand for love of status, conformism, and fame. Both Williams and Kierkegaard gazed fixedly on the paradoxical authority of the Christ of the Gospels. The parallel does not go much further. Kierkegaard was essentially a writer, an artist; Williams was a man of action, a frustrated (and sometimes not so frustrated) politician; he was not a prey to the kind of anguish that racked Kierkegaard. Once Williams had chosen the wilderness he resolutely accepted the consequences. He could endure the shortcomings of Christendom because he deliberately stood outside it.

What is meant by saying that Williams the Bible-loving Puritan was a herald of the ideas of secularity and the secular state? He gave no hint of the secular idealism of a later America. He never suggested that man is intrinsically noble and has inalienable natural rights. Williams saw man as fallen, depraved, estranged from personal union with the Creator. He thought of the lot of society and the individual as hellish except for the predestinate few who were saved by Christ. The Lord had nevertheless set limits to the damage the unregenerate could do to one another. God had located the source of tolerably decent government in the people, as a defence against tyrants. By this divinely ordained means they would be protected from the consequences of their depravity and madness. Citizens should therefore respect and obey civil authorities, but not because of belief in the natural excellence of man and his institutions. The reason for a citizen's loyalty was acceptance of God's mercy in providing government as an alternative to the horrors his neighbours might devise if left to themselves.

Having said which, Williams was prepared to work out reasonable solutions within the political framework thus laid down. He became aware that political order rested on mistrust of excessive power and could be maintained by building realistic relationships. "Who knows not how full the world is of admirable men and women that are not Christians?"[2] he asked. He became a forerunner of the theory of the secular state by taking a low view of human nature, especially when he found ambitious faces wearing religious masks.

By trying to disengage the Church from Christendom Williams became a radical thinker about the Church itself and about its mission. In one way he was as unrealistic about the Church as he was realistic about politics. Where the Church was concerned he was a primitivist and a perfectionist. He took an unwarrantably rosy view of the Church of the first century. He then made it his stereotype for the Church as he expected it to be at the second coming of Christ. He separated Church and State and tried to keep the Church pure. But he appears to have been credulous in thinking that a Church composed of sinners could be like a garden rid of weeds. He looked so eagerly for a pure visible Church that the kind of Church he looked for became increasingly invisible to him. At the same time, what he said and did became a prophetic comment on the need of static and conformist churches to be renewed. Williams could not accommodate himself to the thought that churches, like other institutions, seem subject to the perils of cumbersome organisation and slow decay. He thought it was his duty to remind the churches that their Founder intended them to be unresting bearers of their message, to the ends of the world and until the end of time. Or, to use terms employed by the World Council of Churches and the Second Vatican Council, he saw the Church as the bearer of the Gospel and the Pilgrim People. One of his descriptions makes the point with startling modernity:

> Blessed be the Father of Lights, who hath shown his people of late times the great difference between the stated and settled national church, the ministry and maintenance thereof, and the ordinary [i.e., normative] afflicted, moving, flying state of the Church and churches of Christ Jesus, all the world over.[3]

Williams said this while looking at the Church from a relatively early vantage point in the modern diffusion of Christian missionaries along the routes of Western exploration and trade. He was surprisingly free of the patronising attitudes taken by many of his contemporaries. He recognised that the little island of Christendom was ringed about by majority cultures of non-Christians and that some of them were subtle and proud. He glimpsed the Church again as a voluntary society in an opposed or indifferent world, which would include a European continent more fully emancipated from the pharisaical attitudes of a nominal Christianity. He regarded the restoration of the Church to its place in the world before the time of the Emperor Constantine as desirable for the clarifying of its message in the eyes of the nations. Meanwhile, the missionary activity he undertook among his Indian neighbours amounted to patient presence. He disdained quick and easy results, respected the integrity of his hearers, and did not want the Church to be considered as the propaganda arm of the colonising power.

Roger Williams understood the practice of religious liberty in much the same way as it has been affirmed in the United Nations Declaration and Covenant on Human Rights. Other liberties, such as the right to criticise governments, were not, for him, in the same category. He agreed that civil freedom was good and desirable, but it belonged to the realm of general providence and was governed by law. Religious liberty, by contrast, was governed by the demands of the Gospel. Jesus had suffered, with the power of Church and State ranged against him. Jesus had insisted that the one weapon to be used to create faith was the Word. What held for Jesus holds for all. The meaning of the Incarnation has general application:

It is the will and command of God that, since the coming of His Son, the Lord Jesus, a permission of the most paganish, Jewish, Turkish, or anti-Christian consciences and worships be granted to all men in all nations and countries; and they are only to be fought against with that sword which is only, in soul matters, able to conquer—to wit, the sword of God's Spirit, the Word of God . . .[4]

and again:

An enforced uniformity of religion throughout a nation or civil state confounds the civil and religious, denies the principles of Christianity and civility, and that Jesus Christ is come in the flesh.[5]

Williams gave reasons derived from the Christian religion, but the principle stated was applicable to all men: faith may be propagated, maintained, changed, or entirely forsaken, so long as methods of religious propaganda do not lead to violence and public disorder. Irreligious people are to concede the rights of all religions to indoctrinate and inform. Religious people need to allow for ready dialogue with the irreligious and for free dialogue between differing religions. Both the World Council of Churches and the Roman Catholic Church have recently asserted that "error has rights" and that those rights are protected by the content of the Christian faith.[6] Williams's argument in his *Bloudy Tenent* has come into its own.

Other thinkers developed Williams's argument and evolved the theory behind modern political democracy and pluralism. At this point Williams lived what he did not write. He showed respect and compassion for Royalists, Republicans, Indians, Turks, Dutch, in his correspondence and personal contacts. At the same time he did not hesitate to attack the opinions of others in public to the limit of his spectacular vocabulary. He had come to the conclusion that the pen was mightier than the sword—and his pen could wound. He believed truth could be best refined by the unimpeded conflict of ideas. John Locke, who lived, after the Restoration, as tutor in the house of the Mashams at High Laver, was a reader of Williams and incorporated his ideas into his case for toleration.[7] But the thoughts of the two men differ widely. Locke works out the theme of toleration in hope that "reason" will triumph and boisterous extremes will be composed by assent to moderate self-evident truths. Williams will have no ideas put to rest by the sedative of "reasonableness." He believed in the rugged pamphlet. We cannot imagine him as a polite essayist. Moreover, his controversial weapons were drawn only secondarily from reason and logic; his main appeal was to the data of the Bible, and within the Bible, Christ.

The Puritan expectation of Christ's second coming was important in the thought of men like Williams and John Cotton. Their fervent (and mistaken) hope that Christ would begin to close the world's history within their own near future contributed substantially to their understanding of life. The conception shaped their "realm of ends." Their own goals, at long and short range, were coloured by this view of history. They became resolute activists who knew, on their own account of themselves, what they were doing and why. Roger Williams set his goals by the belief that the man who was killed on the Cross was coming to judge the world. He used the simile of an archer firing at a target to indicate that all men had ultimate aims, fixed by their stance vis-à-vis the meaning of the universe, if any. He saw his own position as defined for him by Christ, who had come and was to come. Nothing else in his large body of writings can be correctly assessed until this overmastering consideration is kept in view. He had many other motives, but this was the purpose he hoped and prayed would dominate the rest.

As Seeker, Roger Williams came to hold a narrow and asocial religious position. He was able to maintain it in old age without incurring serious frustrations because of the undimmed hope he found outside himself, in his faith about Christ's coming to set all wrongs right in the churches and the world. This hope tided him over many years of apparent compromise and barrenness. It was not accompanied by escape into disembodied piety. There was no postponement of action until kingdom come. As in the case of Milton and Cromwell, the measure of light that seemed to shine already, a kind of millennial false dawn, nerved him for orgies of public service, action, speech, and writing. The anchor which still appears on the crest of the state of Rhode Island appears to have its Puritan ancestry in a text in *Hebrews* (*6.19-20*) which calls this hope "an anchor of the soul." The strange location of this "anchor" in heaven turned the imagination of the Puritans upside down. While on earth they seemed to labour on a stormy sea, but they believed they were on the end of a line that held them fast and would finally guarantee them anchorage in a haven beyond all storms. The very narrowness of their heavenly religion gave them scope for action on a broad earthly horizon. They thought all they did had meaning for eternity. In October 1675 Williams wrote to Governor Leverett in Massachusetts and reminisced about Sir Arthur Haselrig, one of the most enterprising political sinners in Cromwell's government and a Puritan who had fought hard to forestall Williams's quest for a charter during his second English journey. The occasion of writing to Leverett was the dark threat of King Philip's War. "I am between fear and hope," wrote Williams, "and humbly wait, making sure, as Haselrig's motto was, sure of my anchor in heaven, *Tantum in Coelis*, only in heaven. Sir, there I long to meet you."[8]

This thirst for eternity is part of Williams the reactionary. He believed in hell, miracles, angels, the election of the saints, and the perdition of the damned. He looked upon himself and all men as under a curse. The Last Judgment was as real to him as a local assize. He sought authority, an apostolic ministry, disciplined sacraments, and the excommunication of the obstinate from the Church. He did not think churches were too strict;

they were not strict enough. In such reactionary intellectual soil he sowed, however, his most revolutionary ideas.

The reactionary was by temperament a revolutionary, but not a social revolutionary. Williams was a prophet, an isolated man who spoke before his time of things to come. He was a revolutionary in his readiness to concede a "civil being" to all his fellow-citizens, including the atheist, who, in his opinion was a person who was blinded, though possibly in good conscience, to the truth. As the revolutionary looked forward on behalf of all men, the reactionary in him looked backward and dug his heels into the familiar narrow Christian track. He thought of "soul liberty" as decreed for all men, but he regarded it as Christ's gift.

Was Roger Williams an Englishman, or already an American? He was both, and neither. His origins and life story are bound together by an allegiance transcending place. He emulated his New Testament predecessor, Paul, in his ability to be all things to all men. Though driven into a forsaken pocket on the rim of civilisation, he was one of the most universally minded of the Puritans. Their insights were usually deep, but provincial; his have come later into their own. How English he was in upbringing and sympathy we may sense by visiting Smithfield, in London, where he lived as a boy, or by pausing in the nearby churches of St. Sepulchre and St. Bartholomew the Great. We may wander through the Inns of Court, remembering Sir Edward Coke, and the boy who took shorthand at his side. The buildings of Sutton's Hospital, once the site of Charterhouse School, still stand; there he began his pathway to learning that led him among the godly preachers at Cambridge as lines of conflict began to form between parliament and king. We may follow him in the fields and woods around High Laver and stand in the church where he was married in 1629. Or we may trace his flight in 1630 as he saw the chimneys of the great house at Stoke on his way down to Bristol, thinking of Sir Edward Coke and finding his parting from his native soil "bitter as death."

We may stand by the grave of John Cotton, a few minutes walk from Boston Common, contemplating the rupture between two men who both believed they were being faithful to truth; or walk the streets of Salem and the pathways of the Pilgrims' cemetery above New Plymouth. But the most moving monument to Williams is the leafy hill of nineteenth century Providence, Rhode Island, with its substantial merchant houses and memorials to men who loved liberty. There we are in the America that was coming to birth before Williams died, in sight of the forests of Connecticut, where a man might "boggle and start as at a Rattle Snake"[9] or muse that "the riches and honour of this world" were "the smoak of a Tobacco-pipe."[10] At Newport and on the islands of the sound, in the stillness of summer nights beside the water, by the house of Richard Smith, Williams's successor in trade among the Narragansetts, we come close to the inwardness of old Roger Williams, who bore within him so much of what America has become.

This young Englishman, this old American, was a citizen of the world, who acted spontaneously in 1653 to obtain the release on parole of the eccentric royalist Scots knight, Sir Thomas Urquhart, the translator of Rabelais and author of a universal language. Sir Thomas had been captured at the Battle of Worcester in September 1651 and imprisoned in Windsor Castle. Somehow Williams arranged for him to return to his castle of Cromarty. Urquhart afterwards expressed his

thankfulness to that reverend preacher, Mr. Roger Williams of Providence in New England, for the manifold favours wherein I stood obliged to him above a whole month before either of us had so much as seen each other, and that by his frequent and earnest solicitation in my behalf of the most special members both of the Parliament and Council of State; in doing whereof he appeared so truly generous, that when it was told him how I, having got notice of his so undeserved respect towards me, was desirous to embrace some sudden opportunity whereby to testify the affection I did owe him, he purposely delayed the occasion of meeting with me till he had, as he said, performed some acceptable office, worthy of my acquaintance; in all which, both before and after we had conversed with one another, and by those many worthy books set forth by him, to the advancement of piety and good order, with some whereof he was pleased to present me, he did approve himself a man of such discretion and inimitably sanctified parts, that an Archangel from heaven could not have shown more goodness with less ostentation.[11]

Williams acted in these ways in response to the "unostentatious goodness" he believed he had received from the hand of "a beggar's brat laid in a manger and a gallows-bird."[12] In the service of Christ he became willing to walk the extra mile, beyond the expectations of conventional Christendom.

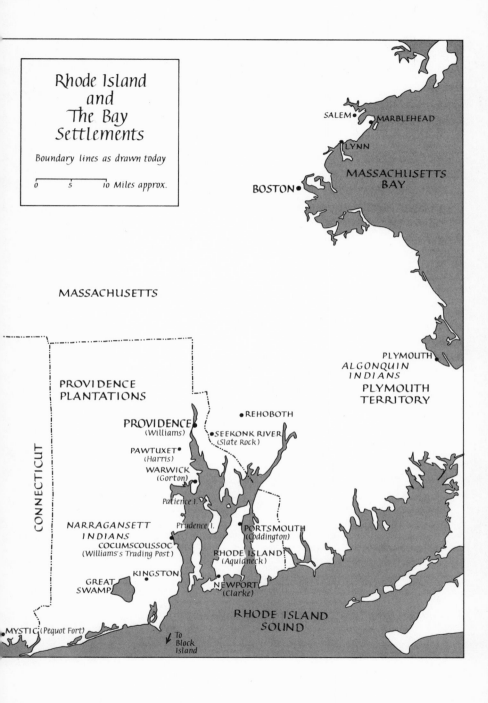

Rhode Island
and
The Bay
Settlements

Boundary lines as drawn today

0   5   10 Miles approx.

SALEM • • MARBLEHEAD

• LYNN

MASSACHUSETTS
BAY

BOSTON •

MASSACHUSETTS

PLYMOUTH
ALGONQUIN
INDIANS

PLYMOUTH
TERRITORY

PROVIDENCE
PLANTATIONS

• REHOBOTH

PROVIDENCE
(Williams)

• SEEKONK RIVER
(Slate Rock)

PAWTUXET •
(Harris)

WARWICK
(Gorton)

Patience I.

CONNECTICUT

Prudence I.

NARRAGANSETT
INDIANS

PORTSMOUTH
(Coddington)

COCUMSCOUSSOC
(Williams's Trading Post)

RHODE ISLAND
(Aquidneck)

KINGSTON •

GREAT
SWAMP

NEWPORT
(Clarke)

RHODE ISLAND
SOUND

MYSTIC (Pequot Fort) •

↙ To
Block
Island

Chronology

1603		Accession of James I
		Probable year of Williams's birth, London
1616		*Williams present when James I came to Court of Star Chamber?*
	June 20	Coke rusticated; and
	November	deprived as Lord Chief Justice
1620		Pilgrims landed at Plymouth Rock
1621		*Williams at Charterhouse*
1625		Death of James I; accession of Charles I
1626–7		*Williams B.A., Cambridge*
1628		Laud preferred to London
		Petition of Right
1629		*Williams at Otes, Essex*
		Massachusetts Bay Company formed
		Remonstrance in Parliament; Dissolution
	December 15	*Williams married Mary Bernard*
1630		Laud enforced conformity to Prayer Book and Articles
		Coke in retirement and under surveillance
		Settlement of Massachusetts Bay
	December 10	*Williams sailed from Bristol*
1631	February 5	*Williams landed at Nantasket*
		Refused Boston and Salem calls
		To Plymouth
1633		Laud elevated to Canterbury
		Williams at Salem
1634		Death of Coke
1635	October 9	*Massachusetts court ordered Williams to leave jurisdiction*
1636		*Williams fled Massachusetts*
	April 20	*Arrival at Slate Rock* (Providence)
	May	John Cotton's book: 'Moses His Judicialls'
		Pequot War
1637		Pequot War continued
		Antinomian crisis in Massachusetts
		Williams received Anne Hutchinson at Providence

1639		*Williams became temporarily a Baptist, then "seeker"*
1640		Long Parliament met, London
1641		Parliament ordered publication of Coke's 'Institutes'
1642		Civil War in England
1643	May	*Williams left for England*
		Publication of 'Key' and 'Mr. Cotton's Letter'
	December 8	Death of Pym
1644	July 15	*Publication of 'Mr. Cotton's Letter . . . Examined'*
		'Bloudy Tenent' published; Williams to Boston
1645	January 10	Laud executed
		Publication of 'Christenings Make Not Christians'
		New Model Army
1647		Publication of Cotton's 'Bloody Tenent Washed . . .'
		Breach between Army and Parliament
1648	December 7	Pride's Purge
1649	January 30	Charles I executed
		Cromwell in Ireland
1650		Cromwell defeated Scots at Dunbar
1651		Cromwell victorious at Worcester
	November	*Williams, Clarke, and Dyer sailed from Boston*
1652		*Publication of 'Experiments,' 'Bloody Tenent Yet More Bloody,' 'Major Butler . . . ,' 'Hireling Ministry,' 'Examiner Defended'*
1653		Cromwell Protector
1654		First Protectorate Parliament
	Spring (May)	Quakers in London
	Summer	*Williams returned to America*
		President of Rhode Island and Providence Plantations (1654–1655)
1655		First Protectorate Parliament dissolved
1656		Second Protectorate Parliament
1657		Cromwell refused kingship
1658		Death of Cromwell; Richard Protector

1660		Restoration in England
1663	July 8	*Rhode Island Charter granted*
1672		*Williams debated with Quakers at New-port and Providence*
1676		*'George Fox Digg'd out of his Burrowes' published at Boston*
1675–6		King Philip's War
		Williams serves with Militia
1676	March 26	Providence burned in Philip's War
1683	January-March (?)	*Death of Williams*

Note on Chronology. Events in New England are omitted in many places to bring out the point that Williams tended to determine his diplomatic and literary activity by reference to what was happening in *old* England.

Notes

Full titles and dates of publication are given in the Bibliography. *C.W.* is used for citations from *The Complete Writings of Roger Williams*.

CHAPTER 1   (Pages 1–6)

1. Hubbard, *General History of New England*, pp. 205–206.
2. Miller, *Roger Williams*; Calamandrei, M., *Neglected Aspects of Roger Williams' Thought*, in *Church History*, Vol. XXI, No. 3, September, 1952, pp. 239–258; Moore, LeRoy, Jr., *Roger Williams and the Historians*, in *Church History*, Vol. XXXII, No. 4, December 1963, pp. 433–451.
3. Background in Miller, *Orthodoxy in Massachusetts*; Miller and Johnson, *The Puritans*; Miller, *Errand into the Wilderness* and *The New England Mind, The Seventeenth Century*.
4. For earlier, especially Tudor, Puritanism: Haller, *The Rise of Puritanism*.
5. Miller, *Roger Williams*, p. v.
6. Haller, *op. cit.*, pp. 56ff.
7. Letters of April (?) and May 2, in Barrington Correspondence, *Egerton MSS.*, 2643–2650, British Museum; facsimile in ed. Chapin, *Letters and Papers*; reprint in *New England Hist. and Geneal. Register*, 1889, Vol. 43, pp. 315–320.
8. Awareness of Chaucer shown in *Bloody Tenent Yet More Bloody*, *C.W.*, IV, p. 423, and n.
9. *Rhode Island Hist. Soc. Pubs.*, *New Series*, Vol. VIII, July 1900, No. 2, pp. 135–136.
10. *C.W.*, V, p. 6.

CHAPTER 2   (Pages 7–34)

1. Known data on birth and family in Winslow, *Master Roger Williams*, pp. 9ff., and notes, pp. 293–294.
2. *George Fox digg'd . . .* , from the preface "To the People Called Quakers," n.p. (first page), *C.W.*, V.
3. Hexter, *Reign of King Pym*; Newton, *Colonising Activities of the English Puritans*; Calder, *The Activities of the Puritan Faction*; Rose-Troup, *John White*; Eusden, *Puritans, Lawyers and Politics*; Brunton and Pennington, *Members of the Long Parliament*; Keeler, *The Long Parliament*.

4. Bowen, *The Lion and the Throne*, pp. 428–433.
5. *C.W.*, VI, pp. 252–253.
6. *Charterhouse Records*, London.
7. Venn, *Matriculations and Degrees . . . University of Cambridge*, 1544–1659, p. 732.
8. Ernst, *Roger Williams*, p. 58.
9. *Egerton MSS.*, 2643–2650, printed in *Hist. MSS. Commission of England* 7th Report, Appendix, p. 546.
10. Stearns, *Congregationalism in the Dutch Netherlands*.
11. Hill, *Society and Puritanism*, pp. 79–123.
12. Keeler, *Long Parliament*, pp. 268–269.
13. *Egerton MSS.* (n. 9, above), printed in *Hist. MSS. Commission of England*.
14. D.N.B., *Barrington*, Sir Thomas; *Egerton MSS.* (above)
15. Easton, *Mary Bernard*, in *R.I.H.S. Colls*, xxix, July 1936, No. 3, pp. 65–80. Cf. marriage register of All Saints Church, High Laver (near the site of Otes), in Essex County Record Office, Chelmsford. The entry appears to be in Williams's own hand.
16. Newton, *Colonising Activities of the English Puritans*; Rose-Troup, *John White*; Andrews, *Colonial Period of American History*, Vol I.
17. Morison, *Builders of the Bay Colony*, p. 65; *C.W.*, IV, p. 65.
18. D.N.B., Supplement, *Cotton*; Ziff, *The Career of John Cotton*.
19. Morgan, *The Puritan Dilemma*, pp. 34–53; Eliot, *Builders*, p. 64.
20. *C.W.*, I, p. 315 (*Cotton's Letter Examined . . .*).
21. *C.W.*, VI, p. 356 (letter of March 25, 1671, to John Cotton, Jr.).
22. *Gods Promise to His Plantation*, London, 1630 (Re-print, *Old South Leaflets*, No. 53); Morgan, *The Puritan Dilemma*, pp. 52–53.
23. *The Writings of Henry Barrow, 1587–1590*, ed. Leland H. Carlson, London, 1962, p. 188.
24. Dexter, *England and Holland of the Pilgrims*; Dale, *History of English Congregationalism*, pp. 165–207.
25. Walker, *Creeds and Platforms of Congregationalism*, pp. 89–91.
26. *C.W.*, VI, p. 3 (letter to Winthrop, Sr., from New Plymouth).
27. Bradford, *History of Plymouth Plantation*, ed. Davies, p. 299 (1633).
28. Knowles, *Memoir*, pp. 108–109.
29. Winthrop, *Journal*, pp. 116ff. (1633); Bradford, *History*, p. 299 (1633).
30. Mather, *Magnalia*, Book VII, p. 431.
31. Dexter, *As to Roger Williams. . .*, p. 75; Morison, *Builders*, p. 97.
32. Winthrop, *Papers*, Vol. III, pp. 146–149 (Winthrop to Endecott).
33. Chapin, *Roger Williams and the King's Colors*.
34. *Ibid.*, pp. 21ff.
35. Hubbard, *General History of New England*, pp. 204–205; cf. *C.W.*, V, pp. 361–362.
36. Morison, *Builders*, p. 65; Dexter, *As to Roger Williams. . .*, p. 54.
37. *C.W.*, I, p. 325.
38. *Op. cit.*, Book VII, 1–6, pp. 430–432.
39. *Ibid.*, p. 431.

40. Winthrop, *Journal*, p. 155, (1635).
41. *Ibid.*, p. 117, (1633).
42. Winthrop, *Journal*, pp. 112–113.
43. *Ibid.*, p. 154.
44. Morton, *New-England's Memorial*, p. 153.
45. Winthrop, *Journal*, pp. 162, 168.
46. *C.W.*, VI, p. 407, (June, 1682); Winthrop, *Journal*, p. 168.
47. Winthrop, *Journal*, p. 168.
48. Baillie, *Disswasive*, p. 63; *Disswasive Vindicated*, p. 30.
49. *Key. . .* , *C.W.*, I, p. 31.
50. *C.W.*, VI, pp. 27–141, *passim*.
51. Winthrop, *Journal*, October 21, 1636–March 22, 1638, *passim*.
52. *Ibid.*, Jan. 20, 1637.
53. Smith, Handy, Loetscher, *American Christianity*, vol. I, pp. 114ff. and bibliography, p. 184.
54. Hexter, *Reign of King Pym*, Ch. I; Wedgwood, *King's Peace*, pp. 363–364.
55. Cotton, *The Churches Resurrection*, pp. 21–22.
56. *C.W.*, VI, p. 262.
57. Miller, *Orthodoxy in Massachusetts*, pp. 263–313; Paul (ed.), *Apologeticall Narration*, pp. 43–56.
58. Hexter, *op. cit.*, pp. 35–36, 151–152.
59. Howell, Roger, Jr., *Newcastle Upon Tyne and the Puritan Revolution*, Oxford, 1967, pp. 153–158.
60. Winthrop, *Journal*, Vol. II, (1644), p. 198.
61. *N.E.H.G.R.*, 1857, Vol. XI, pp. 41–43; Stearns, *Strenuous Puritan*, p. 172.
62. *C.W.*, VI, pp. 392–393.
63. Answer of *Roger Williams to Harris*, 1677, (MS. in library of American Antiquarian Society, Worcester, Mass.).
64. *Bloudy Tenent*, *C.W.*, III, pp. 298–300.
65. *Rhode Island Colonial Records*, Vol. I, p. 45; *C.W.*, VI, p. 142.
66. *C.W.*, VI, pp. 332–333.
67. D.N.B., *Gorton*; Janes, *Samuell Gorton*; Gorton, *Simplicities Defence*; Winslow, *Hypocrisie Unmasked*.
68. Richman, *Rhode Island*, Ch. VII, pp. 197ff.
69. D.A.B., *Clarke*.
70. D.A.B., *Coddington*; Richman, *op. cit.*, pp. 276, 281.
71. D.N.B., *Gorton*.
72. *R.I.H.S. Tracts*, No. 14, Providence, 1881.
73. Richman, *Rhode Island*, p. 276.
74. D.A.B., *Clarke*; King, *A Summer Visit . . .*
75. Clarke, *Ill Newes*, in *Mass. Hist. Soc. Colls*, Fourth Series, Vol. 2, Boston, 1854.
76. *Ibid.*
77. Dexter, *As To Roger Williams. . .*, Chronological Table, and pp. 120–121; cf. King, *Summer Visit. . .*, p. 33.

78. Brown, *Political Activities of Baptists and Fifth Monarchy Men*; Rogers, *Some Account of the Life and Opinions of a Fifth-Monarchy Man.*
79. Winslow, *Master Roger Williams*, p. 230.
80. *C.W.*, VII, pp. 42–114.
81. *Ibid.*, pp. 115–141.
82. *C.W.*, IV.
83. *C.W.*, VI, p. 262; pp. 270, 307.
84. *C.W.*, VI, pp. 237–253.
85. Baillie, *Letters and Journals*, Vol. II, p. 212.
86. Braithwaite, *Beginnings of Quakerism*, Ch. VIII, pp. 153–176.
87. Swan, *Case of Richard Chasmore.*
88. *C.W.*, VI, p. 308.
89. Winslow, *Master Roger Williams*, pp. 261–264; *C.W.*, VI, pp. 387–394.
90. *C.W.*, VI, p. 384.
91. *Ibid.*, and cf. *C.W.*, VI, p. 197.
92. Jones, *Quakers in the American Colonies*, pp. 84–89.
93. *C.W.*, V.
94. London, 1659.
95. By Fox and Burnyeat, 1679.
96. Moffatt, *Life of John Owen*; D.N.B., *Owen.*
97. Nuttall, *Richard Baxter; Reliquiae Baxterianae.*
98. *C.W.*, V, pp. 314–316.
99. Fox, G., *Something in Answer to a Letter.* . . , p. 1.
100. *C.W.*, VI, pp. 363–394.
101. Giddings, *The Indians and Roger Williams*, (MS.), p. 23.
102. Winslow, *Master Roger Williams*, p. 283, and n. 19, p. 311.
103. *MS.*, Mass. Historical Society; cf. *C.W.*, VI, pp. 404–405.
104. Winslow, *Master Roger Williams*, p. 283, and n. 19, p. 311.
105. *C.W.*, VI, p. 399.
106. *Ibid.*, p. 404.
107. *Ibid.*, p. 406.
108. Winslow, *Master Roger Williams*, p. 287.

CHAPTER 3 (Pages 35–68)

1. Hubbard, *General History of New England*, p. 204.
2. Burrage, *Early English Dissenters*, Vol. I, pp. 313–326.
3. Burgess, *John Smith.*
4. MacLear, *Making of the Lay Tradition*, in *Journal of Religion*, Vol. XXIII, No. 2, April 1953, pp. 113–136; Wilson, *Studies in Puritan Millenarianism* (unpublished dissertation).
5. Wilson, *op. cit.*, Ch. VII, pp. 201ff.
6. *Writings of Robert Harrison and Robert Browne* (ed. Peel and Carlson).
7. Ibid., *A True and Short Declaration*, p. 404.
8. *Writings of Henry Barrow and John Greenwood.*

9. Haller, *Rise of Puritanism*; Miller, *The New England Mind, The Seventeenth Century*.
10. Notestein, *The English People on the Eve of Colonization, 1603–1630*, p. 262.
11. *C.W.*, V, p. 146.
12. Notestein, *op. cit.*, pp. 250–266.
13. Hill, *Economic Problems of the Church*, pp. 307–337.
14. Babbage, *Puritanism and Richard Bancroft*, London, 1962.
15. Trevor-Roper, *Archbishop Laud*.
16. Hill, *Economic Problems of the Church*, pp. 338–352.
17. Winslow, *Master Roger Williams*, notes on p. 294.
18. Cf. Winslow, *Master Roger Williams*, pp. 31–33.
19. *C.W.*, VI, pp. 1–2.
20. *Ibid.*, p. 2.
21. Wedgwood, *The King's Peace*, p. 140.
22. *C.W.*, V, n. p.
23. *C.W.*, I, p. 383, *Mr. Cotton's Letter Examined*; *C.W.*, IV, p. 145.
24. *C.W.*, V, pp. 338–339.
25. *C.W.*, VI, p. 212.
26. Miller, *Roger Williams*, pp. 33–38.
27. *Bloody Tenent Yet More Bloody*, *C.W.*, IV, pp. 185–186.
28. *C.W.*, VI, pp. 11, 125.
29. Wilson, *Studies in Puritan Millenarianism* (dissertation); Haller, *Foxe's Book of Martyrs*.
30. Wilson, *op. cit.*
31. Williams, G.H., *Wilderness and Paradise*, p. 75; Haller, *Foxe's Book of Martyrs*, p. 64.
32. *Ibid.*, Ch. V.
33. D.N.B., *Brightman*.
34. D.N.B., *Mead, or Mede*.
35. *C.W.*, VI, p. 8.
36. *Ibid.*, p. 10.
37. *Ibid.*, pp. 10–11.
38. *Ibid.*, p. 12.
39. Mather, *Magnalia*, VII, 7, p. 432.
40. Baxter, *Plain Scripture Proof of Infants Church-Membership and Baptism*, p. 147.
41. Brightman, *Works*, pp. 979ff. (1644 edn.).
42. *Op cit.*, p. 981.
43. Bernard, *Key of Knowledge*, p. 351. Further on Bernard, pp. 63f. and 103–4.
44. *Bloody Tenent Yet More Bloody, To the Reader*, *C.W.*, IV., p. 46; cf. *Queries. . .*, *C.W.*, II, p. 28.
45. Newton, *Colonising Activities*, p. 46.
46. Williams, G.H., *The Pilgrimage of Thomas Hooker*, in *Bulletin of the Congregational Library*, Vol. 19, Nos. 1 and 2, 1967–1968, esp. No. 1, pp. 7–10.

47. *Bloody Tenent Yet More Bloody, C.W.,* IV, p. 64.
48. *Ibid.,* p. 64.
49. *Ibid.,* p. 64.
50. *Bloudy Tenent, C.W.,* III, p. 69, n. (ed. Caldwell); cf. *Oxford Dictionary of the Christian Church,* entry, *Sarpi.*
51. *A Reply of Mr. Roger Williams, C.W.,* II, p. 10.
52. Burrage, *Early English Dissenters,* Vol. I, p. 171.
53. Cf. Foster, *Alumni Oxonienses,* Vol. IV—Early Series, entry, *Staresmore.*
54. Burrage, *Early English Dissenters,* Vol. I, pp. 171–175, 317–318.
55. Bradford, *Of Plimoth Plantation* (Boston edn., 1901), pp. 49–51.
56. Baillie, *Disswasive,* p. 17.
57. *C.W.,* I, pp. 314ff.
58. Cotton, *A Reply. . . , C.W.,* II, pp. 9–10.
59. Ed. Paul, *An Apologeticall Narration,* pp. 81–112.
60. *Cotton's Letter Examined, C.W.,* I, p. 391.
61. *Ibid.*
62. *Ibid.;* D.N.B., *Lathrop.*
63. *C.W.,* I, p. 392.
64. *Ibid.,* p. 395.
65. *Bloody Tenent Yet More Bloody, C.W.,* IV, p. 29.
66. *Ibid.,* p. 30.
67. *Cotton's Letter Examined, C.W.,* I, p. 308.
68. *Ibid.,* p. 380.
69. Wilson, *Another Look at John Canne,* in *Church History,* Vol. XXXIII, No. 1, March, 1964.
70. In *Hanserd Knollys Society Pbns.,* Vol. V.
71. Cotton's *Answer, C.W.,* II, p. 198.
72. *Cotton's Letter Examined. . . , C.W.,* I, p. 381.
73. *Ibid.,* p. 382.
74. *Cotton's Answer, C.W.,* II, p. 195.
75. *George Fox digg'd. . . , C.W.,* V, *To the Quakers* (n. p.), (2).
76. *Bloody Tenent Yet More Bloody, C.W.,* IV, p. 331.
77. Jessop, *A Discovery of the Errors of the English Anabaptists* (1623), p. 77; cf. Burrage, *Early English Dissenters,* Vol. I., pp. 192–193.
78. *Exposition of the 13. Chapter of Revelation,* p. 31.
79. *Ibid.,* p. 17.
80. Written in prison at Colchester, dated 1613. What appears to be further information on Wilkinson's "illegal conventicle" at Coggeshall, Essex, and his trial, is in *Assize File* 35/53a/H 10 (2 March 1612), in Transcript, p. 87, Essex County Records Office, Chelmsford; also 35/54/H 38 and 35/54/T 22. It appears that Wilkinson was a weaver from the London parish of St. Dunstan-in-the-East.
81. Burrage, *Early English Dissenters,* Vol. I, pp. 192–194.
82. Amsterdam (?), 1615. Reprinted in *Tracts on Liberty of Conscience* (Hanserd Knollys Society).
83. *Bloudy Tenent, C.W.,* III, p. 61.
84. *Cotton's Letter Examined. . . , C.W.,* I, p. 341.

85. *Ibid.*, p. 343.
86. Burgess, *John Smith*, p. 257.
87. Easton, *Mary Barnard*, in *R.I.H.S. Colls.*, XXXIX, July 1936, No. 3, pp. 65–80. See also pp. 13 and 49.
88. Burgess, *op. cit.*, pp. 74–80.
89. London, 1608.
90. *Winthrop Papers*, May 1637, p. 399, letter attributed to John White of Dorset by Rose-Troup, *John White*, p. 228.
91. London, 1610.
92. Grindal, *Remains* (Parker Society), pp. 372ff.
93. *The Last Booke of Iohn Smith*, in Burgess, *John Smith*, pp. 259–260.
94. *C.W.*, VI, p. 188.
95. Winthrop, *Journal*, March 16, 1639, p. 297; July, 1639, p. 309; Backus, *An Abridgment of the Church History of New England*, p. 45.
96. *C.W.*, VI, p. 188.
97. Mennonite Encyclopaedia, *Collegiants*; Burrage, *Early English Dissenters*, Vol. II, pp. 302ff.
98. Lindeboom, *The Parish of Austin Friars.*
99. Nuttall, *Visible Saints*, p. 19.
100. *Bloody Tenent Yet More Bloody*, *C.W.*, IV, pp. 47–48.

CHAPTER 4 (Pages 69–91)

1. E.g., *C.W.*, VI, p. 124; IV, p. 337.
2. *Hireling Ministry*, *C.W.*, VI, p. 153.
3. Winslow, *Master Roger Williams*, pp. 45–64, *passim*.
4. Bowen, *The Lion and the Throne*, p. xiii.
5. *Ibid.*, p. 251.
6. Wedgood, *King's Peace*, p. 136.
7. Bowen, *op. cit.*, p. 257.
8. D.N.B., *Coke*.
9. Bowen, *op. cit.*, pp. 322–323.
10. *C.W.*, VI, pp. 333–351.
11. *Ibid.*, p. 345.
12. Benedict, *General History of the Baptist Denomination in America*, I, p. 474.
13. Bowen, *Lion and Throne*, p. 304.
14. Sykes, *Old Priest and New Presbyter*, pp. 1–117.
15. Bowen, *op. cit.*, pp. 428–433.
16. *C.W.*, VI, pp. 237–253.
17. Bowen, *op. cit.*, p. 145.
18. *C.W.*, VI, p. 237.
19. *Ibid.*, pp. 237–238.
20. *Ibid.*, p. 239.
21. *Ibid.*
22. *Ibid.*, pp. 239–240.

23. Bowen, *Lion and Throne*, pp. 383–384.
24. Wedgwood, *King's Peace*, p. 136.
25. *Ibid.*, p. 430, and D.N.B., *Coke*.
26. Wedgwood, *op. cit.*, p. 430.
27. *C.W.*, VI, p. 240.
28. *Ibid.*, p. 241.
29. *Ibid.*
30. *Ibid.*, p 248.
31. *Ibid.*, p. 249.
32. *Ibid.*, p. 246.
33. *Ibid.*, p. 250.
34. *Ibid.*, p. 251.
35. *Ibid.*, p. 252.
36. *Ibid.*
37. *Ibid.*, pp. 252–253.
38. *Charterhouse Records*, London.
39. Trevor-Roper, *Archbishop Laud.*
40. Hill, *Puritanism and Revolution*, pp. 239ff.
41. *Bloody Tenent Yet More Bloody*, *C.W.*, IV, p. 301.
42. *Hireling Ministry*, *C.W.*, VII, p. 153.
43. *Ibid.*, p. 172.
44. *C.W.*, VI, p. 262.
45. *Ibid.*
46. *C.W.*, I, pp. 77–282.
47. Winslow, *Master Roger Williams*, p. 146.
48. *Key*, *C.W.*, I, p. 85.
49. *Ibid.*, p. 89.
50. *C.W.*, VII, pp. 142–191.
51. D.N.B., *Owen.*
52. *Ibid.*, *Goodwin.*
53. *Hireling Ministry*, *C.W.*, VII, p. 169.
54. *Ibid.*, pp. 169–170.
55. Winslow, *Master Roger Williams*, pp. 79ff.
56. *C.W.*, VII, p. 170.
57. *Ibid.*
58. *C.W.*, IV, pp. 1–22.
59. Haller, *Rise of Puritanism*, pp. 55–56; pp. 56–62.
60. Haller, *op. cit.*, pp. 130–144; Miller, *New England Mind, The Seventeenth Century*, pp. 300–362.
61. Miller, *New England Mind. . .* , pp. 116–153.
62. D.N.B., Supplement, *Cotton.*
63. *C.W.*, VI, p. 309.
64. *George Fox digg'd. . .* , *C.W.*, V, p. 202.
65. *C.W.*, VI, p. 312.
66. *C.W.*, IV, pp. 34–35.
67. *C.W.*, VI, p. 319.
68. *Bloody Tenent Yet More Bloody*, *C.W.*, IV, p. 4.

69. *C.W.*, VI, pp. 397–398.
70. *Experiments of Spiritual Life and Health*, *C.W.*, VII, p. 113.
71. *C.W.*, VI, p. 384.
72. *C.W.*, VI, p. 192.
73. *C.W.*, IV, p. 523.
74. *C.W.*, VI, p. 373.
75. *Examiner Defended*, *C.W.*, VII, p. 234.
76. *Bloody Tenent Yet More Bloody*, *C.W.*, IV, pp. 103–104.
77. *Ibid.*, p. 206.
78. *Ibid.*, p. 185.
79. *Ibid.*, p. 211.
80. *Ibid.*, p. 301.
81. *Ibid.*, p. 304.
82. *Ibid.*, pp. 381–382.

CHAPTER 5 (Pages 92–118)

1. Venn, *Matriculations and Degrees*, p. 732.
2. Gee and Hardy, *Documents*, pp. 482–483.
3. Calder, *Activities of the Puritan Faction. . .* , p. xi.
4. *Ibid.*, p. xix.
5. Trevelyan, *England under the Stuarts*, p. 166.
6. In *Egerton MSS.* 2643–2650 (British Museum), re-printed in N.E.H.G.R., 1889, Vol. 43, pp. 316–320.
7. Morison, *Builders of the Bay Colony*, pp. 31–32.
8. Winslow, *Master Roger Williams*, pp. 79ff.
9. Stearns, *Strenuous Puritan*.
10. N.E.H.G.R., (n. 6, above), p. 316.
11. Keeler, *Long Parliament, Dictionary of Parliament Men, Barrington, Sir Thomas*.
12. Hexter, *Reign of King Pym*; Keeler, *op. cit.*; Brunton and Pennington, *Members of the Long Parliament*.
13. Keeler, *op. cit.*, p. 29.
14. N.E.H.G.R. (n. 6, above), p. 316.
15. *C.W.*, VI, p. 237.
16. On Hooke, A.G. Matthews, in *Congregational Historical Society Transactions*, IX, pp. 263–265.
17. May 2, 1629, in N.E.H.G.R. (n. 6, above), p. 318.
18. Keeler, *Long Parliament*, p. 269; D.N.B., *St. John, Oliver*.
19. Easton, Emily, in R.I.H.S. Colls., XXXIX, July 1936, No. 3, p. 67.
20. *Ibid.* Cf. pp. 49 and 63f.
21. Rose-Troup, *John White*; D.N.B., *Bernard*.
22. *Winthrop Papers*, Vol. III, p. 399.
23. Easton, (n. 19, above), pp. 67ff.
24. Berins, M.A., *Descendants of Roger and Mary (Barnard) Williams*, MS. in R.I.H.S. Library, Providence, R.I. (n. d.),

25. *C.W.*, VII, pp. 45ff.
26. *Ibid.*, p. 113.
27. D.N.B., *Laud*.
28. Stearns, *Congregationalism in the Dutch Netherlands*.
29. Paul (ed.), *Apologeticall Narration*.
30. D.A.B., *Hooker*.
31. Morison, *Builders of the Bay Colony*, pp. 289–319.
32. Stearns, *Strenuous Puritan*.
33. Miller, *Orthodoxy in Massachusetts*, Ch. IV.
34. *Bloody Tenent Yet More Bloody*, *C.W.*, IV, p. 409.
35. *C.W.*, III, p. 3, *(Bloudy Tenent)*.
36. *C.W.*, IV, p. 266 (and mg.).
37. *I Peter* 2.5; cf. *C.W.*, VI, p. 10.
38. *Revelation 11.3*.
39. *C.W.*, VI, pp. 10–11.
40. Miller and Johnson, *The Puritans*, Vol. I, pp. 290–291; Skelton, p. 126 (and n.).
41. Miller, *New England Mind, The Seventeenth Century*, pp. 438–439.
42. Andrews, *Colonial Period of American History*, Vol. II, pp. 144–194.
43. Miller and Johnson, *op. cit.*, pp. 117–118.
44. Hubbard, *General History of New England*, pp. 205, 207–208.
45. Morison, *Builders of the Bay Colony*, p. 65.
46. Mather, *Magnalia*, Book ii, V, 1.
47. Bradford, *History* (ed. Davis), p. 299.
48. *Ibid.*
49. Prefatory notice to Hubbard, *General History of New England*, p. iii.
50. Hubbard, *op. cit.*, p. 181.
51. *Ibid.*, pp. 189–190.
52. *Ibid.*, p. 202
53. *Ibid.*, pp. 202–203.
54. *Ibid.*, pp. 205–206.
55. *Magnalia*, Book VII, pp. 429–430.
56. *Ibid.*, p. 430.
57. *Ibid.*
58. *Ibid.*
59. *Ibid.*, p. 431.
60. *Ibid.*
61. *Ibid.*, p. 432.
62. *Ibid.*, p 431.
63. *Ibid.*, p. 433.
64. Morison, *Builders of the Bay Colony*, p. 68.
65. *C.W.*, VI, pp. 70–71; p. 78.
66. Baillie, *Disswasive*, p. 63.
67. *C.W.*, VI, p. 142.
68. *C.W.*, VI, p. 13.
69. *Ibid.*, p. 145.
70. D.A.B., *John Winthrop, Jr.*

71. *C.W.*, VI, pp. 306–307.
72. D.A.B., *Winthrop, Jr.*
73. *C.W.*, VI, p. 319.
74. *Ibid.*, cf. *Key, C.W.*, I, p. 193.
75. *C.W.*, VI, pp. 342–345.
76. *C.W.*, VI, p. 335; cf. p. 317.
77. *Ibid.*, p. 335.
78. *Ibid.*, pp. 337–338.
79. Winthrop, *Journal*, 1635, p. 162.
80. *C.W.*, VII, pp. 195ff.
81. *Ibid.*, (Perry Miller), p. 192.
82. *Ibid.*, p. 225.

CHAPTER 6 (Pages 119–144)

1. Williams, G.H., *Wilderness and Paradise*.
2. *C.W.*, VII, p. 29.
3. *Christenings Make Not Christians, C.W.*, VII, p. 38.
4. Cf. *Key, C.W.*, I, p. 221.
5. *C.W.*, VII, p. 28; cf. Baillie, *Disswasive, The Testimonies*, pp. 69, 70.
6. Baillie, *loc. cit.*
7. *Christenings. . . , C.W.*, VII, p. 34; cf. Baillie (n. 5, above).
8. *C.W.*, VII, p. 37; cf. Baillie, *op. cit., Testimonies*, p. 70.
9. *Hireling Ministry. . . , C.W.*, VII, p. 168.
10. *Key. . . , C.W.*, I, p. 79.
11. *Ibid.*, p. 80.
12. *C.W.*, VI, pp. 407–408.
13. *C.W.*, VI, p. 256.
14. *C.W.*, I, p. 91.
15. *Ibid.*, p. 106.
16. *Ibid.*
17. *Ibid.*, p. 125.
18. *Ibid.*, p. 137.
19. *Ibid.*, p. 141.
20. *Ibid.*, p. 203.
21. *Ibid.*, p. 220.
22. *Ibid.*, p. 218.
23. *Ibid.*, p. 245.
24. *Christenings. . . , C.W.*, VII, p. 35.
25. *Key. . . , C.W.*, I, p. 83.
26. *Letter to Winthrop, C.W.*, VI, p. 172.
27. Ed. Chapin, *Letters and Papers of Roger Williams* (facsimile), no. 2; On Eliot and his work, Kellaway, W., *The New England Company*.
28. *Hireling Ministry, C.W.*, VII, p. 160.
29. *C.W.*, VI, p. 404.

30. *Experiments.* . . , *C.W.*, VII, pp. 39–41.
31. *Bloody Tenent Yet More Bloody*, *C.W.*, IV, pp. 371–374; cf. *C.W.*, VI, p. 172, and *Christenings.* . . , *C.W.*, VII, pp. 39–41.
32. *C.W.*, IV, p. 373, n.
33. Knappen, *Tudor Puritanism*, Ch. XXIV, pp. 442ff.
34. *Clear Sun-shine*, p. 31 (quoted *C.W.*, IV, p. 373 n.); cf. Kellaway, *New England Company*, pp. 12–13.
35. *C.W.*, VI, pp. 346–347. The reference is probably to Calvin, *Institutes*, III, viii, 34. Cf. *Colossians 2, 16*.
36. *C.W.*, VI, p. 361.
37. *C.W.*, VI, p. 327.
38. *C.W.*, VI, p. 269.
39. *Ibid.*, p. 270.
40. *Ibid.*, p. 271.
41. *Ibid.*
42. *Ibid.*, p. 272.
43. *Ibid.*, p. 275.
44. *Ibid.*, pp. 275–276.
45. *Ibid.*, p. 276.
46. *C.W.*, VI, p. 35.
47. *Ibid.*, p. 36.
48. *C.W.*, VI, pp. 338–339.
49. *C.W.*, VI, p. 369.
50. *Ibid.*
51. *C.W.*, VI, p. 323.
52. *C.W.*, VI, p. 364.
53. *C.W.*, VI, p. 376.
54. MS. letter in possession of American Antiquarian Society, Worcester, Mass., (1677). I am grateful to Mr. Bradford F. Swan for a copy in facsimile.
55. *Ibid.*
56. *Ibid.*
57. *C.W.*, VI, p. 104.
58. Winslow, *Master Roger Williams*, pp. 261–264.
59. MS. letter (1677); see n. 54 (above).
60. *C.W.*, VI, pp. 305–306.
61. *C.W.*, VI, p. 332.
62. *Ibid.*
63. *Key.* . . , *C.W.*, I, p. 133.
64. *C.W.*, VI, p. 261.
65. *C.W.*, VI, p. 333.
66. *C.W.*, VI, p. 296.
67. *Historical Discourse*, p. 111.
68. *Key.* . . , *C.W.*, I, p. 87.
69. *Christenings.* . . , *C.W.*, VII, p. 36.
70. *Ibid.*, pp. 36–37; cf. *Hireling Ministry.* . . , *C.W.*, VII, p. 163.

71. *C.W.*, I, p. 109.
72. *Ibid.*, pp. 86–87.
73. Giddings, *The Indians and Roger Williams* (MS.), p. 1.
74. *C.W.*, VI, p. 17.
75. *Hireling Ministry. . . , C.W.*, VII, p. 174.

CHAPTER 7 (Pages 145–175)

1. Ed. Abbott, *Writings and Speeches of Cromwell*, Vol. I, p. 416.
2. Braithwaite, *Beginnings of Quakerism*, p. 25 (quotes Penn's Preface to Fox's *Journal*).
3. Ed. Paul, *Apologeticall Narration*, p. 47 (and n.).
4. Baillie, *Anabaptism. . .* , pp. 96–97 (and mg.).
5. Baillie, *Disswasive*, pp. 57, 63, 72.
6. *Ibid., The Testimonies*, pp. 117, 118.
7. Baillie, *Letters and Journals*, Vol. II, p. 212.
8. Baillie, *Anabaptism*, pp. 96–97.
9. *Ibid.*, p. 97.
10. *Gangraena*, Part II, p. 11.
11. *Ibid.*, Part I, p. 77.
12. *Cotton's Letter Examined. . . , C.W.*, I, p. 316.
13. Nuttall, *James Nayler*, pp. 11–12.
14. *C.W.*, I, p. 317.
15. E.g., *C.W.*, VI, p. 90, p. 125.
16. *C.W.*, I, p. 317, mg.
17. *Ibid.*
18. *Ibid.*
19. *Ibid.*, p. 318.
20. Cook, *op. cit.*, p. 8.
21. *Ibid.*
22. Baxter, *Plain Scripture Proof. . .* , p. 147.
23. *Cotton's Answer. . . , C.W.*, II, p. 11; cf. *C.W.*, II, p. 19.
24. *Ibid., C.W.*, II, pp. 11–12; cf. Williams, *Cotton's Letter Examined. . .* , *C.W.*, I, p. 322.
25. Moffatt, *Life of John Owen*, p. 26.
26. Nuttall, *Holy Spirit in Puritan Faith and Experience*, pp. 108–112.
27. Wilson, *Studies in Puritan Millenarianism* (Union Theological Seminary, N.Y., unprinted dissertation), Ch. VII, pp. 201ff.
28. Maclear, *The Puritan Party*, 1603–1643 (Chicago Ph.D. unprinted dissertation), p. 160 and refs.; Baillie, *Letters and Journals*, I, p. 287; D'Ewes, *Journal*, pp. 313–314; Edwards, *Antapologia*, p. 242, p. 226; cf. also Vicars, *Schismatick Sifted*, pp. 15–18.
29. Nuttall, *James Nayler*, pp. 11–12. I am indebted to Dr. Nuttall for having given me the following provisional elucidation of the bewildering family pedigree of the Wrays:

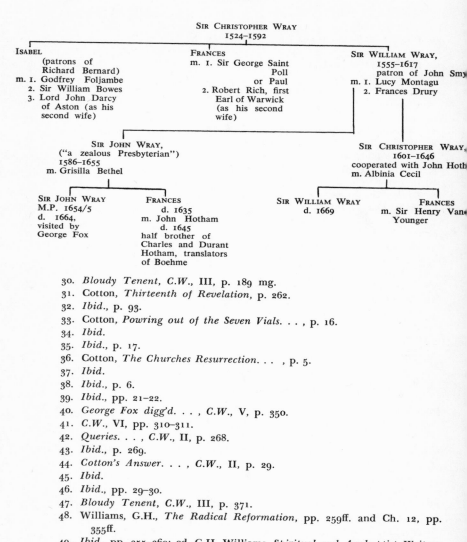

SIR CHRISTOPHER WRAY
1524–1592

ISABEL
(patrons of
Richard Bernard)
m. 1. Godfrey Foljambe
2. Sir William Bowes
3. Lord John Darcy
of Aston (as his
second wife)

FRANCES
m. 1. Sir George Saint
Poll
or Paul
2. Robert Rich, first
Earl of Warwick
(as his second
wife)

SIR WILLIAM WRAY,
1555–1617
patron of John Smy
m. 1. Lucy Montagu
2. Frances Drury

SIR JOHN WRAY,
("a zealous Presbyterian")
1586–1655
m. Grisilla Bethel

SIR CHRISTOPHER WRAY,
1601–1646
cooperated with John Hoth
m. Albinia Cecil

SIR JOHN WRAY
M.P. 1654/5
d. 1664,
visited by
George Fox

FRANCES
d. 1635
m. John Hotham
d. 1645
half brother of
Charles and Durant
Hotham, translators
of Boehme

SIR WILLIAM WRAY
d. 1669

FRANCES
m. Sir Henry Van
Younger

30. *Bloudy Tenent, C.W.*, III, p. 189 mg.
31. Cotton, *Thirteenth of Revelation*, p. 262.
32. *Ibid.*, p. 93.
33. Cotton, *Powring out of the Seven Vials. . .* , p. 16.
34. *Ibid.*
35. *Ibid.*, p. 17.
36. Cotton, *The Churches Resurrection. . .* , p. 5.
37. *Ibid.*
38. *Ibid.*, p. 6.
39. *Ibid.*, pp. 21–22.
40. *George Fox digg'd. . .* , *C.W.*, V, p. 350.
41. *C.W.*, VI, pp. 310–311.
42. *Queries. . .* , *C.W.*, II, p. 268.
43. *Ibid.*, p. 269.
44. *Cotton's Answer. . .* , *C.W.*, II, p. 29.
45. *Ibid.*
46. *Ibid.*, pp. 29–30.
47. *Bloudy Tenent, C.W.*, III, p. 371.
48. Williams, G.H., *The Radical Reformation*, pp. 259ff. and Ch. 12, pp. 355ff.
49. *Ibid.*, pp. 355–360; ed. G.H. Williams, *Spiritual and Anabaptist Writers*, pp. 204–206.
50. Williams, G.H., *Wilderness and Paradise in Christian Thought*, p. 75; Haller, *Foxe's Book of Martyrs and the Elect Nation*, p. 64.
51. Barrow, *Four Principall and Waighty Causes for Separation*, pp. 15, 16.
52. Lawne, *Prophane Schisme of the Brownists*, p. 55. See also pp. 6of. above.

53. Jessop, *A Discovery of the Errors of the English Anabaptists*, p. 77.
54. *Ibid.*, pp. 88–89.
55. *The Sealed Fountaine. . . ; An Exposition of the 13. Chapter of the Revelation. . .*
56. Jessop, *A Discovery. . .* , pp. 88–89.
57. To Winthrop, 1646, *C.W.*, VI, p. 141.
58. *C.W.*, I, p. 387; *C.W.*, II, pp. 272–273; *C.W.*, III, pp. 106 (mg.), 288–289, 293–294, 307 (and mg.), 363, 368.
59. Vendettuoli, *The English Seekers. . .* , (unprinted Harvard Ph.D. thesis). Dr. Vendettuoli has also given me much direct help, but I am unable to attribute more than the three works I have listed in the bibliography to this particular John Jackson.
60. William Allen to Baxter, in *Reliquiae Baxterianae*, Appendix IV, p. 93 (and cf. p. 95). I owe this reference to Dr. Geoffrey Nuttall.
61. *Sober Word*, Preface, p. 2.
62. *Ibid.*, p. 3.
63. *Cotton's Letter Examined. . .* , *C.W.*, I, p. 385.
64. Jackson, *Sober Word*, pp. 10–11.
65. *Ibid.*, p. 4.
66. *Ibid.*, p. 15.
67. *C.W.*, III, p. 294 (mg.); cf. *Hireling Ministry*, *C.W.*, VII, p. 162, *Bloody Tenent Yet More Bloody*, *C.W.*, IV, p. 64.
68. *Sober Word*, p. 15; cf. *ibid.*, p. 18.
69. *Ibid.*, p. 4.
70. *Ibid.*, p. 36; Williams, *Cotton's Letter Examined. . .* , *C.W.*, I, pp. 350–351.
71. *Sober Word*, p. 18.
72. *Ibid.*, p. 37.
73. *Ibid.*, p. 39.
74. *Ibid.*, p. 60.
75. E.g., *C.W.*, VI, p. 247; VII, pp. 151, 199, 201.
76. *Key for Catholicks*, p. 334; cf. Baxter's Correspondence with Allen, *Reliquiae Baxterianae*, App. IV, (n. 60, above).
77. Wilson, *Another Look at John Canne*, in Church History, Vol. XXXIII, No. 1, March, 1964; *Cotton's Letter Examined. . .* , *C.W.*, I, p. 386.
78. Archer, *The Personall Reign of Christ. . .* ; *C.W.*, IV, p. 221.
79. D.N.B., *Saltmarsh*.
80. Saltmarsh, *Sparkles of Glory*, p. 292.
81. Braithwaite, *The Beginnings of Quakerism*, Ch. VIII.
82. *George Fox digg'd. . .* , *C.W.*, V, p. 43.
83. *Strength in Weakness*, p. 12 (error in pagination, 20 in sequence).
84. Braithwaite, *Beginnings of Quakerism*, Ch. XI.
85. *Strength in Weakness*, The Publisher to the Reader.
86. *Ibid.*
87. *Ibid.*, p. 7.
88. *Sober Word*, title page.
89. *C.W.*, VII, p. 194

90. *George Fox digg'd. . .* , C.W., V, p. 84.
91. C.W., V, pp. 427–443.
92. *Hosannah to the Son of David, To the Reader.*
93. *Ibid.*
94. *Fourth Paper Presented by Major Butler,* C.W., VII, p. 122.
95. *Bloody Tenent Yet More Bloody,* C.W., IV, p. 279.

CHAPTER 8 (Pages 176–209)

1. Abbott, *Writings and Speeches of Cromwell,* Vol. III, pp. 864–865.
2. C.W., VI, p. 240 (to Mrs. Sadleir).
3. *Ibid.*
4. C.W., VI, p. 350.
5. *Ibid.*, p. 344.
6. *Ibid.*, p. 343.
7. C.W., IV, p. 337; C.W., VI, p. 124.
8. C.W., VI, p. 350.
9. C.W., VI, p. 333; cf. pp. 143, 287, 379, 403 ("so called").
10. Cf. Woodhouse, *Puritanism and Liberty,* pp. 84–86.
11. *Cotton's Answer. . .* , C.W., II, p. 11.
12. *Bloudy Tenent,* C.W., III, pp. 249–250.
13. *Bloody Tenent Yet More Bloody,* C.W., IV, p. 333.
14. E.g., C.W., VI, p. 408.
15. *Bloudy Tenent,* C.W., III, pp. 249–250
16. *Ibid.*, p. 343.
17. C.W., V, p. 143.
18. *Bloody Tenent Yet More Bloody,* C.W., IV, pp. 138–140, 220, 249, 480.
19. *Bloudy Tenent,* C.W., III, p. 367 (and mg.).
20. *Bloody Tenent Yet More Bloody,* C.W., IV, p. 222.
21. *Ibid.*, p. 414.
22. *Bloudy Tenent,* C.W., III, p. 298; *Bloody Tenent Yet More Bloody,* C.W., IV, p. 112; C.W., VI, p. 392.
23. C.W., VI, pp. 219–220.
24. *Queries. . .* , C.W., VII, p. 232.
25. E.g., *Bloudy Tenent,* C.W., III, pp. 97–118; *Bloody Tenent Yet More Bloody,* C.W., IV, pp. 115f. (*passim*).
26. Ed. Underhill, *Tracts on Liberty of Conscience,* pp. 189–231.
27. C.W., III, p. 61.
28. *Bloudy Tenent,* C.W., III, p. 36 (quoting Luther as cited in *Humble Supplication*).
29. *Bloody Tenent Yet More Bloody,* C.W., IV, p. 122.
30. *Bloudy Tenent,* C.W., III, p. 225.
31. *Ibid.*, p. 129; *Bloody Tenent Yet More Bloody,* C.W., IV, p. 201.
32. *Examiner Defended,* C.W., VII, p. 204.
33. *Ibid.*, p. 212 (mg.).
34. *Ibid.*, pp. 212–213 (and mg.).

35. *C.W.,* III, p. 334.

36. *Bloody Tenent Yet More Bloody, C.W.,* IV, p. 213; cf. *C.W.,* IV, p. 151, and *Examiner Defended, C.W.,* VII, p. 227.

37. *Bloody Tenent Yet More Bloody, C.W.,* IV, pp. 290–291.

38. *Ibid.,* p. 238.

39. Letter to Mason, *C.W.,* VI, p. 350 (1670).

40. *Bloody Tenent Yet More Bloody, C.W.,* IV, p. 365.

41. *Bloudy Tenent, C.W.,* III, p. 251.

42. Shaw, *History of the English Church,* Vol. I, Ch. II, Vol. II, Ch. III.

43. *Ibid.,* Vol. II, Ch. IV.

44. Brown, *Political Activities of Baptists and Fifth Monarchy Men.*

45. D.A.B., *Coddington.*

46. Eusden, *Puritans, Lawyers and Politics,* p. 6; Trevelyan, *English Social History,* pp. 103–105.

47. Eusden, *op. cit.,* p. 42 (and n.).

48. See notes 11, 12, to Ch. 5 (above).

49. *Historical MSS. Commission Seventh Report,* Appendix, Sir Thomas Barrington to Lady Joan Barrington, May, 1630.

50. Hexter, *Reign of King Pym,* p. 63.

51. Gee and Hardy, *Documents. . . ,* p. 536.

52. Winthrop, *Journal,* p. 116.

53. *Bloody Tenent Yet More Bloody, C.W.,* IV, pp. 461–462.

54. *Op. cit.,* Vol. II, vii, 9, p. 433.

55. *Ibid.,* p. 431.

56. Morison, *Builders of the Bay Colony,* p. 97.

57. *Cotton's Letter Examined. . . , C.W.,* I, pp. 324–325.

58. *Cotton's Answer, C.W.,* II, p. 184.

59. *Bloudy Tenent, C.W.,* III, p. 172.

60. *C.W.,* VI, pp. 3–7.

61. Stearns, *Strenuous Puritan,* Ch. VII, esp. p. 172.

62. *Bloody Tenent Yet More Bloody, C.W.,* IV, p. 104.

63. Stearns (n. 61, above), *loc. cit.*

64. Winthrop, *Journal,* 1644, p. 198.

65. *Ibid.,* pp. 197–198.

66. D.N.B., *Percy.*

67. D.N.B., *Wharton;* Jones, *Saw-Pit Wharton.*

68. D.N.B., *Harley.*

69. D.N.B., *Gurdon.*

70. D.N.B., *Holland.*

71. D.N.B., *Blakiston;* Howell, *Newcastle upon Tyne and the Puritan Revolution,* pp. 88–89, 125–128, 139–140.

72. D.N.B., *St. John.*

73. D.N.B., *Pennington, Sir Isaac* (1587?–1661).

74. D.N.B., *Pickering.*

75. D.N.B., *Corbet.*

76. Walker, *Compleat History of Independency,* Part II, *Address to Reader,* p. 1.

77. *Magnalia*, II, vii, 8, p. 433.
78. *C.W.*, VI, pp. 168, 179, 374.
79. To Mason, 1670, *C.W.*, VI, p. 342.
80. *C.W.*, VI, p. 181.
81. *C.W.*, VI, pp. 199–200.
82. *C.W.*, VI, pp. 216–217.
83. *C.W.*, VI, p. 259.
84. *C.W.*, VI, p. 319.
85. *C.W.*, VI, p. 253.
86. *C.W.*, VI, pp. 351–357.
87. *C.W.*, IV, pp. 502–529.
88. *C.W.*, VI, p. 297.
89. *Bloody Tenent Yet More Bloody*, *C.W.*, IV, p. 51.
90. *Ibid.*, p. 81.
91. *Ibid.*, p. 107.
92. *Ibid.*, p. 337.
93. *Ibid.*, p. 240 (mg.).
94. *Ibid.*, p. 431.
95. *Ibid.*, p. 388.
96. *Hireling Ministry. . .* , *C.W.*, VII, p. 167, cf. p. 198; on How, see Tindall, *John Bunyan*, pp. 72–73, 84, 86, 87, 104; Burrage, *Early English Dissenters*, Vol. II, pp. 311ff., 328ff.
97. *Examiner Defended*, *C.W.*, VII, p. 199.
98. Hexter, *Reign of King Pym*, pp. 168–171.
99. Mather, *Magnalia*, II, vii, 8, p. 433.
100. *Bloody Tenent Yet More Bloody*, *C.W.*, IV, p. 437.
101. *Bloudy Tenent*, *C.W.*, III, p. 178.

CHAPTER 9 (Pages 210–239)

1. Jones, *Quakers in the American Colonies*, pp. 114–118.
2. Winthrop, *Journal*, March 27, 1638; cf., *C.W.*, VI, pp. 90–92. The credibility of the story has been doubted (Jones, *Quakers in American Colonies*, p. 21), but an abnormal birth is well attested, despite early accretions to the story. See Rogers, *Mary Dyer*, Appendixes I–IV, for documents.
3. Rogers, *op. cit.*
4. Richman, *Rhode Island*, p. 362; Bishop, *New England Judged*, Parts I and II.
5. *George Fox digg'd. . .* , *C.W.*, V, pp. 60–62.
6. *C.W.*, V, p. 42.
7. Fox, *Journal*, Vol. II, pp. 216–220 (letter of John Stubbs recounting challenge); Edmundson, *Journal*, pp. 73–74; Burnyeat, *Journal*, p. 211. Camp, *Roger Williams vs. "The Upstarts". . .* , in *Quaker History*, Autumn, 1963, Vol. 52, No. 2, pp. 69–76.
8. *Bloody Tenent Yet More Bloody*, *C.W.*, IV, p. 286.

9. *Ibid.*, p. 266.
10. *C.W.*, V, p. 1.
11. *Ibid.*
12. *Ibid.*
13. *Ibid.*, (third of prefatory dedications, n. p.).
14. *Great Mistery, Epistle*, n. p. (7).
15. *Ibid.*
16. *Ibid.*
17. *Ibid.*
18. *Ibid.*, (9)
19. *Ibid.*, (15).
20. *Ibid.*, (28).
21. *Great Mistery*, p. 61.
22. *Ibid.*, p. 114.
23. *Ibid.*, p. 120.
24. *Ibid., To the Reader*, (24).
25. *C.W.*, V, pp. 3–5.
26. Cf. *C.W.*, V, p. 7.
27. *C.W.*, V, Introduction (ed. Diman), pp. xxii–xxvii, 6–7, 35; cf. Fox and Burnyeat, *New England Fire-brand Quenched*, p. 1.
28. *C.W.*, V, p. 7.
29. *Ibid.*, p. 6.
30. *Ibid.*, p. 37.
31. *Ibid.*, p. 286.
32. *Ibid.*, p. 38.
33. *Ibid.*, p. 39.
34. *Ibid.*, pp. 213–214.
35. *Ibid.*, preface, *To The People called Quakers*, n. p., (3), and cf. p. 56.
36. *Ibid.*, p. 38.
37. *Ibid.*, p. 65.
38. *Ibid.*, p. 57.
39. *Ibid.*, p. 67.
40. *Ibid.*, p. 65.
41. *Ibid.*, p. 213 (mg.).
42. *Ibid.*, p. 213.
43. *Ibid.*, pp. 217–218.
44. *Ibid.*, p. 218.
45. *Ibid.*, p. 220.
46. *Ibid.*, pp. 315–317.
47. *Ibid.*, pp. 8–34.
48. *New England Fire-Brand Quenched*, Part II, p. 249.
49. *Ibid.*, p. 35.
50. *Ibid.*, p. 322.
51. *Ibid., Epistle Dedicatory to King*.
52. *Ibid.*
53. Latin edn. London, 1676; English edn., 1678; Braithwaite, *Second Period of Quakerism*, pp. 385–394.

54. Barbour, *The Quakers in Puritan England*, p. xi.
55. Nuttall, *James Nayler*, p. 2.
56. *C.W.*, V. pp. 42–43.
57. *Ibid.*, p. 343.
58. *Ibid.*, p. 217.
59. *Ibid.*, p. 494.
60. *Ibid.*, pp. 495–496.
61. Nuttall, *James Nayler*, p. 16.
62. *Ibid.*
63. Nuttall, *Holy Spirit in Puritan Faith and Experience*, p. 163.
64. *C.W.*, V, p. 253.
65. *Ibid.*, p. 200.
66. *Ibid.*, pp. 200–202.
67. *Ibid.*, p. 183.
68. *Ibid.*, p. 366.
69. *Ibid.*
70. *Ibid.*, p. 69.
71. *Ibid.*, p. 421 (mg.).
72. *Ibid.*, pp. 69–70 (and mg.).
73. *Ibid.*, pp. 192–193.
74. *Ibid.*, p. 470.
75. *Ibid.*, pp. 143, 149–150, 203.
76. *Ibid.*, pp. 95–96.
77. Nuttall, *Holy Spirit in Puritan Faith and Experience*, p. 163.
78. *C.W.*, V, pp. 329–330, p. 481.
79. *Ibid.*, p. 147.
80. Nuttall, *Holy Spirit in Puritan Faith and Experience*, p. 131.
81. Nuttall, *Welsh Saints*, p. 58.
82. *C.W.*, V, p. 134.
83. Barbour, *Quakers in Puritan England*, p. 16.
84. *C.W.*, V., p. 60.
85. *Ibid.*, p. 14.
86. *Ibid.*, p. 81.
87. *Ibid.*, p. 117.
88. *Ibid.*, p. 148.
89. *Ibid.*, p. 345 (and mg.).
90. Quoted (from *Journal*) in Nuttall, *Holy Spirit in Puritan Faith and Experience*, p. 131.
91. Quoted Nuttall, *ibid.*
92. *C.W.*, V, pp. 210, 359–363.
93. *Ibid.*, pp. 408–413.
94. *Ibid.*, pp. 412–413.
95. *Ibid.*, p. 210.
96. *Ibid.*, pp. 211–212.
97. *Ibid.*, p. 368.
98. *Ibid.*, pp. 278–279, 357, 359, 492–493.
99. *Ibid.*, p. 279.

100. *Ibid., Preface* to Baxter, Owen and others.
101. *Ibid.*, p. 424.
102. *Ibid.*, p. 234.
103. *Ibid.*, pp. 102, 165, 177.
104. *Ibid.*, pp. 102–103, cf. p. 165.
105. *Ibid.*, p. 503, cf. pp. 236, 489.
106. *C.W.*, VI, p. 362.
107. Fox, *Something in Answer to a Letter*, p. 1.
108. *C.W.*, V, pp. 53–54.
109. Fox, *Short Journal* (ed. Penney), p. 235.
110. *New England Fire-Brand Quenched*, pp. 246–247.
111. *Ibid.*
112. *Ibid.*, p. 3.
113. *Ibid.*, p. 25.
114. *Ibid.*, Part II, p. 152 (mg.).
115. *Ibid.*, Part II, p. 144.
116. The fine copy in the Massachusetts Historical Society's Library is dated 1679.
117. *Something in Answer. . .* , p. 2.
118. *Ibid.*, p. 6.
119. *Ibid.*, p. 7.

CHAPTER 10 (Pages 240–250)

1. *George Fox digg'd out of His Burrowes*, *C.W.*, V, Epistle Dedicatory to King (3).
2. *Ibid.*, p. 356.
3. *Hireling Ministry*, *C.W.*, VII, p. 165.
4. *Bloudy Tenent*, *C.W.*, III, p. 3.
5. *Ibid.*, p. 4.
6. *Christian Witness, Proselytism and Religious Liberty in the Setting of the World Council of Churches—A Provisional Report*, in *The Ecumenical Review*, Vol. IX, No. 1, October, 1956, pp. 48–56; Carrillo De Albornoz, *Roman Catholicism and Religious Liberty*; *Declaration on Religious Freedom*, in *Documents of Vatican II* (ed. Abbott).
7. Hudson, Winthrop S., *John Locke: Heir of Puritan Political Theorists*, in *Calvinism and the Political Order* (ed. Hunt).
8. *C.W.*, VI, p. 376.
9. *C.W.*, V, p. 209.
10. *Ibid.*, p. 262.
11. Urquhart, *Works* (Maitland Club), pp. 408–409, cited in R.I.H.S. Pubns., New Series, Vol. VIII, July, 1900, No. 2, pp. 135–136.
12. *C.W.*, V, p. 294.

Bibliography

ABBREVIATIONS

C.W. *The Complete Writings of Roger Williams,* New York, 1963, vols. I-VII
D.N.B. *Dictionary of National Biography*
D.A.B. *Dictionary of American Biography*
M.H.S. *Massachusetts Historical Society* (Collections and Publications)
N.E.H.G.R. *New England Historical and Genealogical Register*
R.I.H.S. *Rhode Island Historical Society*

BIBLIOGRAPHICAL AND REFERENCE

Gillett, Charles R., *Catalogue of the McAlpin Collection of British History and Theology,* New York, 1928. (Union Theological Seminary)
Fortescue, G.K., *Catalogue of the Pamphlets, Books, Newspapers, and Manuscripts . . . Collected by George Thomason, 1640–1661,* London, 1908. (British Museum)
Wing, Donald, *Short Title Catalogue . . . 1641–1700,* New York, 1945.
Smith, Joseph, *Bibliotheca Antiquakeriana,* London, 1873.

SOURCES

Allen, William, *A Doubt Resolved, or Satisfaction for the Seekers . . . ,* London, 1655
Archer, Henry, *The Personall Reign of Christ Upon Earth,* London, 1642
Baillie, Robert, *A Disswasive from the Errours of the Time . . . ,* London, 1646; *Anabaptism, the True Fountaine of Independency . . . ,* London, 1647; *The Disswasive from the Errors of the Time, Vindicated . . . ,* London, 1655; *Letters and Journals* (3 vols.), ed. Laing, Edinburgh, 1841
Ball, John, *A Friendly Triall,* Cambridge, 1640; *An Answer to Two Treatises of Mr. Iohn Can,* London, 1642
Barrow, Henry: *The Writings of Henry Barrow and John Greenwood, 1587–1590,* ed. Albert Peel and Leland H. Carlson, London, 1966;

Four Principall and Waighty Causes for Separation, 1593 (?), ed.
T.G. Crippen, London, 1906

Bastwick, John, *The Utter Routing of the whole Army of all the
Independents & Sectaries* . . . , London, 1646

Baxter, Richard, *Plain Scripture Proof of Infants Church-Membership
and Baptism,* (Fourth Edition), London, 1656; *A Key for
Catholicks,* London, 1659; *Reliquiae Baxterianae* . . . , London,
1696

Benedict, David, *General History of the Baptist Denomination in
America,* Boston, 1813

Bernard, Richard, *Christian Advertisements and Counsels of Peace,*
London, 1608; *Plaine Evidences: The Church of England is
Apostolicall, and the Separation Schismaticall,* London, 1610;
*A Key of Knowledge for the Opening of the Secret Mysteries of
St. Johns Mysticall Revelation,* London, 1617; *The Seven Golden
Candlesticks,* London, 1621; *Looke beyond Luther* . . ., London,
1624

Bishop, George, *New-England Judged By The Spirit of the Lord,* 1661

Bradford, William, *Of Plimoth Plantation,* reprinted Boston, 1901;
History of Plymouth Plantation, 1606–1646, ed. Davies, W.T.,
reprinted New York, 1908

Bradshaw, William, *The Unreasonableness of the Separation,* London,
1640

Bridge, William, *Christs Coming Opened,* London, 1648

Brightman, Thomas, *Workes,* London, 1644

Browne, Robert: *The Writings of Robert Harrison and Robert Browne,*
ed. Peel, Albert, and Carlson, Leland H., London, 1953

Burnyeat, John, *Journal,* ed. Barclay, John, London, 1839

Canne, John, *A Necessitie of Separation* . . . , 1634; *The Snare is
Broken,* London, 1649; *A Voice from The Temple,* London,
1653; *A Second Voice from The Temple,* London, 1653; *Truth
With Time,* London, 1656

Clapham, Henoch, *Three Partes of Salomon his Song of Songs, ex-
pounded,* London, 1603; *A Chronological Discourse,* 1609; *Errour
On the Right hand* . . . , 1608; *Errour on the Left Hand* . . . ,
London, 1608

Clarke, John, *Ill Newes from New-England,* reprint in M.H.S. Colls.,
Fourth Series, vol. 2, Boston, 1854

Cook, John, *What The Independents Would have,* London, 1647

Cotton, John, *God's Promise To His Plantation,* London, 1630; *A Brief
Exposition of the whole Book of Canticles,* London, 1642; *The
Powring out of the Seven Vials,* London, 1642; *The Churches
Resurrection* . . . , London, 1642; *The Keyes of the Kingdom of*

Heaven, London, 1644; *The Way of the Churches of Christ in New England,* London, 1645; *The Bloudy Tenent, Washed, And Made white in the bloud of the Lambe . . . ,* London, 1647; *An Exposition upon the Thirteenth Chapter of The Revelation,* London, 1655

Cromwell, Oliver, *The Writings and Speeches of Oliver Cromwell,* 4 vols., ed. Abbott, W.C., Cambridge (Mass.), 1937

Edmundson, William, *A Journal . . .* (second edition), London, 1774

Edwards, Thomas, *Gangraena. . . .* (third edition), London, 1646, *Antapologia: Or, A Full Answer to the Apologeticall Narration,* London, 1646

Erbery, William, *The Lord of Hosts . . . ,* London, 1646

Fairlambe, Peter, *The Recantation of a Brownist,* London, 1606

Firmin, Giles, *Separation Examined . . . ,* London, 1652

First Publishers of Truth, The, ed. Penney, Norman, London, 1907

Fox, George, *The Great Mistery of the Great Whore Unfolded,* London, 1659 (with Edward Burrough)

Fox, George, *Something in Answer to a Letter,* 1677

Fox, George (and Burnyeat, John), *A New England Fire-Brand Quenched,* 1679; *The Journal,* ed. Penney, Norman, 2 vols., Cambridge (England), 1911; *The Journal,* (short version) ed. Penney.

Foxe, John, *Acts and Monuments,* ed. Townsend, London, 1843

Gee, Henry, and Hardy, William J., (eds.) *Documents Illustrative of English Church History,* London, 1914

Goodwin, Thomas (et al.) *An Apologeticall Narration . . . ,* London, 1643

Gorton, Samuel, *Simplicities Defence . . . ,* London, 1646

Grindal, Edmund, *The Remains of Edmund Grindal,* ed. Nicholson, W., Parker Society, 1843

How, Samuel, *The Sufficiency of the Spirits Teaching . . . ,* London, 1639

Hubbard, William, *A General History of New England from the Discovery to MDCLXXX,* (M.H.S. edn.), Cambridge (Mass.), 1815

Jackson, John, *A Sober Word to A Serious People . . . ,* London, 1651; *Strength in Weakness . . . ,* London, 1655; *Hosannah to the Son of David,* London, 1657

Jessop, Edmond, *A Discovery of the Errors of the English Ana-baptists . . . ,* London, 1623

Johnson, Edward, *The Wonder-Working Providence of Sions Saviour in New England,* London, 1654, ed. Jamison, J. Franklin, New York, 1910

Lawne, Christopher (et al.), *The Prophane Schisme of the Brown-ists* . . . [Amsterdam?], 1612

Mather, Cotton, *Magnalia Christi Americana, or, The Ecclesiastical History of New England* . . . , London, 1702, Hartford edn., 1820, 2 vols.

Morton, Nathaniel, *New Englands Memorial*, 1669, ed. Davis, John, Boston, 1826

Murton, John, *Objections Answered by way of Dialogue* . . . , [Amster-dam?], 1615

Pagitt, Ephraim, *Heresiography* . . . , London, 1654

Powell, Vavasor, *God the Father Glorified* . . . , London, 1650; *Christ Exalted Above All Creatures* . . . , London, 1651

Rogers, Edward, *Some Account of the Life and Opinions of a Fifth-Monarchy Man. Chiefly extracted from the Writings of John Rogers, Preacher,* London, 1867

Saltmarsh, John, *Sparkles of Glory* . . . , London, 1647

(Underhill, E.B., ed.), *Tracts on Liberty of Conscience and Persecution,* Hanserd Knollys Society, London, 1846

Urquhart, Sir Thomas, *Works,* (Maitland Club edn.), ed. Maitland, G., Edinburgh, 1834

Vane, Sir Henry the younger, *The Retired Mans Meditations* . . . , London, 1655

Vicars, John, *The Picture of Independency Lively (yet Lovingly) Delineated,* London, 1645; *The Schismatick Sifted, or, The Picture of Independents, Freshly and Fairly Washt-over again,* London, 1646

(Walker, Williston, ed.), *The Creeds and Platforms of Congregation-ism,* reprinted, Boston, 1960

Walker, Clement, *The Compleat History of Independency* . . . , London, 1661

Weld, Thomas (et al.), *The Perfect Pharisee under Monkish Holi-nes* . . . , London, 1654

Wilkinson, John, *An Exposition of The 13 Chapter of the Revelation of Jesus Christ,* (London?), 1619; *The Sealed Fountaine opened to the Faithfull, and their Seed,* 1646

Williams, Roger, *The Complete Writings of Roger Williams,* 7 vols., reproducing the Narragansett edn. of Williams, with new material in vol. 7., which contains an Essay in Interpretation by Perry Miller. New York, 1963.
Vol. I
    Biographical Introduction by Guild, R.A.
    Key into the Language of America, ed. Trumbull, J.H.

Letter of Mr. John Cotton
Mr. Cotton's Letter Examined and Answered, ed. Guild
Vol. II
John Cotton's Answer to Roger Williams
Queries of Highest Consideration, ed. Guild
Vol. III
The Bloudy Tenent of Persecution, ed. Caldwell, S.L.
Vol. IV
The Bloody Tenent Yet More Bloody, ed. Caldwell
Vol. V
George Fox Digg'd out of His Burrowes, ed. Diman, J.L.
Vol. VI
Letters, ed. Bartlett, J.R.
Vol. VII
Publisher's Foreword
Roger Williams: An Essay in Interpretation, by Perry Miller
Christenings make Not Christians
Experiments of Spiritual Life and Health
The Fourth Paper Presented by Major Butler
The Hireling Ministry None of Christs
The Examiner—Defended in a Fair and Sober Answer
Note: Introductions and notes in this edition are often valuable, but
need revision, as does the text. The *Letters* have been cut in
places and need to be compared with surviving mss., many of
which appear in:
  Chapin, Howard M., ed., *Letters and Papers of Roger Wil-
    liams, 1629–1682,* Massachusetts Historical Society, 1924.
This work contains photo-copies of mss.
Mss. of Williams's correspondence with Lady Joan Barrington are
among the *Egerton MSS.* in the British Museum and the originals
of his letters to Mrs. Sadleir are at Trinity College, Cambridge.
Well edited items of his letters to the Winthrops are in the
Winthrop Correspondence (Mass. Hist. Soc.). Other specimens
of Williams's handwriting and shorthand are in the John Carter
Brown Library, Providence, R.I.
Winslow, Edward, *Hypocrisie Unmasked . . . ,* London, 1646
Winthrop, John, *Journal, History of New England, 1630–1649,* ed.
    Hosmer, James K., 2 vols., New York, 1908; *Papers,* Vol. III,
    1631–1637, M.H.S., 1943
Wood, William, *New Englands Prospect,* London, 1634
Zeal Examined . . . , (anon.), London, 1652

LATER WORKS

Abbott, Walter M., ed., *The Documents of Vatican II*, London-Dublin, 1966

Andrews, Charles M., *The Colonial Period of American History*, 4 vols., New Haven, 1934–1938

Babbage, S.B., *Puritanism and Richard Bancroft*, London, 1962

Backus, Isaac, *A History of New-England, With Particular Reference to the Denomination of Christians called Baptists*, 3 vols., Boston, 1777, Providence, 1784, Boston, 1796; *An Abridgment of the Church History of New England from 1602 to 1804*, Boston, 1804

Bainton, R.H., *The Travail of Religious Liberty*, Philadelphia, 1951

Barbour, Hugh, *The Quakers in Puritan England*, New Haven and London, 1964

Barclay, Robert, *The Inner Life of the Religious Societies of the Commonwealth*, London, 1876

Barker, Arthur E., *Milton and the Puritan Dilemma, 1641–1660*, Toronto, 1942

Berins, M.A., *Descendants of Roger and Mary (Barnard) Williams*, MS. in R.I.H.S. Library, Providence, R.I., n.d.

Bowen, Catherine Drinker, *The Lion and the Throne. The Life and Times of Sir Edward Coke, 1552–1634*, London, 1957

Braithwaite, William C., *The Beginnings of Quakerism*, second edn., revised by Cadbury, Henry J., Cambridge (England), 1955

Brockunier, Samuel Hugh, *The Irrepressible Democrat—Roger Williams*, New York, 1940

Brown, Louise Fargo, *The Political Activities of the Baptists and Fifth Monarchy Men in England During the Interregnum*, Washington, 1912

Brunton, P., and Pennington, D.H., *Members of the Long Parliament*, London, 1954

Burgess, Walter H., *John Smith the Se Baptist*, London, 1911.

Burrage, Champlin, *The Early English Dissenters in the Light of Recent Research* (1550–1641), 2 vols., Cambridge University Press, 1912

Calder, Isabel M., ed., *The Activities of the Puritan Faction of the Church of England, 1625–33*, London, 1957

Callender, John, *An Historical Discourse on the Civil and Religious Affairs of the Colony of Rhode Island . . .* , Boston, 1739. Reprint in R.I.H.S. Colls., Vol. IV, Providence, 1838

Carpenter, Edmund J., *Roger Williams; a study of the Life, Times and Character of a Political Pioneer*, New York, 1909

Carrillo de Albornoz, A.F., *Roman Catholicism and Religious Liberty,* Geneva, 1959

Chapin, Howard M., *Documentary History of Rhode Island,* 2 vols., Providence, 1916; *List of Roger Williams' Writings,* Providence, 1918, revised by Kane, Hope (MS. annotations), in R.I.H.S. Library, Providence; *The Trading Post of Roger Williams . . . ,* Providence, 1933; *Roger Williams and the King's Colors,* Providence, 1928

Covey, Cyclone, *The Gentle Radical: a biography of Roger Williams,* New York, 1966

Dale, R.W., *History of English Congregationalism* (Completed and ed. by A.W.W. Dale), London, 1907

Dexter, Henry Martyn, *As to Roger Williams and his 'Banishment' from the Massachusetts Plantation,* Boston, 1876; *The Congregationalism of the Last Three Hundred Years . . . ,* New York, 1880; (with Dexter, Morton), *The True Story of John Smyth the Se-Baptist,* Boston, 1881; *The England and Holland of the Pilgrims,* Boston and New York, 1905

Duncan, Pope A., *Hanserd Knollys: Seventeenth-Century Baptist,* Nashville, 1965

Easton, Emily, *Roger Williams, Prophet and Pioneer,* Boston and New York, 1930

Elton, Romeo, *Life of Roger Williams,* Providence, 1853

Emerson, Everett H., *John Cotton,* New York, 1965

Ernst, James, *Roger Williams, New England Firebrand,* New York, 1932

Eusden, John D., *Puritans, Lawyers and Politics in Early Seventeenth-Century England,* New Haven, 1958

Foster, Joseph, *Alumni Oxonienses,* 1500–1714, Vol. IV—Early Series, Oxford, 1892

Gammell, William, *Life of Roger Williams, Founder of the State of Rhode Island,* Boston, 1846

Giddings, James L., *The Indians and Roger Williams* (typescript, lecture before R.I.H.S., Oct. 24, 1957; in R.I.H.S. Lib., Providence)

Glass, H.A., *The Barbone Parliament,* London, 1899

Haller, William, *The Rise of Puritanism,* New York, 1938; *Foxe's Book of Martyrs and the Elect Nation,* London, 1963

Hexter, J.K., *The Reign of King Pym,* Cambridge (Harvard), 1941

Hill, Christopher, *Economic Problems of the Church from Archbishop Whitgift to the Long Parliament,* Oxford, 1956; *Puritanism and Revolution,* London, 1958; *Society and Puritanism in Pre-Revolutionary England,* New York, 1964

Howell, Roger, Jr., *Newcastle upon Tyne and the Puritan Revolution,* Oxford, 1967

Hudson, Winthrop S., *John Locke: Heir of Puritan Political Theorists,* in Hunt, George L. (ed.), *Calvinism and The Political Order,* Philadelphia, 1955

Janes, Lewis G., *Samuell Gorton, First Settler of Warwick, R.I.,* Providence, 1896

Jones, G.F.T., *Saw-Pit Wharton,* Sydney, 1967

Jones, Rufus M., *The Quakers in the American Colonies,* London, 1923

Keeler, Mary F., *The Long Parliament, 1640–1641, A Biographical Study of its Members,* Philadelphia, 1954

Kellaway, William, *The New England Company, 1649–1776,* London, 1961

King, Henry Melville, *A Summer Visit of Three Rhode Islanders to the Massachusetts Bay in 1651,* Providence, 1896

Knappen, M.M., *Tudor Puritanism,* Chicago and London, re-print, 1965

Knowles, James D., *Memoir of Roger Williams,* Boston, 1834

Lindeboom, Johannes, *The Parish of Austin Friars,* The Hague, 1950

Maclear, James F., *The Puritan Party, 1603–1643: A Study in a Lost Reformation* (unprinted Ph.D. dissertation, Univ. of Chicago), 1947

Masson, D., *Life of John Milton,* 4 vols., London, 1894

Miller, Perry, *Errand into the Wilderness,* New York, 1964; *The New England Mind, The Seventeenth Century,* Boston, 1961; *Orthodoxy in Massachusetts, 1630–1650: A Genetic Study,* Cambridge (Mass.), 1961; *Roger Williams, His Contribution to the American Tradition,* New York, 1962

Miller, Perry, and Johnson, Thomas H., *The Puritans,* 2 vols., revised edn., New York, 1963

Moffat(t), James, *The Life of John Owen,* London, Congregational Union of England and Wales, n.d.

Morgan, Edmund S., *The Puritan Dilemma, The Story of John Winthrop,* Boston, 1958; *Roger Williams: The Church and the State,* New York, 1967; *Visible Saints, The History of a Puritan Idea,* Ithaca (N.Y.), 1965

Morison, Samuel Eliot, *Builders of the Bay Colony,* Boston and New York, 1930

Mozley, J.F., *John Foxe and His Book,* London, 1940

Murdock, Kenneth B., *Literature and Theology in Colonial New England,* Cambridge (Mass.), 1949

Newton, A.P., *The Colonising Activities of the English Puritans,* New Haven, 1914

Notestein, Wallace, *The English People on the Eve of Colonization, 1603–1630,* New York and Evanston, 1962

Nuttall, Geoffrey F., *The Holy Spirit in Puritan Faith and Experience,* Oxford, 1946; *James Nayler, A Fresh Approach,* Supplement No. 26, *Journal of the Friends' Historical Society,* London, 1954; *Visible Saints, The Congregational Way, 1640–1660,* Oxford, 1957; *The Welsh Saints, 1640–1660,* Cardiff, 1957; *Richard Baxter,* London, 1965

Paul, Robert S., *Historical Introduction* to facsimile edn. of *An Apologeticall Narration,* Philadelphia and Boston, 1963

Pearl, Valerie, *London and the Outbreak of the Puritan Revolution. City Government and National Politics, 1625–43,* Oxford, 1961

Richman, I.B., *Rhode Island, Its Making and Meaning, 1636–1683,* New York and London, 1908

Rose-Troup, Frances, *John White, The Patriarch of Dorchester (Dorset) and the Founder of Massachusetts, 1575–1648,* New York and London, 1930

Rogers, Horatio, *Mary Dyer of Rhode Island, The Quaker Martyr,* Providence, 1896

Schenk, W., *The Concern for Social Justice in the Puritan Revolution,* London, 1948

Shakespeare, J.H., *Baptist and Congregational Pioneers,* London, 1906

Shaw, William A., *A History of the English Church During The Civil Wars and Under the Commonwealth, 1640–1660,* 2 vols., London, 1900

Sippell, Theodor, *Zur Vorgeschichte des Quäkertums,* Giessen, 1920; *Werdendes Quäkertum,* Stuttgart, 1937

Smith, H. Shelton; Handy, Robert T.; Loetscher, Lefferts A., eds., *American Christianity, An Historical Interpretation with Representative Documents, Vol. I, 1607–1820,* New York, 1960

Stearns, Raymond P., *Congregationalism in the Dutch Netherlands, The Rise and Fall of The English Congregational Classis, 1621–1635,* Chicago, 1940; *The Strenuous Puritan, Hugh Peter, 1598–1660,* Urbana (Ill.), 1954

Straus, Oscar S., *Roger Williams, The Pioneer of Religious Liberty,* New York, 1894

Swan, Bradford F., *The Case of Richard Chasmore, alias Long Dick,* Providence, 1944; *Gregory Dexter of London and New England, 1610–1700,* Rochester, 1949

Sykes, Norman, *Old Priest and New Presbyter,* Cambridge (England), 1956

Tindall, William York, *John Bunyan, Mechanick Preacher,* New York, 1934

Trevelyan, G.M., *England under the Stuarts,* Pelican reprint, Harmondsworth, 1960; *English Social History,* Vol. II, London, 1942

Trevor-Roper, Hugh, *Archbishop Laud,* London, 1940

Vendettuoli, James A., Jr., *The English Seekers: John Jackson, The Principal Spokesman,* (Harvard Ph.D. Thesis), unprinted, 1958

Venn, John, and Venn, J.A., *Matriculations and Degrees . . . University of Cambridge, 1544–1569,* Cambridge, 1913

Walzer, Michael, *The Revolution of the Saints,* Harvard, 1965

Wedgwood, C.V., *The King's Peace, 1637–1641,* New York, 1955

Williams, G.H., *The Radical Reformation,* Philadelphia, 1962; ed., *Spiritual and Anabaptist Writers,* Library of Christian Classics, Vol. XXV, London, 1957; *Wilderness and Paradise in Christian Thought,* New York, 1962

Wilson, John F., *Studies in Puritan Millenarianism under the Early Stuarts* (unprinted Union Theological Seminary Th.D. dissertation), New York, 1962

Winslow, Ola F., *Master Roger Williams,* New York, 1957

Woodhouse, A.S.P., *Puritanism and Liberty,* London, 1951

Wroth, Lawrence C., *Roger Williams,* Brown University Papers, Providence, 1937

Yule, George, *The Independents in the English Civil War,* Cambridge (England) and Melbourne, 1958

Ziff, Larzer, *The Career of John Cotton, Puritanism and the American Experience,* Princeton, 1962

PERIODICALS

Burrage, Champlin, *The Antecedents of Quakerism,* in *English Historical Review,* Vol. XXX, No. 117, January 1915

Calamandrei, Mauro, *Neglected Aspects of Roger Williams' Thought,* in *Church History,* Vol. XXI, No. 3, September 1952, pp. 239–258

Camp, Leon R., *Roger Williams vs. "The Upstarts": The Rhode Island Debates of 1672,* in *Quaker History,* Autumn, 1963, Vol. 52, No. 2, pp. 69–76

Easton, Emily, *Mary Barnard,* in *R.I.H.S. Colls.,* XXIX, July 1936, No. 3, pp. 65–80

Hardacre, P.H., *William Allen, Cromwellian Agitator and 'Fanatic',* in *The Baptist Quarterly,* New Series, Vol. XIX, London, 1961–1962, pp. 292–308

Hudson, Winthrop S., *Baptists Were Not Anabaptists,* in *The Chronicle,* Vol. XVI, October 1953, No. 4, pp. 171ff.

Kerr, Norman, *John Clarke—Architect of Freedom,* in *The Chronicle,* Vol. XIX, October 1956, No. 4, pp. 147ff.

Matthews, A.G., *A Censored Letter* in *Congregational Historical Society Transactions,* IX, pp. 263–5

Mosteller, James D., *Baptists and Anabaptists,* in *The Chronicle,* Vol. XX, January 1957, No. 1, and Vol. XX, July 1957, No. 3

Maclear, J.F., *The Making of the Lay Tradition,* in *The Journal of Religion,* Vol. XXIII, No. 2, April 1953, pp. 113–136

Moore, LeRoy, Jr., *Roger Williams and the Historians,* in *Church History,* Vol. XXXII, No. 4, December 1963, pp. 433–451; *Religious Liberty: Roger Williams and the Revolutionary Era,* in *Church History,* Vol. XXXIV, No. 1, March 1965

Whitley, W.T., *The Hubbard-How-More Church,* in *Transactions of the Baptist Historical Society,* Vol. II, 1910–1911, pp. 31–52 (London)

Williams, G.H., *The Pilgrimage of Thomas Hooker (1586–1674),* in *Bulletin of the Congregational Library,* Boston, Vol. 19, Nos. 1 and 2, October 1967 (pp. 5–15) and January 1968, (pp. 9–13)

Wilson, John F., *Another Look at John Canne,* in *Church History,* Vol. XXXIII, No. 1, March 1964

(World Council of Churches), *Christian Witness, Proselytism and Religious Liberty . . . ,* in *The Ecumenical Review,* Vol. IX, No. 1, October 1956, pp. 48–56

Index

Index

DATE DUE

OCT 1 8 1979			
NOV 8 1979			
NOV 2 9 1979			